PREFACE

For approximately 400 years, Japanese mothers have been
handing on to their children the traditional methods of folding paper,
which we call origami. In this period, the handicraft developed
and spread, and today people all over Japan practice it
with pleasure. Origami is not merely a traditional amusement,
it is also a scientific handicraft that anyone, anywhere, and
at any time can learn. It is, however, necessary to select and use
traditional origami works of some antiquity in presenting the handicraft
to the peoples of the world. Because we were afraid some of the
ancient ceremonial folds and some of the traditional folds
of an exclusively Japanese nature might be difficult to understand,
in our discussion of origami history we have eliminated all
but an essential few such works. We have included a number of bird
and animal forms of our own in the more modern works, but
we should like to remark that all of them depend on traditional
folding methods for their forms.

Origami, for which all you need is a sheet of paper, transcends
differences of wealth, station, or race and makes all equal. It serves to
guide children into a world of future art, craft, and invention.

We earnestly hope that, like the impartial sunlight, this work will
bring an equal measure of happiness to adults and children alike
all over the world.

ISAO HONDA

September, 1965

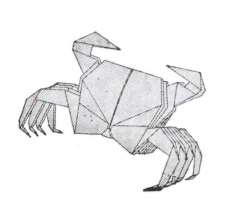

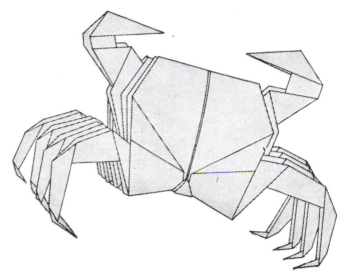

CONTENTS

The World of ORIGAMI

The World of

ORIGAMI

Isao Honda

JAPAN PUBLICATIONS, INC.

THIS IS AN ABRIDGED POPULAR EDITION OF *The World of Origami*
BY THE SAME AUTHOR AND PUBLISHER.

© 1965 by Isao Honda

First edition,1965. Reprinted 1966,1967,1968,1969,1970,1971,
1972,1973.

Popular edition:
First printed in August 1976
Twenty–second printing: November 1998

Library of Congress Catalog Card No. 65–27101
ISBN 0–87040–383–4

Published by
JAPAN PUBLICATIONS, INC. TOKYO

Distributors:
UNITED STATES: Kodansha America, Inc., through Oxford University Press,
198 Madison Avenue, New York, N.Y. 10016. CANADA: Fitzhenry & Whiteside
Ltd., 195 Allstate Parkway, Markham, Ontario L3R 4T8. UNITED KINGDOM AND
EUROPEAN CONTINENT: Premier Book Marketing Ltd., 1 Gower Street, London
WC1E 6HA . AUSTRALIA AND NEW ZEALAND: Bookwise International,
54 Crittenden Road, Findon, South Australia 5023. ASIA AND JAPAN: Japan
Publications Trading Co., Ltd., 1–2–1, Sarugaku–cho, Chiyoda–ku, Tokyo 101   Japan

Printed in U.S.A.

EXPLANATORY SYMBOLS

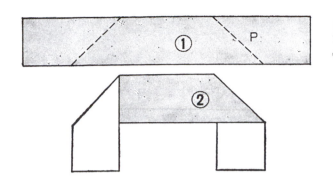

A plain dotted line indicates a valley (concave) fold. A dotted line with the letter "p" indicates a peak (convex) fold.

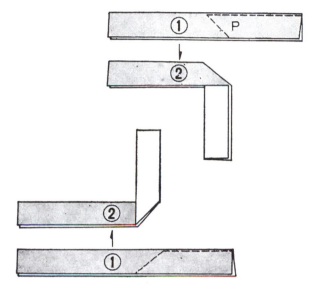

By making a long horizontal valley fold and a short diagonal peak fold, we can reverse fold the paper so that the outside is in.

By making a long horizontal valley fold and a short diagonal valley fold, we can reverse fold the paper so that the inside is out.

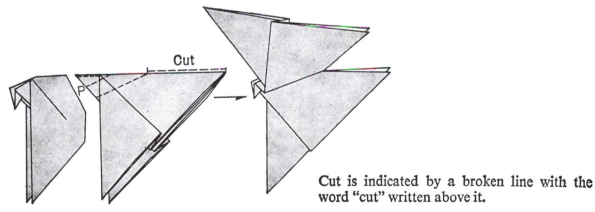

Cut is indicated by a broken line with the word "cut" written above it.

---

① Begin folding.   ② ③ ④ Folding order.   ❺ The finished product.

⟹ ◯ Folding method up to this point is as in . . . .

THE ORIGINS OF ORIGAMI

■ What is Origami?

The definitions of "origami" in *Webster's Third New International Dictionary* are: 1. The art of Japanese paper folding. 2. Something (as a representative of a bird, insect, flower) made by origami. Since in the Japanese language the word "origami" means merely folding paper as well as the specialized folding done in the art of origami, we cannot consider origami, in its most basic sense, to be a uniquely Japanese pastime. All countries that use paper have formal paper folding methods, and in general, we can say that wherever there is paper there is paper folding.

On the other hand, in Japan, mothers have taught their children origami in all ages over the centuries until paper folding, at some stage or another, became a handicraft. Because the techniques and methods used in constructing Japanese origami are distinctive to this country and because origami is a part of the daily lives of people all over Japan, when we began to publish English-language explanatory charts explaining paper folding methods, we decided to use the name "origami."

Since a Buddhist priest brought paper-making methods into Japan from China through Korea in 538 A.D., some historians use this historical fact as a basis for insisting that paper-folding methods must naturally have come in then too. None of the ancient origami works, however, provides us with material for asserting their Chinese or Korean origin, and no documents to that effect have turned up.

Even after the manufacture of paper had spread all over the country, its price prevented its use for a pastime like origami. Because of paper's value, the people used it carefully for special origami for ceremonial occasions. The folding styles for ceremonialized origami were rigidly fixed. To learn them it was necessary to study with a specialist. Because all of this was troublesome the ceremonial styles never attained general distribution, and later, particularly after the cultural exchanges with the West in the nineteenth century and the resulting social revolutions, the ancient difficult ceremonial styles fell from favor until today they are practically extinct. On the other hand, since there are a number of modern origami that developed from the geometric styles of the ancient folds, we include illustrations and explanations of some of the older ones which resemble modern origami.

The period in which ceremonial origami was most common was also a glorious period of brilliant development in painting, literature, architecture, and other arts and crafts, and a period in which the aristocrats indulged in luxurious living.

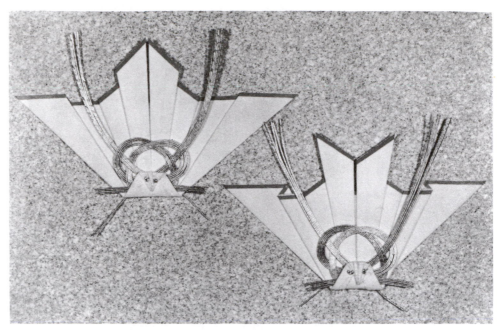

Figure 1. Male and female butterflies.

These abstract representations of a male and a female butterfly were used to decorate sake bottles at wedding ceremonies. The fold on the left is the male and that on the right is the female. In weddings today, these ancient butterfly ornaments appear, though the ones used now are much more splendid and their folding method is somewhat different.

This is one of the oldest examples of formative creative origami.

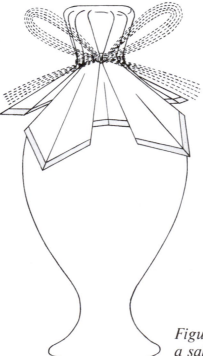

From ancient times, it has been a custom to place a bottle of sake on the altar during Japanese religious ceremonies. An origami ornament of this type is used at the mouth of the sake bottle. It resembles modern origami in that is systematically folded.

The ornamental knot in silver and gold is called a *mizuhiki*. Although it, too, is ceremonially stylized, since it is not origami we will omit an explanation of its tying methods.

Figure 2. Flower ornament for the mouth of a sake container.

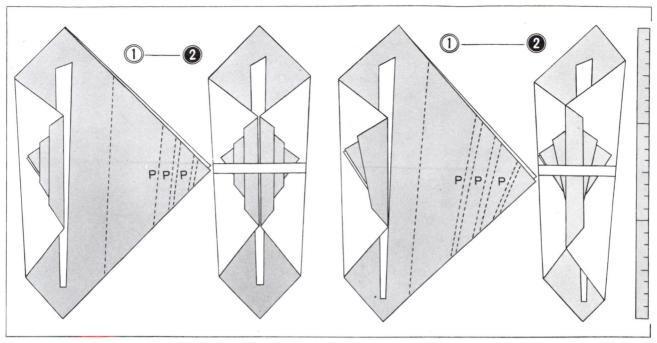

Figure 3. Noshi.

Though, as we said earlier, ceremonial origami have all but vanished from the modern scene, the *noshi* is one example of its surviving to become a part of the daily lives of all Japanese people.

Explaining the form and the ancient custom of *noshi* is somewhat difficult, but as I have already said in an earlier work on them (*NOSHI-Classic Origami in Japan*) a *noshi* is a folded paper ornament which all shops attach to purchases when the purchaser tells them he is buying a gift for someone. The *noshi* itself signifies the hope of the giver that the recipient will enjoy good fortune. The origin of the custom dates back to the end of the twelfth century when it was said, "When you send a gift to someone, always wrap it in pure white paper." The *noshi*, a folded bit of paper, is an abbreviation of the earlier custom.

Since making simple *noshi* was the work of every housewife the presence for this purpose in the home of lovely papers in colors and printed patterns naturally served to create interest in making other origami and in spreading this interest.

In the center of the paper ornament is the actual *noshi* itself. The word "*noshi*" is an abbreviation of *noshi-awabi*, a thin strip of dried abalone attached in the middle of the paper fold. The use of abalone on *noshi* for gifts dates back to the twelfth century, though its significance is no longer known.

■ *Kan-no-Mado*

As we have already noted, origami was handed down from age to age and from person to person so that the folds that were too difficult or those that lost favor were naturally eliminated. The bulk of the folds that have a long tradition and that continue in use today are superior works that have passed the judgement of the people of Japan. Oddly enough, a photoduplication of an old origami instruction book, called the *Kan-no-mado*, which is not too well known in Japan, has been published in the United States. From this book we can get an idea of some of the more complicated and difficult Japanese folds. The book was issued by the Library of Congress photoduplication service, Washington 25, D.C., in July 23, 1934. After the noted American specialist on paper folding Gerson Legman included the title in his own *Bibliography of Paper-Folding* and used some of its illustrations on the cover, the heretofore obscure *Kan-no-mado* suddenly became well known. Legman labels his illustrations with the following remark:

> *Kan-no-mado* (Japan, c. 1950) vol. 233, pt. 1, 56p.
> A reproduction of the magnificent Dragon-fly (*tombo*) from this manuscript encyclopedia is given by Starr (q.v.) in 1922 as then in the possession of the newspaper Asahi in Osaka.

Unfortunately the Osaka Asahi Newspaper is in the process of rebuilding, and they have transferred their library to another location making an examination of the original manuscript impossible. We feel sure, however, that the title of the work is actually *Kan-no-mado* and that the scholar Katsuyuki Adachi compiled the fragments of documentary material together into 233 small volumes and recopied them himself.

The single volume concerning origami contains over ten ceremonial folds and over thirty of the folds that belong to the pastime class. All of them are illustrated with brush drawings. The author of the *Kan-no-mado* remarks:

Origami spread as an amusement for friends. Since such folds as the (1) the thousand cranes (2) the boat (3) the vehicle, (4) the lotus flower, (5) the *sambo*, (6) the *komoso* (?), (7) the thread container, and (8) a variety of types of helmets are all generally known there is no need to illustrate them. We will illustrate only the folds with complicated folding methods.

Note In this book the above folds are numbered:

1. Thousand cranes   see pp. 5 and 6)
2. Ship   sailboat 27, double boat 28
3. Vehicles   *kago* 54
4. Lotus blossom   38
5. *Sambo*   43
6. *Komoso* (?)   We suppose that this might be the man-servant in 40.
7. Thread container   115
8. Helmet   10

The author then drew illustrations for the folds just as he said he would. The parts of the folds that were too difficult he failed to illustrate; consequently, some of the illustrations are difficult even for Japanese trained in origami to understand. We have chosen in this book to eliminate all of the examples that are too exotically Japanese (human shapes in ancient costumes, etc.).

We are unable to give a clear answer concerning the meaning of the term "*kan-no-mado*. Though the literal meaning seems to be "a window for the cold season," the usage is not conventional in the Japanese language. In addition, we cannot understand what such a phrase might mean as the title of a book. Some people interpret the title as a possible misreading of classical characters meaning "a winter window." For instance, there are instances in ancient writings in which the phrase "rays of light from the window" means "to study." If this is the case, we might attach the modest meaning of "knowledge, meagre like the light that comes through the window in wintertime," to the title of the book.

We have made our illustrations of the folding methods for the *Kan-no-mado* dragonfly and monkey as easy to follow as possible, but we call attention to the fact that these methods are only our own suppositions.

In the proper origami tradition one uses a square piece of paper as a basis and avoids the use of scissors as much as possible. Since, in *Kan-no-mado* folds like the dragonfly and the monkey, we use the scissors quite a lot and since, though the folding techniques are most complicated, the finished form is flat, these folds are really not among the finest as far a true origami goes.

In answer to the question, "Who thought up these elaborate folding techniques?" we might point out a book published in 1797 called *Chushingura Orikata*, ($18\frac{1}{2}$ by 13 inches) in which origami representations of the activities of the main characters in all eleven acts of the famous play *Chushingura* appear in woodcut-print illustrations. The folding techniques required to reproduce all of these complicated costumed figures would have been impossible with paper shapes in use up to that time, and the author had to devise new ones. Because the basic paper shape used in the *Kan-no-mado* dragonfly is the same as that used in *Chushingura Orikata*, we suppose that the dragonfly was a by-product of the illustrations for the book. The author of *Chushingura Orikata* and of the *Sembazuru Orikata*, about which we shall speak next, was the head priest at a temple called the Rokoan.

■ Sembazuru Orikata

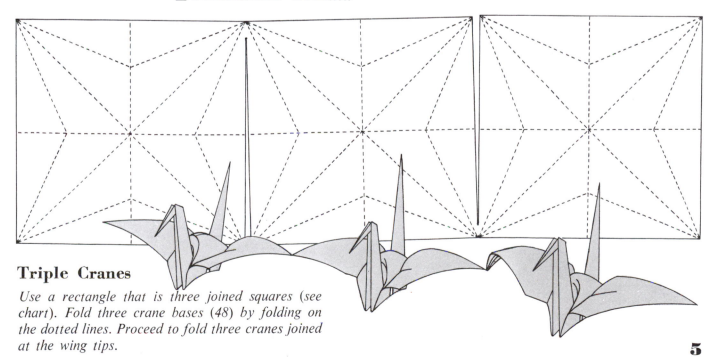

Triple Cranes

Use a rectangle that is three joined squares (see chart). Fold three crane bases (48) by folding on the dotted lines. Proceed to fold three cranes joined at the wing tips.

The crane is not only the most representative of all Japanese origami, it is also the senior and the fold with the most truly nationwide distribution. Though, from the viewpoint of origami craft, the crane seems to have come about accidentally, because of the long tradition of regarding the bird itself as an omen of "a life of a thousand years," the fold, which resembles the Roundhead Crane, is very popular as a symbol of good fortune and long life.

The homeland of the Roundhead Crane is actually northeastern Asia, and the bird has long been considered migratory in this country, but there is an area in Hokkaido where about 200 of them have settled and one other area to which they migrate yearly. Both areas are special crane sanctuaries.

The book *Sembazuru Orikata* (*Folding the Thousand Cranes*) contains the most widely known crane folding method and makes skilful use of the appeal of the bird as an auspicious symbol. The folding method calls for the use of one sheet of origami paper in which one makes a number of slits to produce a fairly good number of mutually connected squares. Each of these squares folded into a crane gives a very virtuoso origami effect. The book illustrates the proper cutting methods and makes full use of the special stiffness of Japanese paper to produce a typically Japanese origami.

You will find details on the folding of the crane in the explanations.

Mother Crane and Babies

Use a square of white paper at least 12 inches to a side. This rather complicated fold is actually less difficult than it looks. To make it, simply make creases to guide your cutting by folding the paper in quarters lengthwise and widthwise. Cut the slits that you see in the chart, and fold a crane (48) with each of the resulting squares. Be sure to fold them so that the heads come where the circle marks are on the chart.

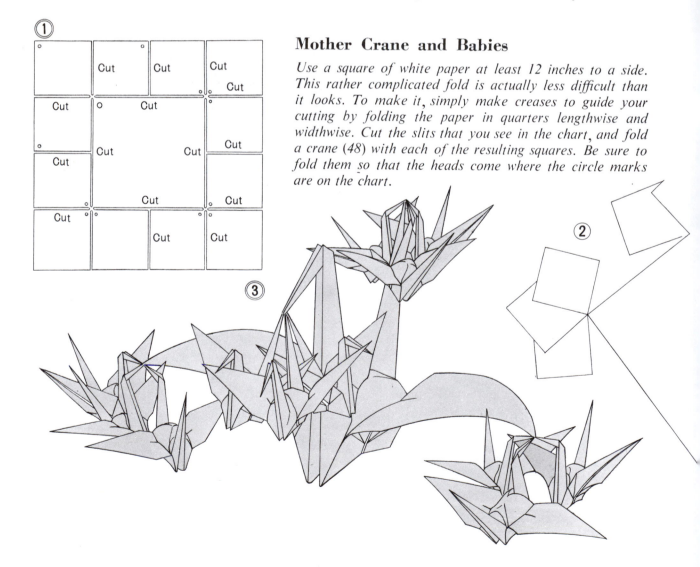

6

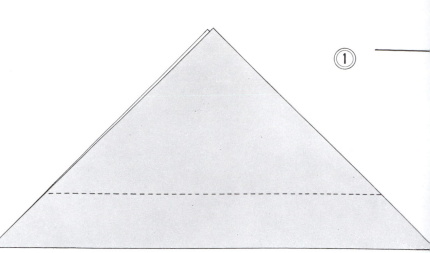

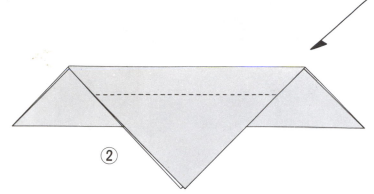

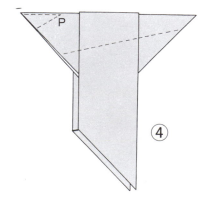

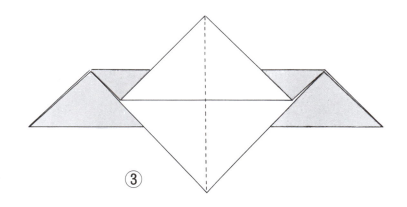

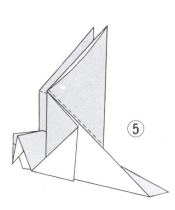

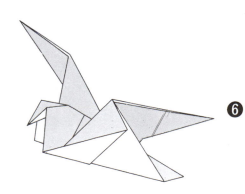

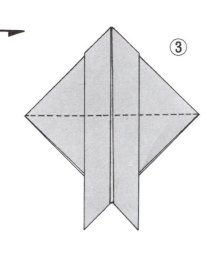

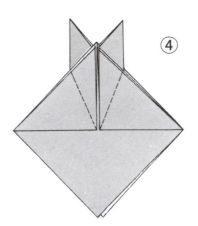 ③

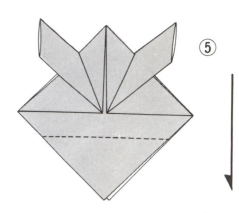 ④

⑤

⑥

10. Japanese Helmet

Use a six-inch square of paper.

1~2. Fold as for work cap (8) to step 3.
3. Valley fold on the dotted line (top two layers only).
4. Valley fold on the dotted lines.
5. Valley fold the bottom point upward (top layer only).
6. Valley fold in numerical order on the dotted lines.
7. Completed front.
8. Turn the model over, and valley fold on the dotted line.
9. Valley fold on the dotted lines in numerical order.
10. Front and rear views of the completed model based on a medieval Japanese helmet which featured long horn-like ornaments in the front.

⑦

underside ⑧

⑨

underside

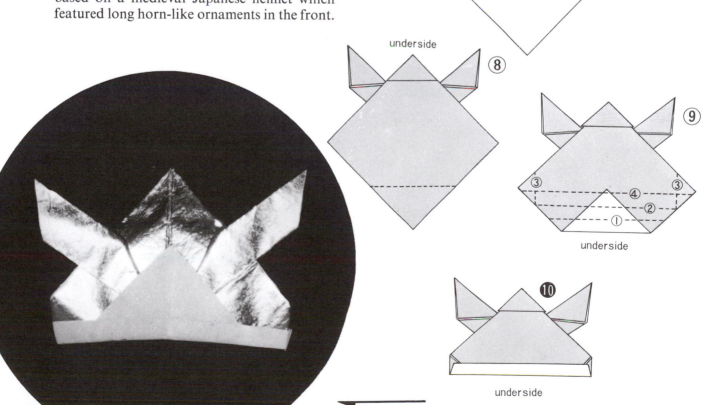

⑩

underside

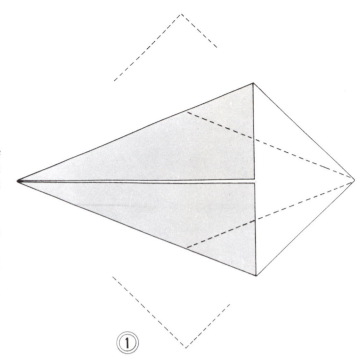

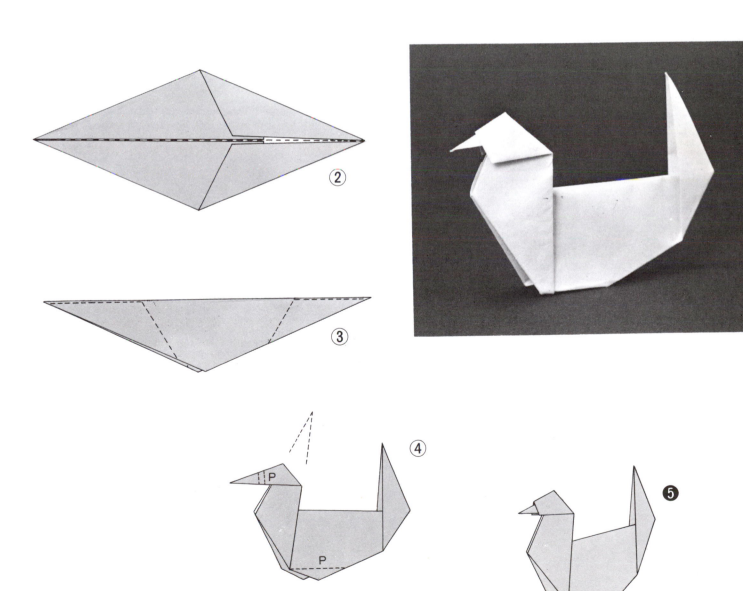

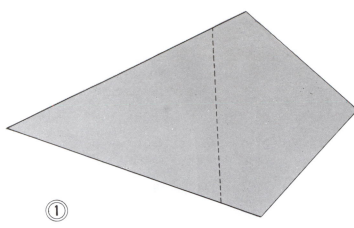

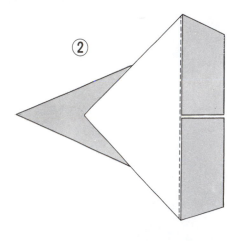

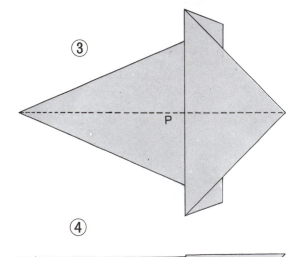

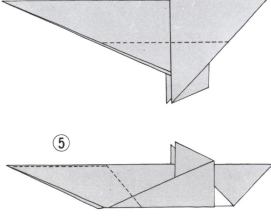

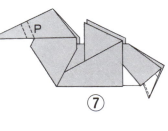

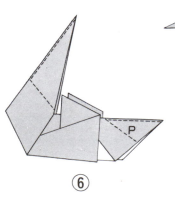

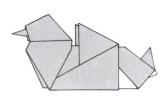

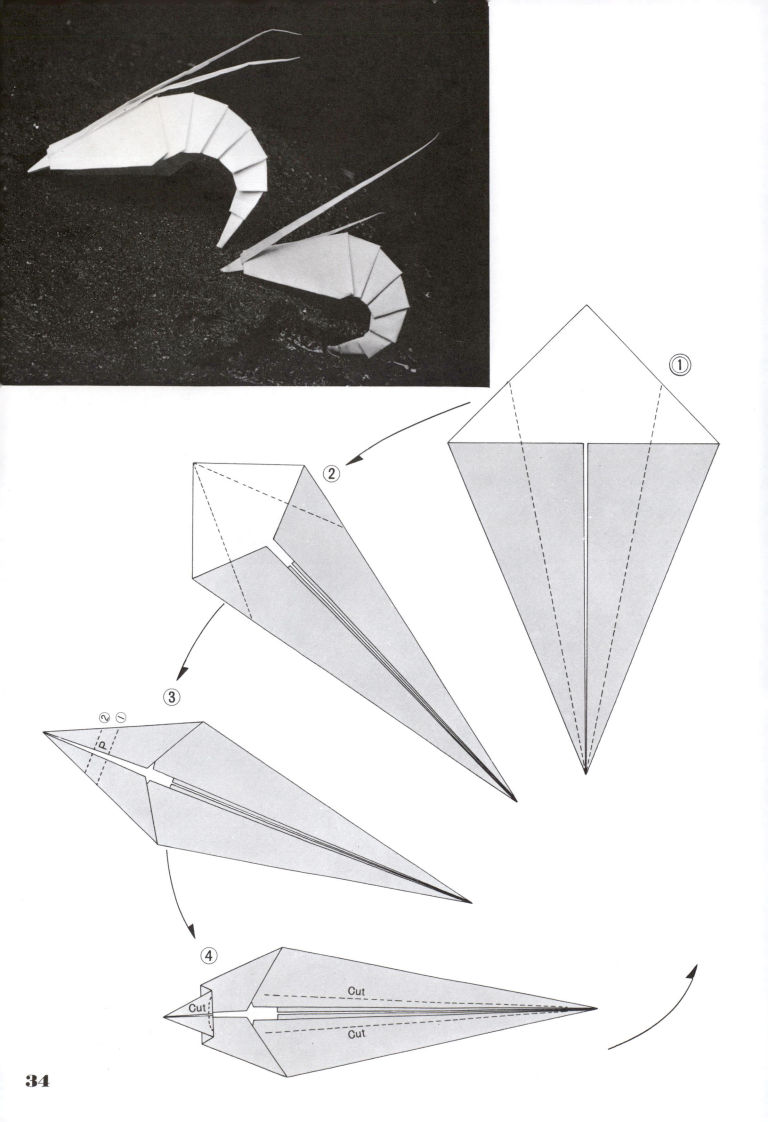

① ② ③ ④

Cut
Cut
Cut

34

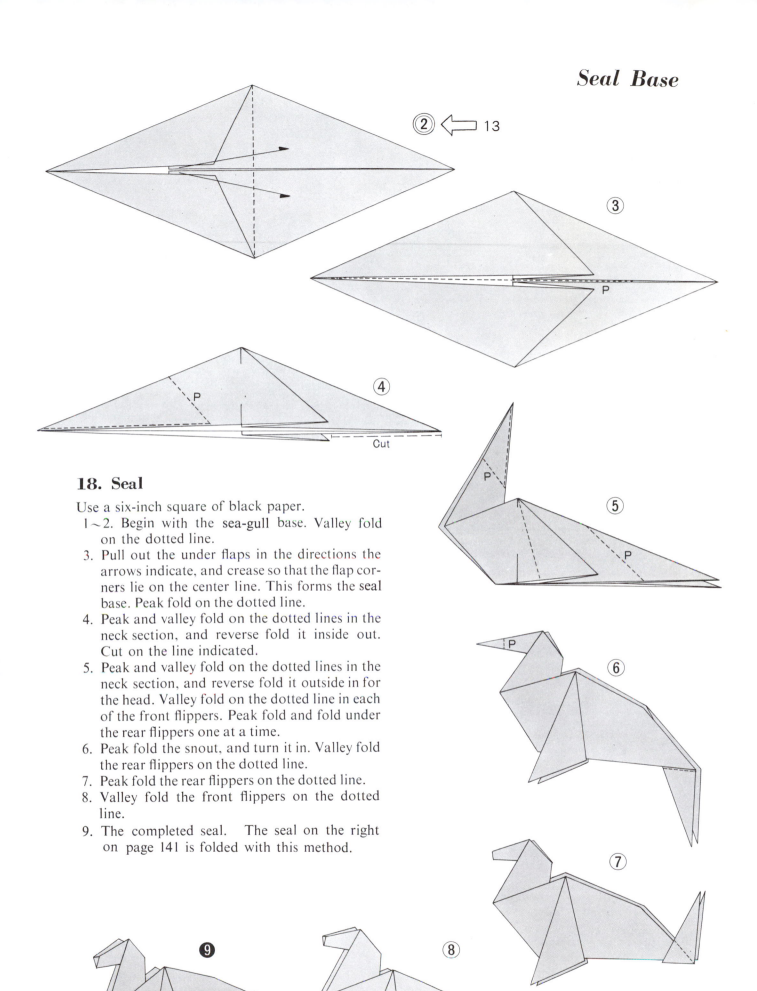

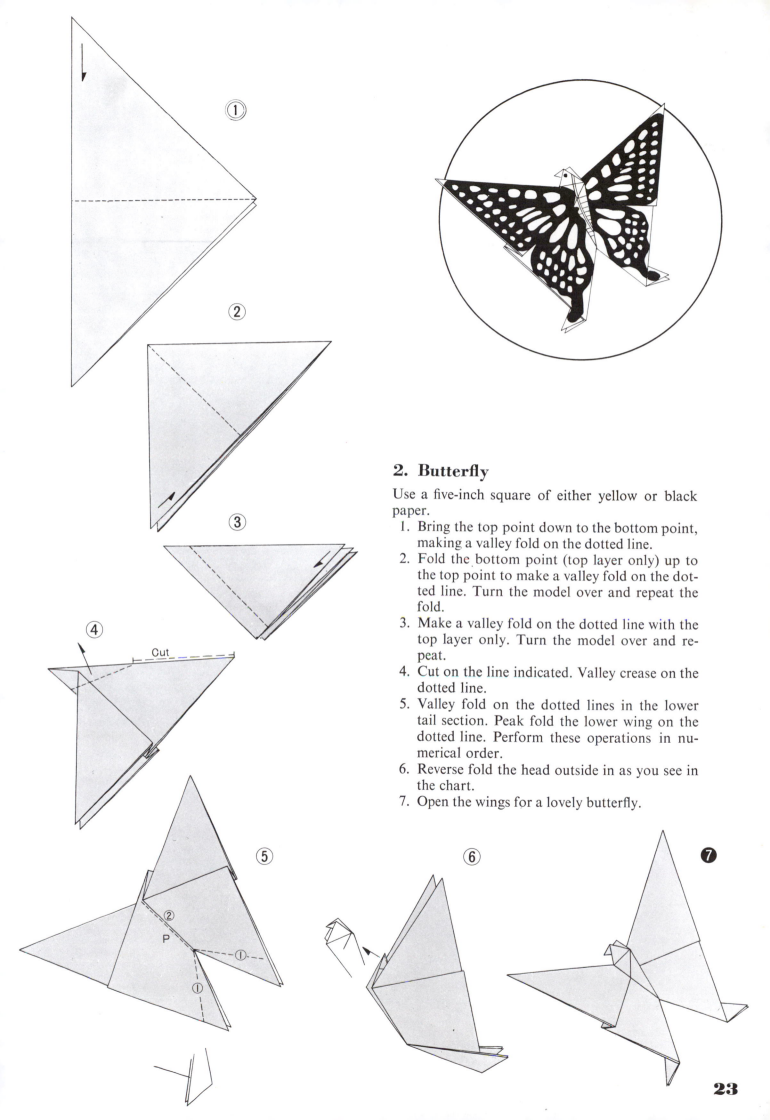

2. Butterfly

Use a five-inch square of either yellow or black paper.

1. Bring the top point down to the bottom point, making a valley fold on the dotted line.
2. Fold the bottom point (top layer only) up to the top point to make a valley fold on the dotted line. Turn the model over and repeat the fold.
3. Make a valley fold on the dotted line with the top layer only. Turn the model over and repeat.
4. Cut on the line indicated. Valley crease on the dotted line.
5. Valley fold on the dotted lines in the lower tail section. Peak fold the lower wing on the dotted line. Perform these operations in numerical order.
6. Reverse fold the head outside in as you see in the chart.
7. Open the wings for a lovely butterfly.

23

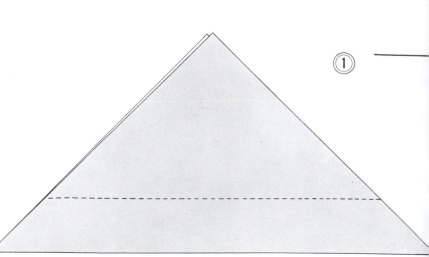

①

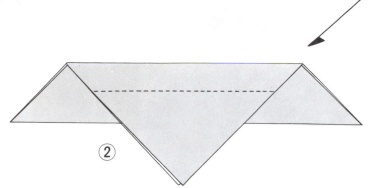

②

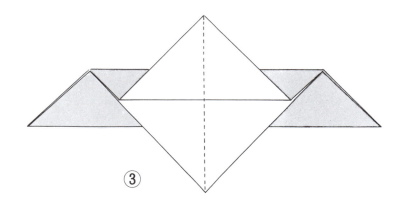

③

3. Dove (1)

Use a five-inch square of white paper.
1. Valley fold the top point (both layers) down on the dotted line.
2. Valley fold the bottom point (top layer only) upward on the dotted line. Be sure that you form a perfect square.
3. Valley fold on the dotted line.
4. Valley fold one wing on the dotted line. Turn the model over and repeat. Reverse fold the head section outside in with one horizontal valley fold and one diagonal peak fold on the dotted lines.
5. Valley fold each wing on the dotted line.
6. Arrange the wings to look as they do in the finished figure.

P

④

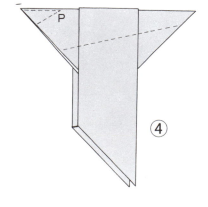

⑤

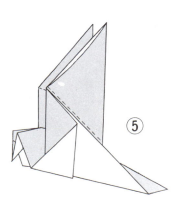

❻

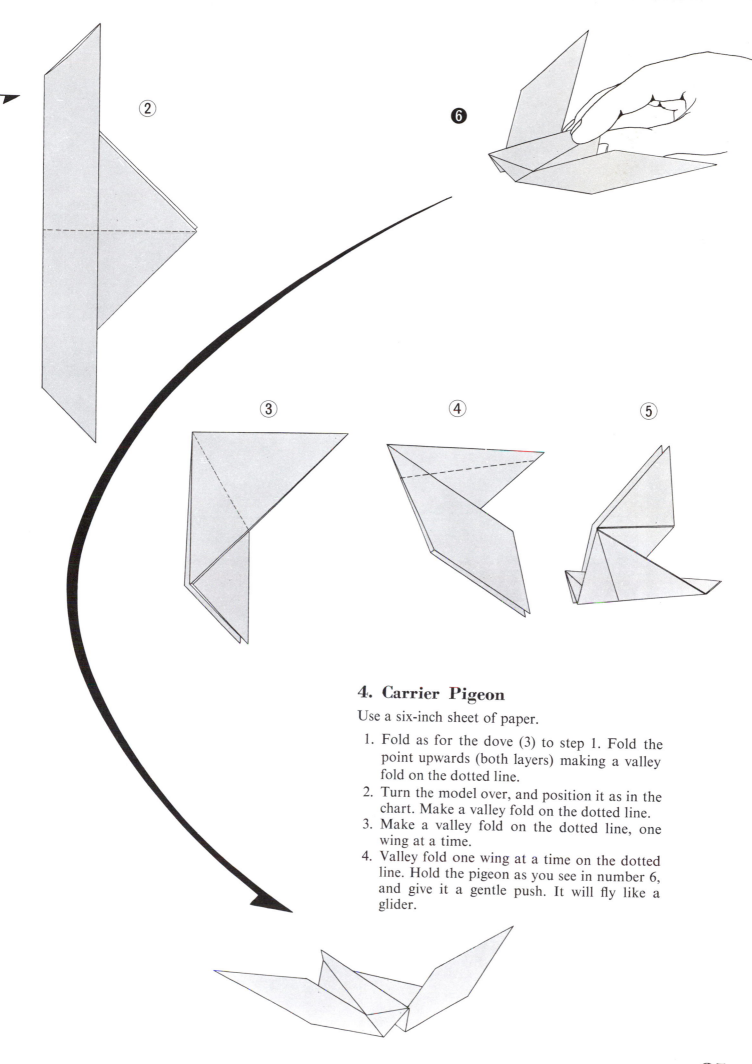

4. Carrier Pigeon

Use a six-inch sheet of paper.

1. Fold as for the dove (3) to step 1. Fold the point upwards (both layers) making a valley fold on the dotted line.
2. Turn the model over, and position it as in the chart. Make a valley fold on the dotted line.
3. Make a valley fold on the dotted line, one wing at a time.
4. Valley fold one wing at a time on the dotted line. Hold the pigeon as you see in number 6, and give it a gentle push. It will fly like a glider.

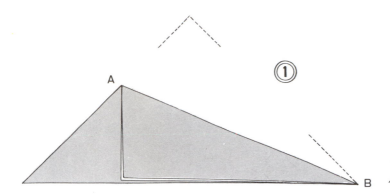

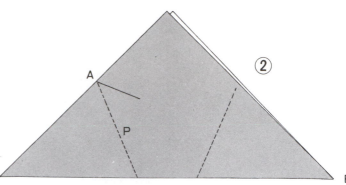

5. Cup

Use a six-inch square of waxed paper.

1. Establish point A by bringing the top point down so that it forms a perpendicular with the base of the triangle. Return the model to its original shape.
2. Join points A and B to make a valley fold on the dotted line on the right. Turn the model over, and repeat the fold to make a peak fold on the dotted line on the left.
3. Tuck the upper layer only of the top point into the pocket formed on that side.
4. Turn the model over, and tuck the remaining layer into the pocket on that side.
5. The completed cup.

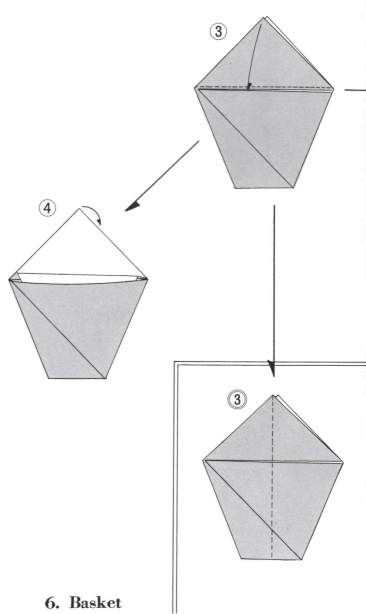

6. Basket

Use a five-inch square of paper.

1~3. Fold as for a cup (5) up to step 3. Make a valley fold on the dotted line.
4. Cut where indicated.
5. Open to the original shape.
6. Tuck in the upper points as in a cup (5), but leave the handle as it is. The basket the stork on page 97 is carrying is folded this way.

7. Hat

Use a five-inch square of paper.

1~3. Fold as for a cup (5) to step 3.
4. Fold the top points downward, one layer to the front and one to the back. Peak fold where indicated. Valley fold the dotted lines on the outside edges.
5. Pull outward on the center fold, and invert the model.
6. Valley fold the bottom points upward on the dotted line.
7. Pull outward on each of the points.
8. The finished hat.

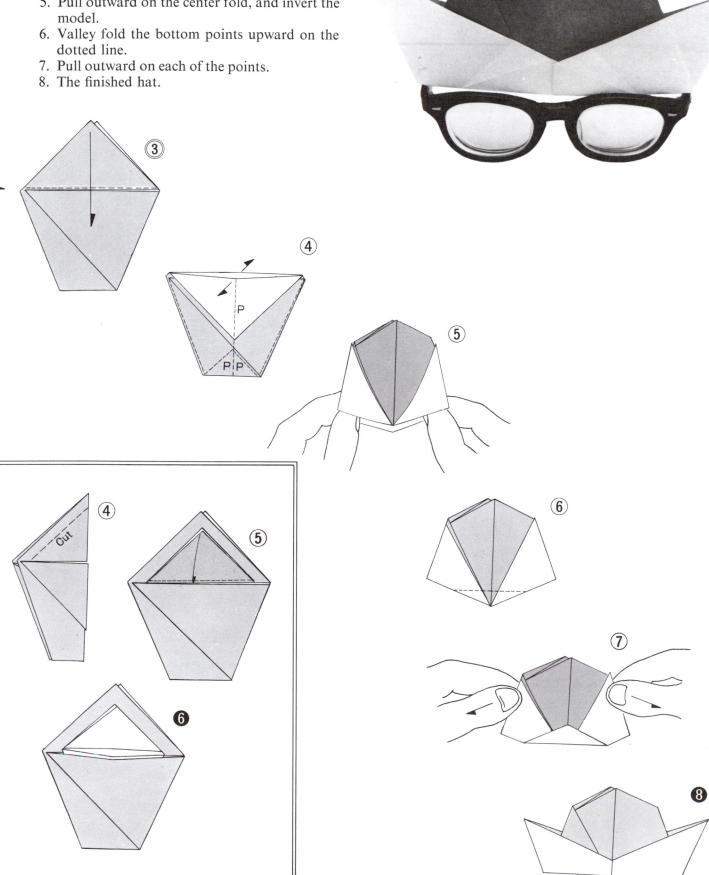

27

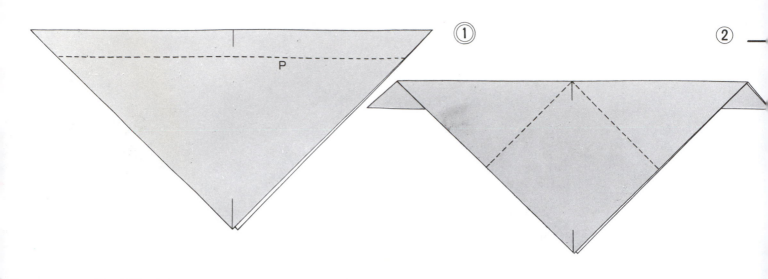

① ②

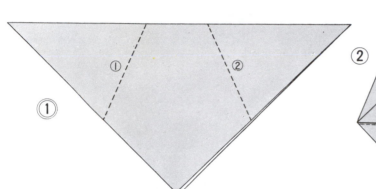

① ② ③

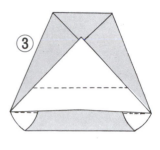

④

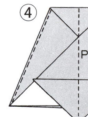

⑤

8. Work Cap

Use a five-inch square of paper.

1. Valley fold on the dotted lines in numerical order.
2. Valley fold only the upper layer of the bottom point upward.
3. Tuck the lower layer of the bottom point inside. Form the brim by valley folding the remaining point on the dotted line.
4. Peak fold on the dotted line. Valley fold on the dotted lines on the outer edges.
5. Turn the model sideways and pull outward.
6. The completed cap.

9. Bird-face Cap

Use a square of wrapping paper or newspaper large enough to make a hat for yourself.
Fold as for a work cap (8) to step 4. Fold the remaining layer of the point completely down.

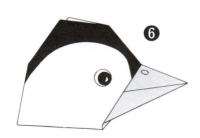

❻

❻

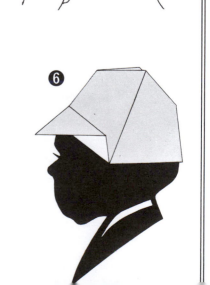

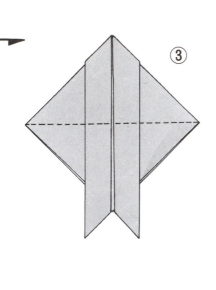

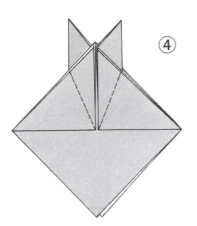

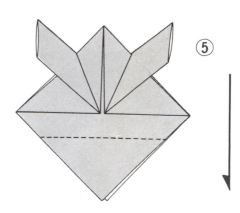

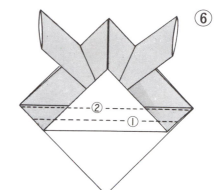

10. Japanese Helmet

Use a six-inch square of paper.

1~2. Fold as for work cap (8) to step 3.
3. Valley fold on the dotted line (top two layers only).
4. Valley fold on the dotted lines.
5. Valley fold the bottom point upward (top layer only).
6. Valley fold in numerical order on the dotted lines.
7. Completed front.
8. Turn the model over, and valley fold on the dotted line.
9. Valley fold on the dotted lines in numerical order.
10. Front and rear views of the completed model based on a medieval Japanese helmet which featured long horn-like ornaments in the front.

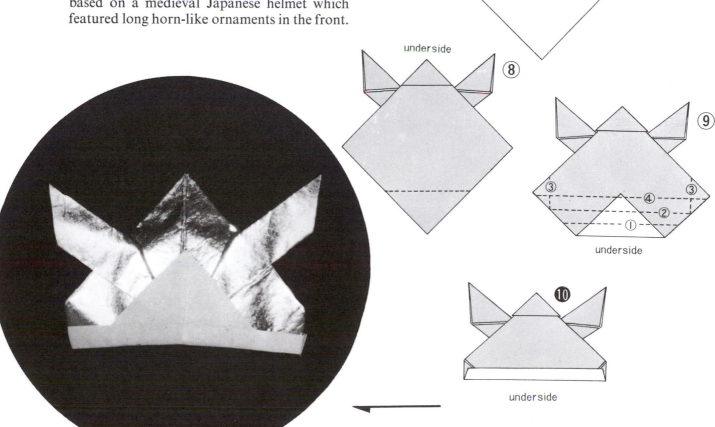

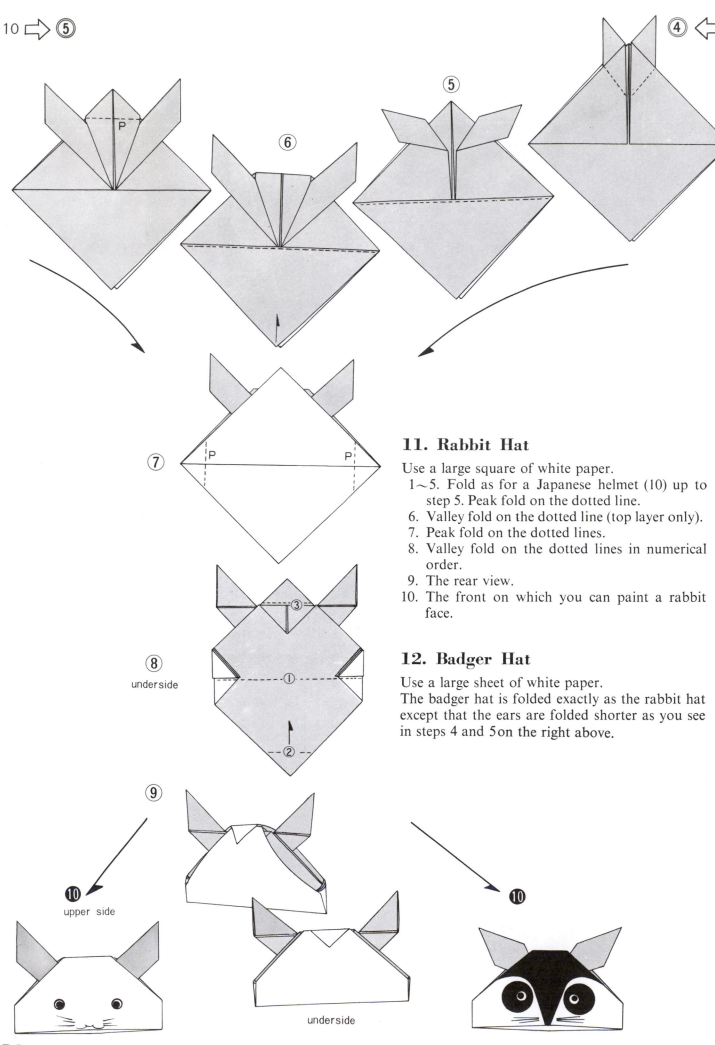

11. Rabbit Hat

Use a large square of white paper.
  1~5. Fold as for a Japanese helmet (10) up to step 5. Peak fold on the dotted line.
  6. Valley fold on the dotted line (top layer only).
  7. Peak fold on the dotted lines.
  8. Valley fold on the dotted lines in numerical order.
  9. The rear view.
  10. The front on which you can paint a rabbit face.

12. Badger Hat

Use a large sheet of white paper.
The badger hat is folded exactly as the rabbit hat except that the ears are folded shorter as you see in steps 4 and 5 on the right above.

⑦ P   P

⑧ underside

③

①

②

⑨

❿ upper side

❿

underside

30

Sea Gull Base

13. Sea Gull (I)

Use a five-inch square of white paper.

1. First determine the center line by folding the paper diagonally in half. Open the paper; then join the outside edges on the center line as you see in step 1. This forms the diamond base. Valley fold on the dotted lines.
2. Valley fold on the dotted line running the length of the paper.
3. Valley fold on the dotted lines, and reverse fold the points outside in.
4. Valley fold and reverse fold the point outside in for the head. Peak and valley fold on the dotted lines, and crimp the paper inward to form the beak.
5. The finished sea gull afloat.

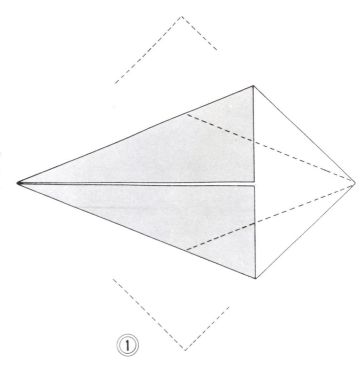

①

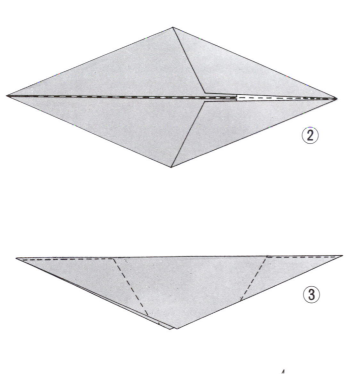

②

③

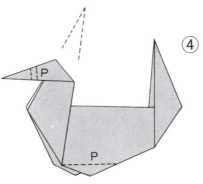

④

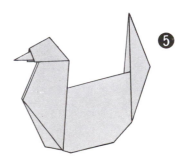

⑤

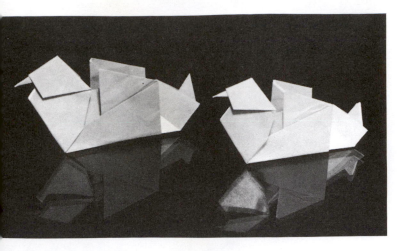

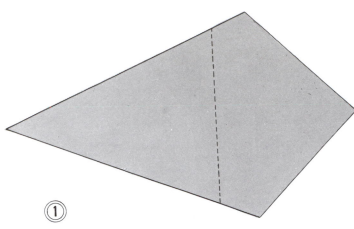
①

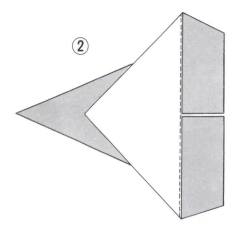
②

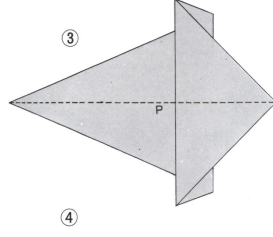
③

④

14. Mandarin Duck

Use a five-inch square of blue or purple paper.
1. Make a sea-gull base. Turn it over and valley fold on the dotted line.
2. Valley fold on the dotted line.
3. Peak fold on the dotted line.
4. Valley fold on the dotted line (one wing only). Turn the model over and valley fold the other wing.
5. Valley fold on the dotted lines, and reverse fold the point inside out for the neck and head section.
6. Valley fold on the dotted lines, and reverse fold the point inside out to form the head. Fold close to the body to keep the neck short. Peak and valley fold on the dotted lines in the tail section, and reverse fold the point outside in.
7. Peak fold on the dotted lines in the head section, and fold inward to make the beak. Valley fold in the tail section on the dotted line, and reverse fold the point inside out to complete the tail.

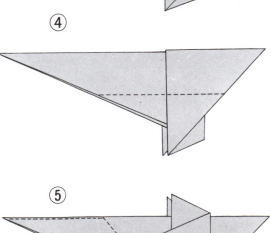
⑤

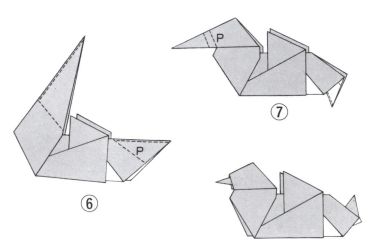
⑥

⑦

❽

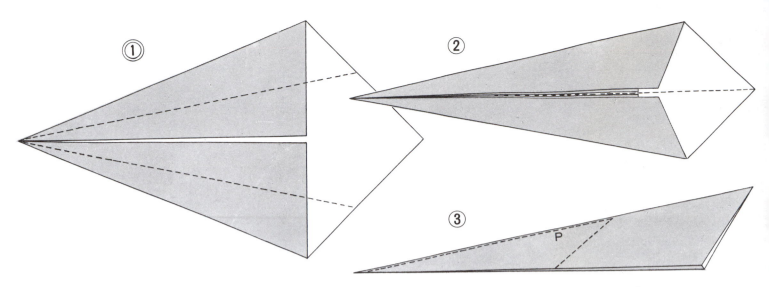

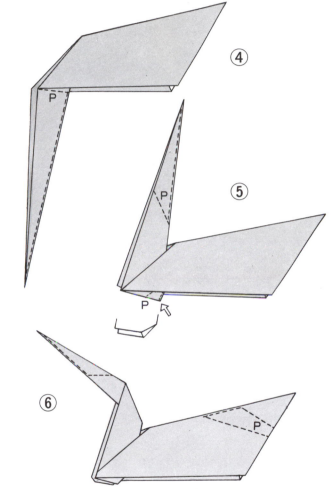

15. Cormorant

Use a six-inch square of black paper.

1. Begin with the sea-gull base. Valley fold on the dotted lines so that the outer edges meet on the center line.
2. Valley fold on the dotted line.
3. Peak and valley fold on the dotted lines, and reverse fold the point outside in.
4. Peak fold on the dotted line, beginning at the body section and folding at an angle. Valley fold on the dotted line, and reverse fold the point outside in.
5. Peak and valley fold for the head section, and reverse fold outside in. Peak and valley fold and turn the corner in at the base of the neck.
6. Valley fold on the dotted lines in the head section, and reverse fold the point inside out. Peak and valley fold on the dotted lines in the tail section, and turn the point in then out again to form the tail.
7. Peak and valley fold on the dotted lines in the head to form the beak. Be careful to bend the tip slightly in to make the correct shape of a cormorant's beak.

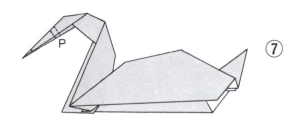

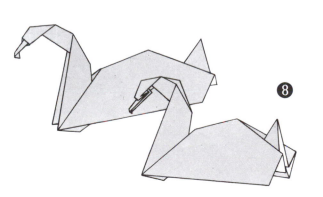

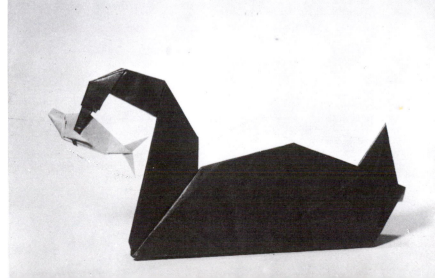

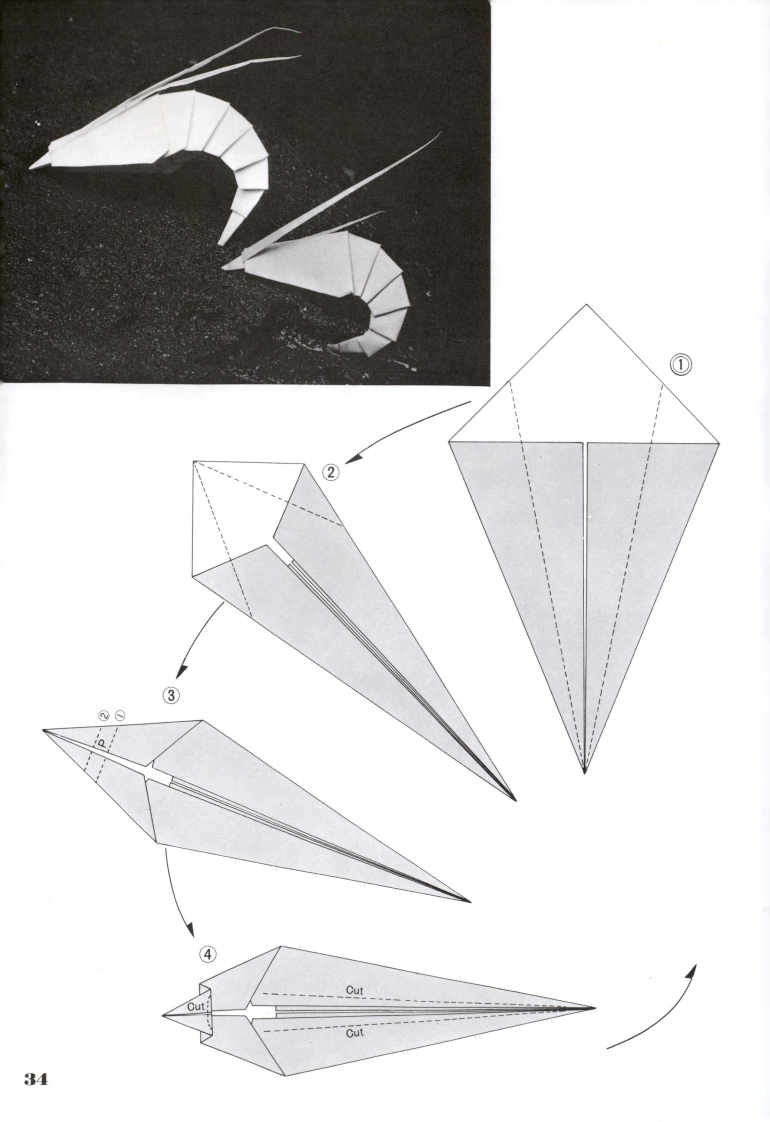

①

②

③

②　①

p

④

Cut

Cut

Cut

34

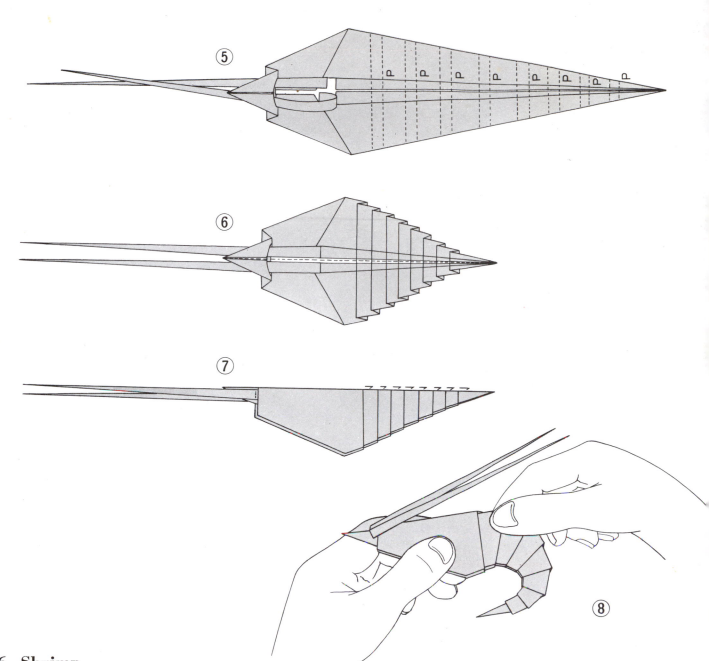

16. Shrimp

Use a six-inch square of red paper.

1. Using the sea-gull base, valley fold on the dotted lines.
2. Valley fold on the dotted lines.
3. Valley and peak fold in numerical order.
4. Cut a slit in the head at the indicated place. Open the model out somewhat for ease, and beginning at the point of the tail section cut (folded layer only) as indicated in the chart to form the antennae.
5. Run the antennae through the slit cut in the head section. Valley and peak fold the tail section.
6. Valley fold on the dotted line running lengthwise the body.
7. Valley fold the antennae on the dotted lines.
8. Hold as you see in the chart, and pull the tail sections out slightly to curve the tail as it is in step 9.
9. The completed shrimp.

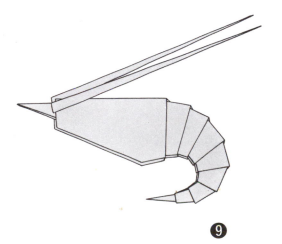

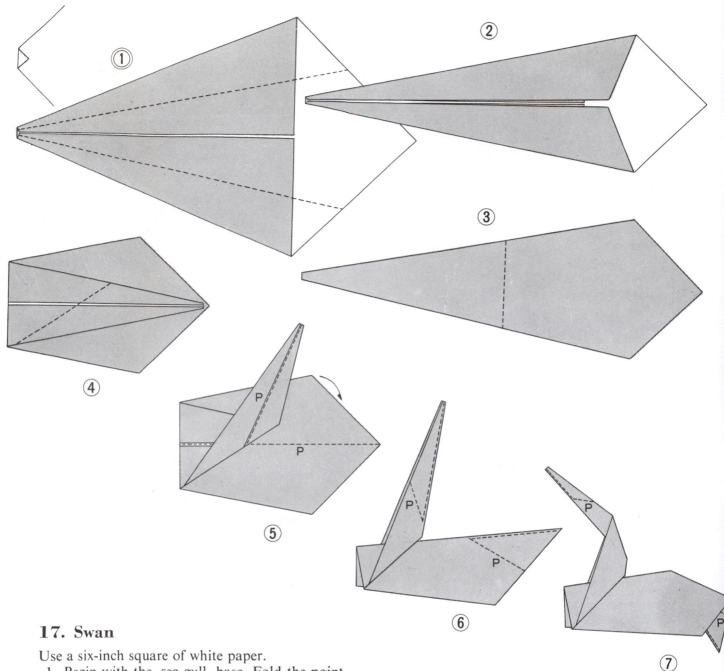

17. Swan

Use a six-inch square of white paper.

1. Begin with the sea-gull base. Fold the point under slightly as you see in the chart. Valley fold on the dotted lines.
2. Invert the model.
3. Valley fold on the dotted line halfway the length of the model.
4. Valley fold on the dotted line.
5. Peak fold on the dotted lines, and the model will naturally assume the proper shape for step 6.
6. Peak and valley fold on the dotted lines in the head and tail, and reverse fold both points outside in.
7. Peak and valley fold on the dotted lines in the tail and head, and reverse fold both points inside out.
8. Peak and valley fold on the dotted lines in the beak, and fold inward. Peak and valley fold the breast in, and reverse fold the point in.
9. The completed swan.

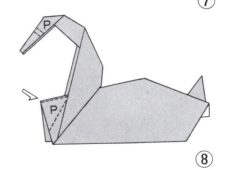

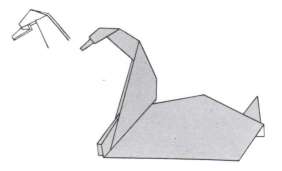

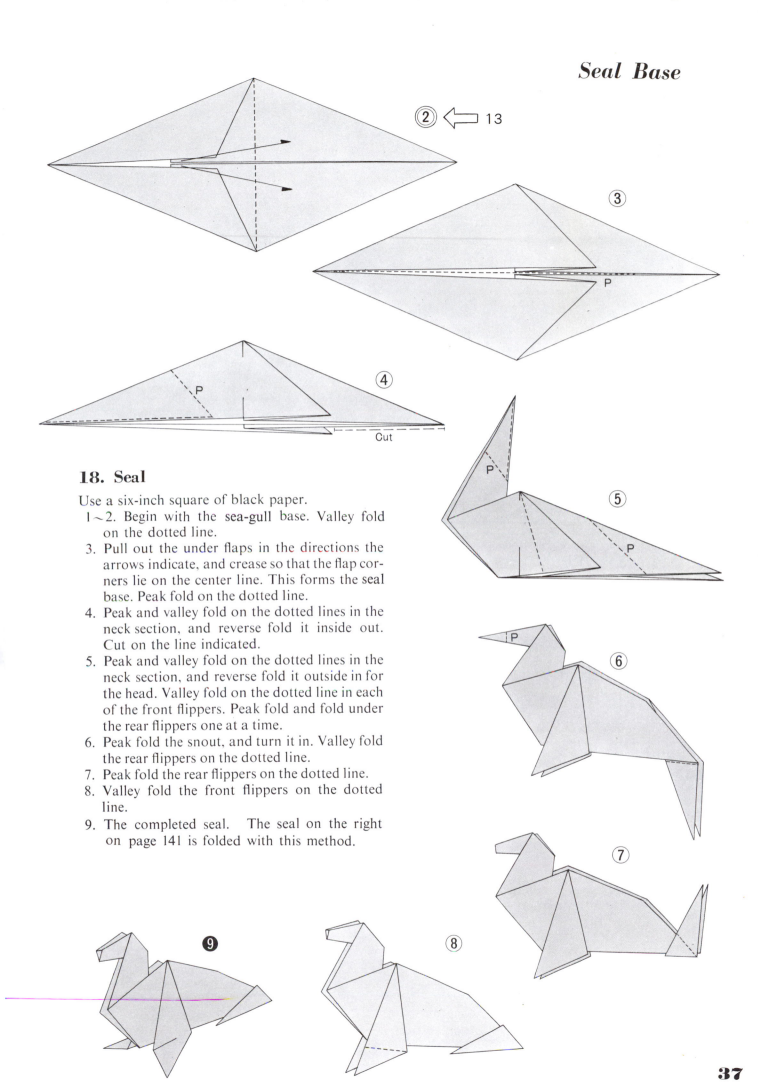

18. Seal

Use a six-inch square of black paper.

1~2. Begin with the **sea-gull** base. Valley fold on the dotted line.

3. Pull out the under flaps in the directions the arrows indicate, and crease so that the flap corners lie on the center line. This forms the seal base. Peak fold on the dotted line.

4. Peak and valley fold on the dotted lines in the neck section, and reverse fold it inside out. Cut on the line indicated.

5. Peak and valley fold on the dotted lines in the neck section, and reverse fold it outside in for the head. Valley fold on the dotted line in each of the front flippers. Peak fold and fold under the rear flippers one at a time.

6. Peak fold the snout, and turn it in. Valley fold the rear flippers on the dotted line.

7. Peak fold the rear flippers on the dotted line.

8. Valley fold the front flippers on the dotted line.

9. The completed seal.   The seal on the right on page 141 is folded with this method.

37

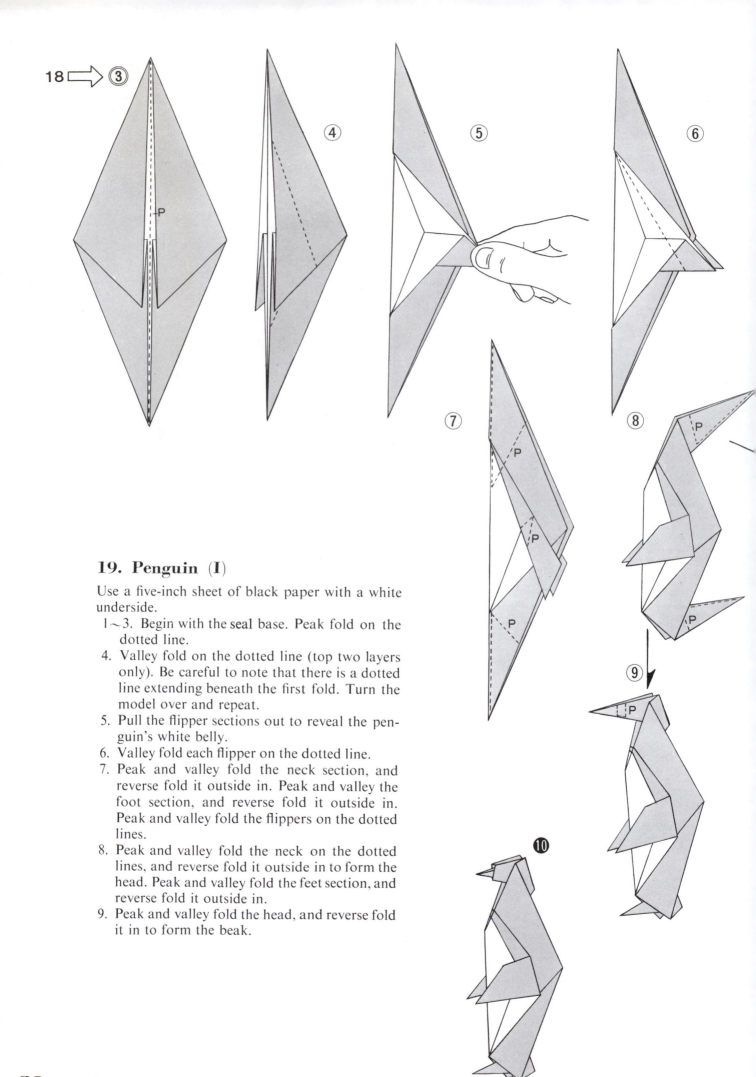

18 ⟹ ③

④ ⑤ ⑥ ⑦ ⑧ ⑨ ⑩

19. Penguin (I)

Use a five-inch sheet of black paper with a white underside.

1~3. Begin with the seal base. Peak fold on the dotted line.

4. Valley fold on the dotted line (top two layers only). Be careful to note that there is a dotted line extending beneath the first fold. Turn the model over and repeat.

5. Pull the flipper sections out to reveal the penguin's white belly.

6. Valley fold each flipper on the dotted line.

7. Peak and valley fold the neck section, and reverse fold it outside in. Peak and valley the foot section, and reverse fold it outside in. Peak and valley fold the flippers on the dotted lines.

8. Peak and valley fold the neck on the dotted lines, and reverse fold it outside in to form the head. Peak and valley fold the feet section, and reverse fold it outside in.

9. Peak and valley fold the head, and reverse fold it in to form the beak.

38

20. Penguin (II)

1~7. Fold as for penguin (I)
    (19) to step 8.
8. Peak and valley fold on the
    dotted lines for a reverse
    fold outside in.
9. Fold the flaps down as the
    arrows indicate.
10. Valley fold on the dotted
    line.
11. Peak and valley fold the
    beak into shape.
12. The completed penguin.

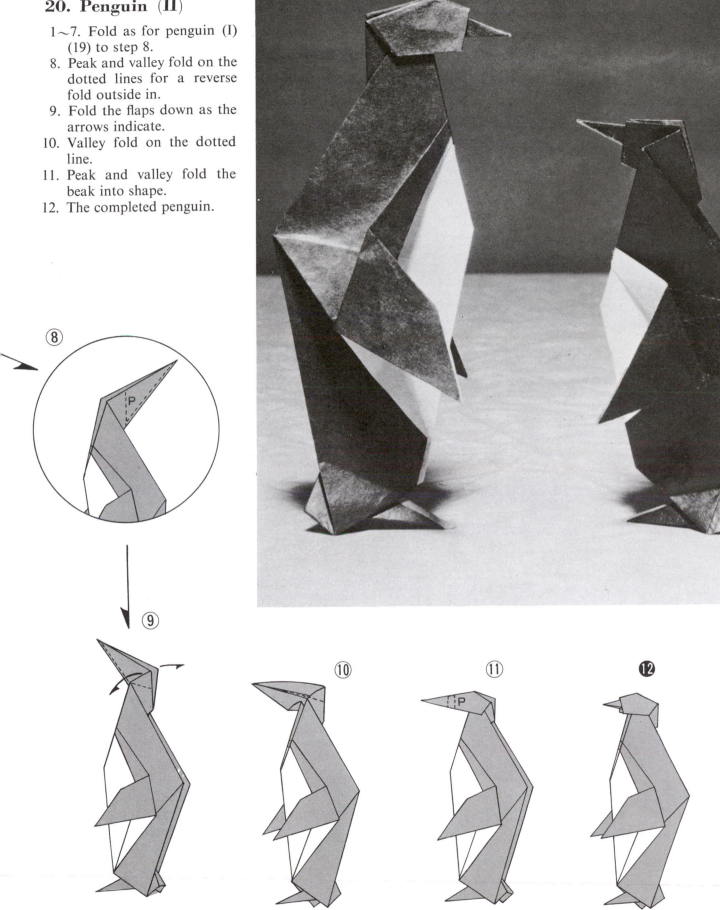

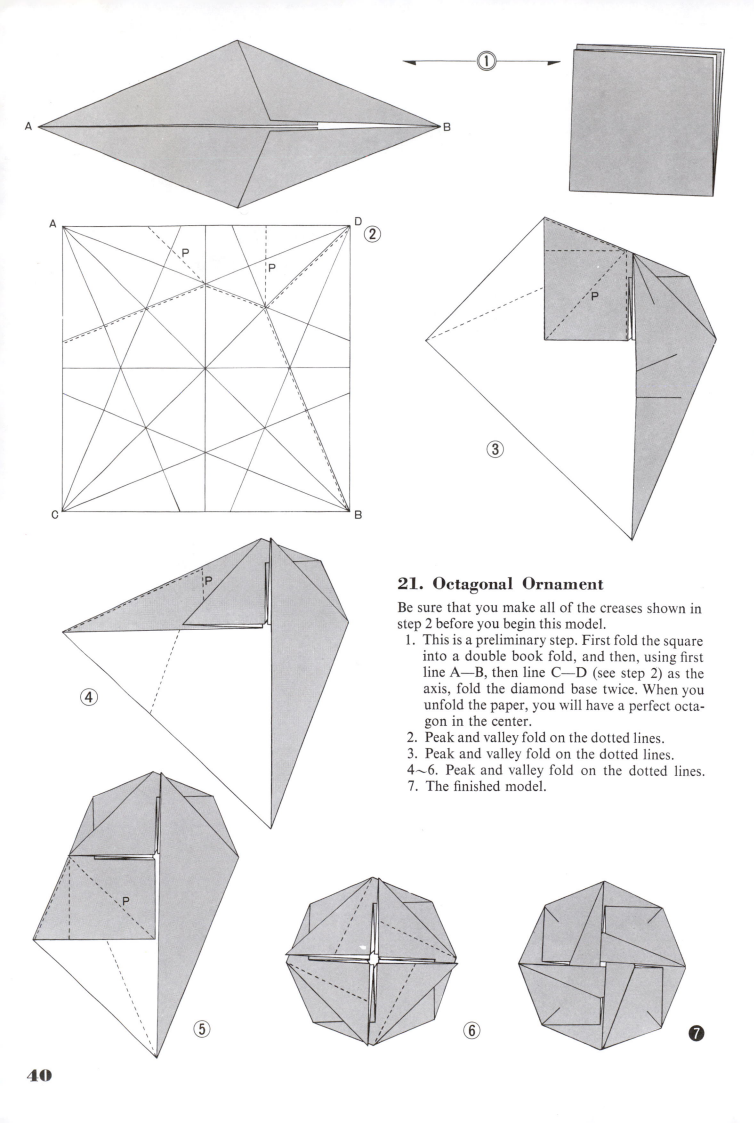

21. Octagonal Ornament

Be sure that you make all of the creases shown in step 2 before you begin this model.

1. This is a preliminary step. First fold the square into a double book fold, and then, using first line A—B, then line C—D (see step 2) as the axis, fold the diamond base twice. When you unfold the paper, you will have a perfect octagon in the center.
2. Peak and valley fold on the dotted lines.
3. Peak and valley fold on the dotted lines.
4~6. Peak and valley fold on the dotted lines.
7. The finished model.

40

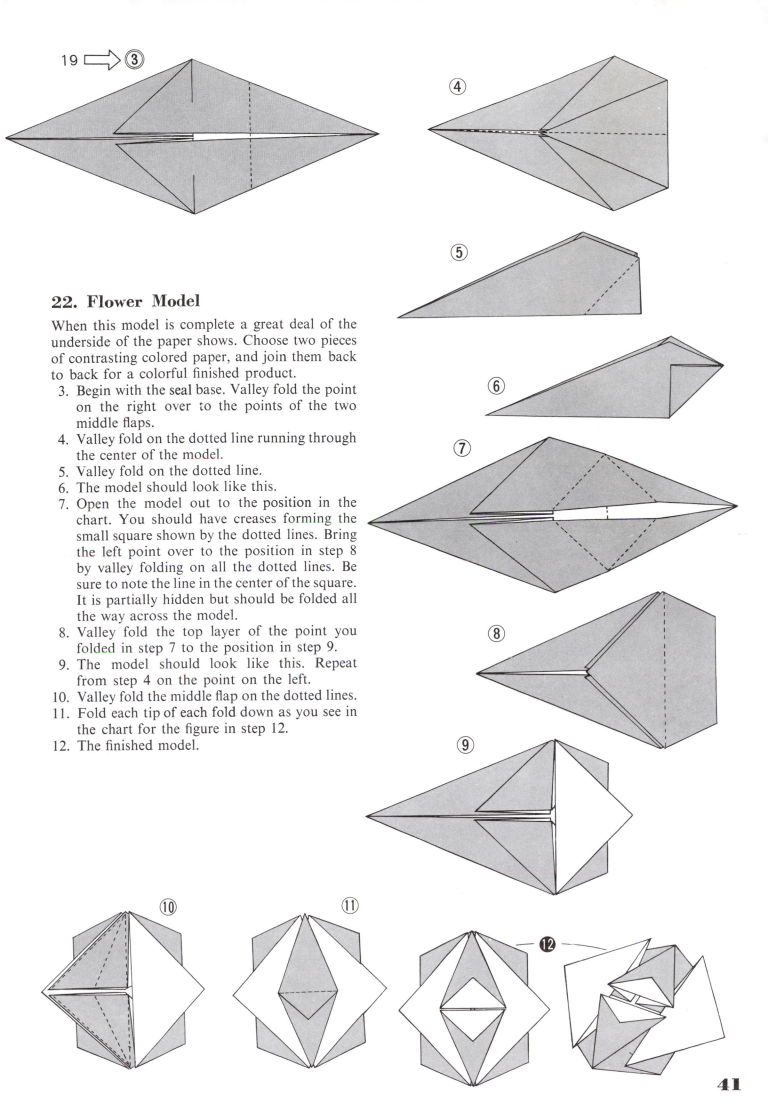

19 ⟹ ③

22. Flower Model

When this model is complete a great deal of the underside of the paper shows. Choose two pieces of contrasting colored paper, and join them back to back for a colorful finished product.

3. Begin with the seal base. Valley fold the point on the right over to the points of the two middle flaps.
4. Valley fold on the dotted line running through the center of the model.
5. Valley fold on the dotted line.
6. The model should look like this.
7. Open the model out to the position in the chart. You should have creases forming the small square shown by the dotted lines. Bring the left point over to the position in step 8 by valley folding on all the dotted lines. Be sure to note the line in the center of the square. It is partially hidden but should be folded all the way across the model.
8. Valley fold the top layer of the point you folded in step 7 to the position in step 9.
9. The model should look like this. Repeat from step 4 on the point on the left.
10. Valley fold the middle flap on the dotted lines.
11. Fold each tip of each fold down as you see in the chart for the figure in step 12.
12. The finished model.

Book Fold

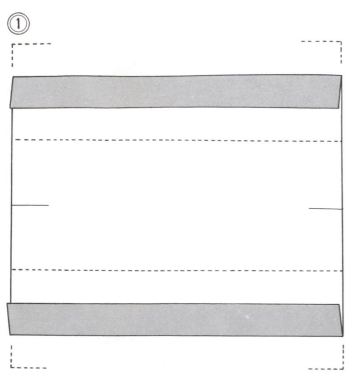

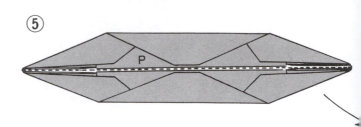

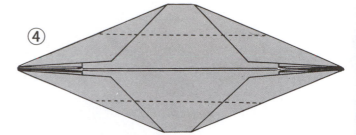

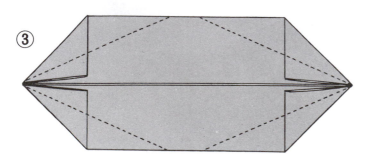

23. Boat

Use a square of waxed paper.

1. Establish the center line by book folding the paper in half. Further divide the paper into quarters by two more book folds parallel to the first. Valley fold the top and bottom quarters in half. Bring the top and bottom folds to the center line and valley fold.
2. Valley fold the four corners (all layers) on the dotted lines.
3. Valley fold on the dotted lines.
4. Valley fold on the dotted lines.
5. Peak fold on the dotted line running the length of the entire model.
6. Spread the boat apart to the position in step 7.
7. Gently turn the boat inside out, peak creasing the fold that runs the length of the model.
8. Step 7 in progress.
9. The finished boat.

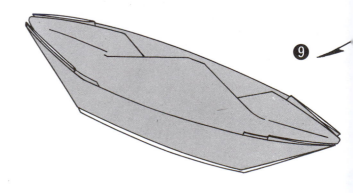

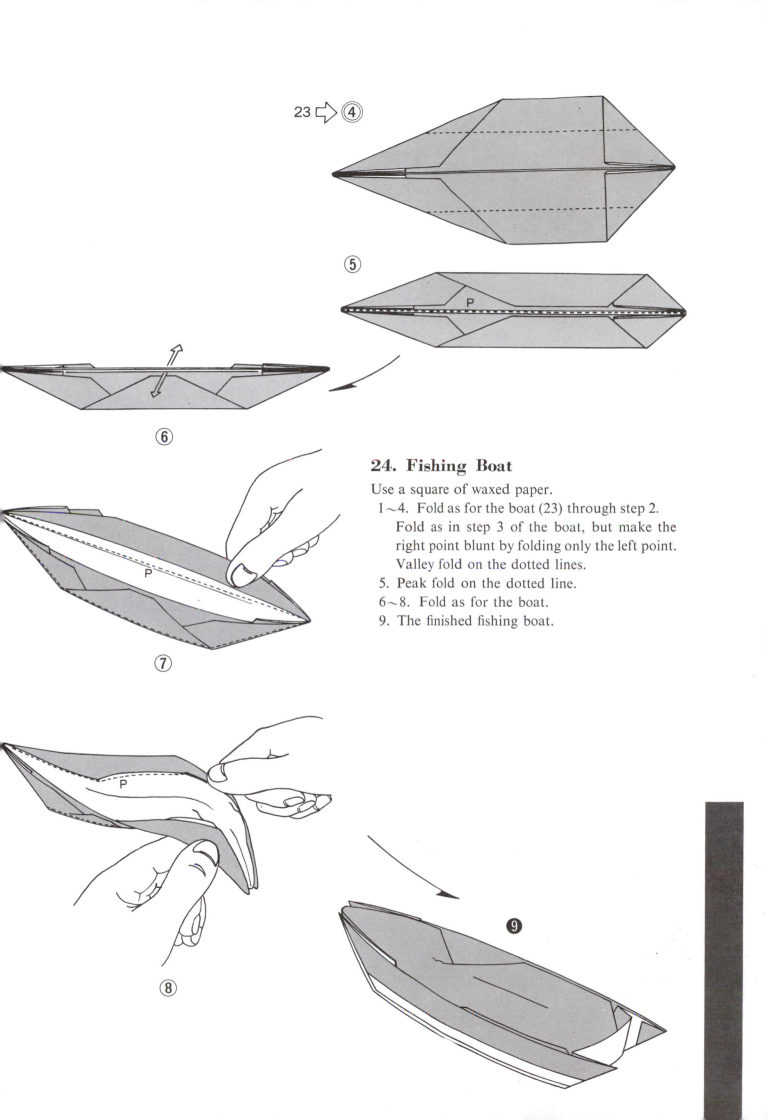

23 ⇨ ④

⑤

⑥

⑦

⑧

❾

24. Fishing Boat

Use a square of waxed paper.

1~4. Fold as for the boat (23) through step 2.
   Fold as in step 3 of the boat, but make the
   right point blunt by folding only the left point.
   Valley fold on the dotted lines.
5. Peak fold on the dotted line.
6~8. Fold as for the boat.
9. The finished fishing boat.

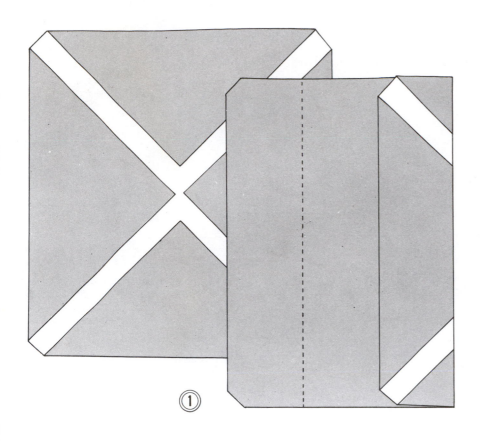

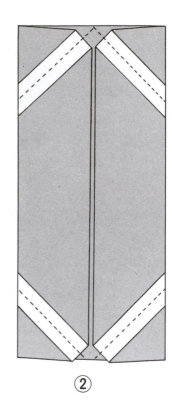

① ②

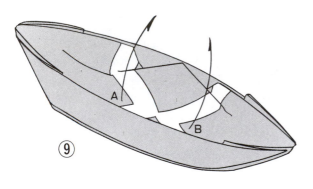

⑨

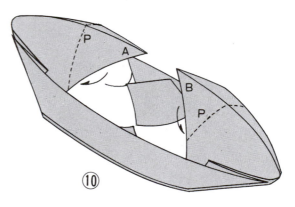

⑩

25. Motorboat

Use a six-inch square of waxed paper.

1. Begin by folding the points of the square in toward, but not to, the center of the paper. Turn the model over, and fold the edges to the center.
2. Valley fold on the dotted lines.
3∼8. Fold as for the boat (23).
9. Lift flaps A and B, and pull them upward.
10. Peak fold on the dotted lines, and tuck the tabs under.
11. The completed motorboat.

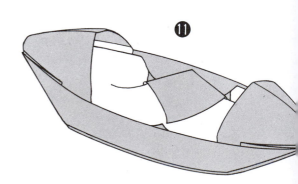

⓫

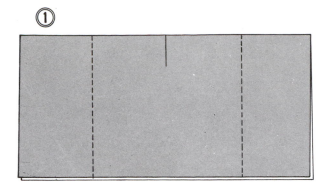

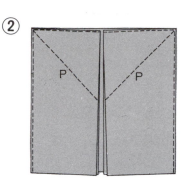

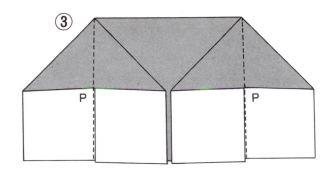

26. Fox Mask

Use a five-inch square of white paper.

1. Book fold the paper in half. Fold the outer edges to the center line.
2. Peak and valley fold on the dotted lines.
3. Open both sides out to the position shown in the chart, and peak fold on the dotted lines.
4. Turn the model into the illustrated position, and valley fold the front flap on the dotted line. Turn the model over and repeat.
5. Valley fold the top flap on the dotted line. Turn the model over, and repeat the fold.
6. Valley fold the top flap on the dotted line. Turn the model over and repeat.
7. Peak fold on the dotted lines, and pull the sides of the mask outward as illustrated.
8. Pull gently until the mask has assumed the proper shape.
9. If you hold the mask with your fingertips as shown, you can make it move its jaws as if it were barking.

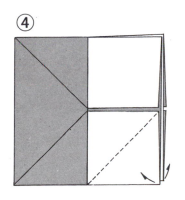

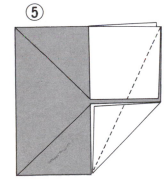

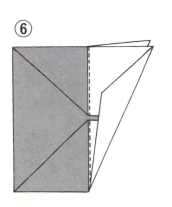

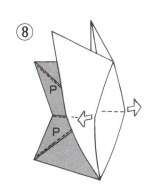

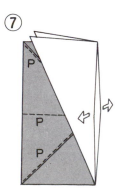

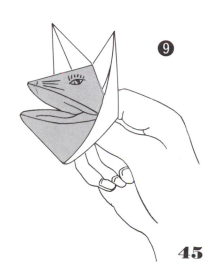

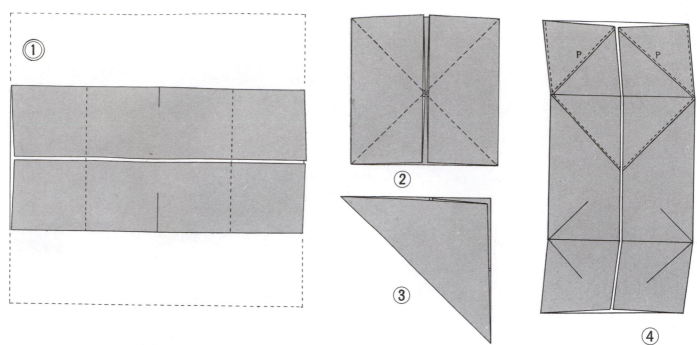

① ② ③ ④

27. Sailboat (II)

Use a five-inch square of paper.
1. Fold the top and bottom edges of the paper to the center. Valley fold on the dotted lines to bring the right and left edges to the vertical center line.
2. Valley fold on the diagonal dotted lines. Crease well.
3. Unfold to the position in the chart.
4. Peak and valley fold on the dotted lines, and open the upper part of the figure to look like step 5.
5. Invert the figure and repeat the process.
6. Valley fold on the dotted line.
7. Fold the top section back, and bend the section that protrudes at the bottom (dotted outline in chart) to make a foot for the boat to stand on.

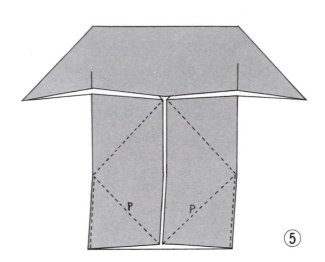

⑤

28. Double Boat

Fold as for the sailboat (27) to step 6. Simply fold the two sections horizontally in half to look like the finished double boat.

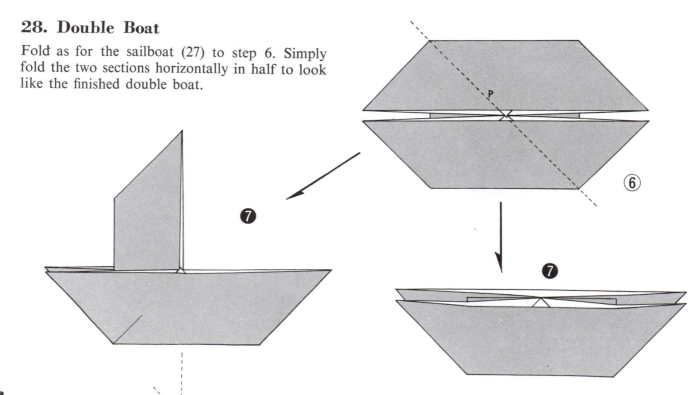

⑥ ❼ ❼

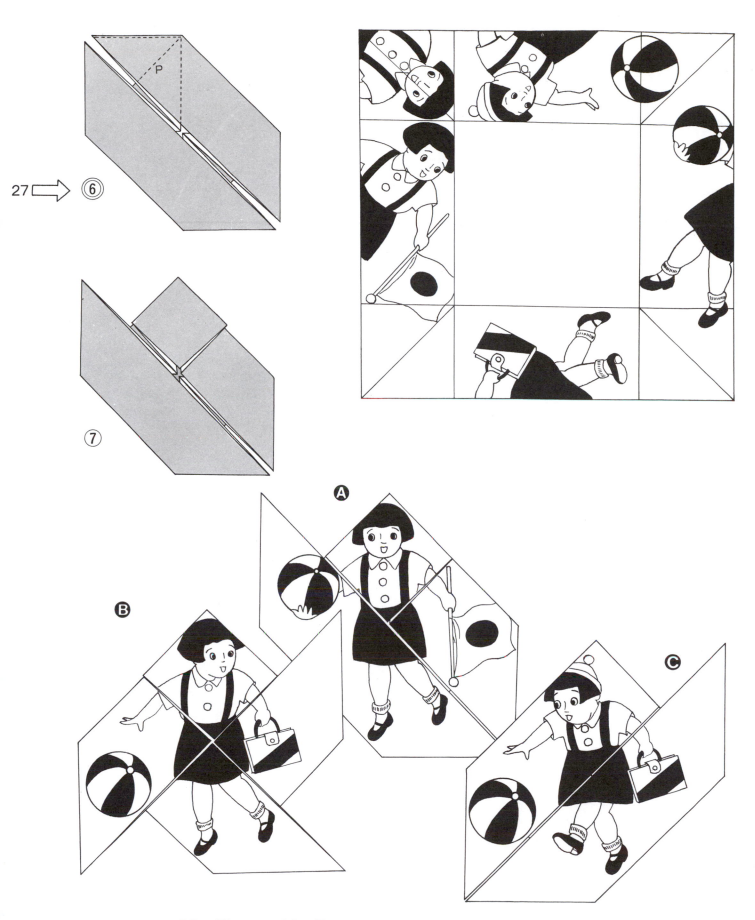

27 ⟹ ⑥

⑦

Ⓐ

Ⓑ

Ⓒ

29. Changeable Picture

Fold as for the double boat (28) to step 6. Peak and valley fold on the dotted lines, and squash the flap square as you see in the chart. Copy the sections of the picture on the paper before you fold it just as you see in the chart. By opening and closing the flaps of the folded model, you can make an origami that will delight your children.

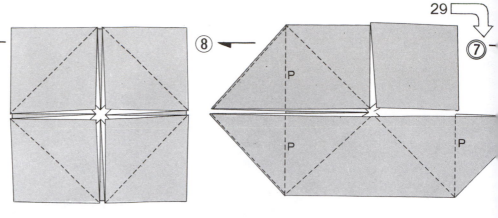

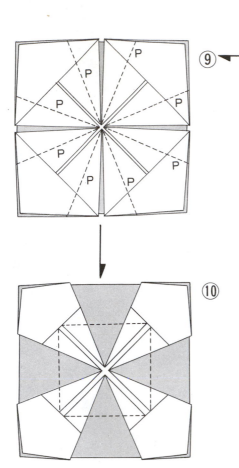

⑨ ←

⑧ ←

29

⑦

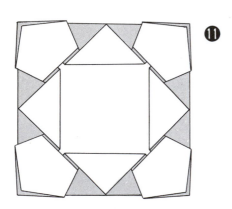

⑩

30. Photograph Frame (I)

Use two six-inch squares of contrasting colored paper lined up back to back.

1~6. Fold as for the changeable picture (29) through step 6.
7. Valley fold on the dotted lines on the edges, and peak fold on the lines indicated, bring the projecting points in to the center, and flatten to form three more squares like the one in the upper right in figure 7.
8. Valley fold on the dotted lines.
9. Peak fold on the dotted lines, and tuck the folded edges under.
10. Valley fold on the dotted lines.
11. The completed picture frame.

31. Photograph Frame (II)

1~7. Fold as for photograph frame (I) through step 7.
8. Valley fold on the dotted lines (two layers).
9. Flatten each of the triangular folds into the position in step 10 by valley folding on the dotted lines.
10. Valley fold each point back on the dotted lines.
11. Valley fold on the dotted lines.
12. The completed photograph frame.

⓫

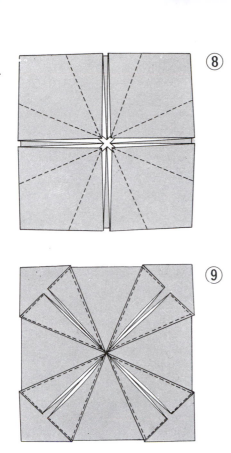

⑧

⑨

⑩

⑪

⑫

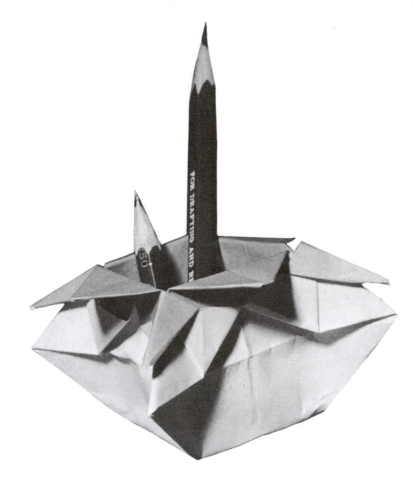

32. Pencil Box

If you take the completed photograph frame (II) and hold it in your left hand, as you see in the chart, and pull each of the corners upward, you can make a box-like model that is good for holding pencils or pens. Pay close attention to the folding method in the preceding three models because the same methods are used in model 42 the Flower-shaped Candy Cup.

⑬

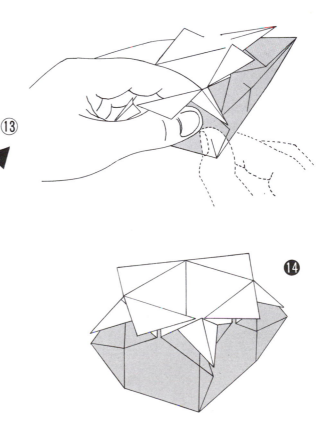

⑭

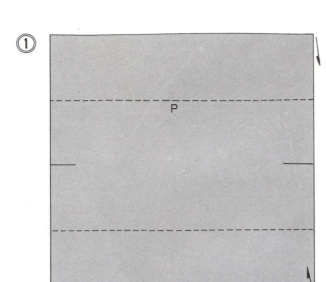

① P

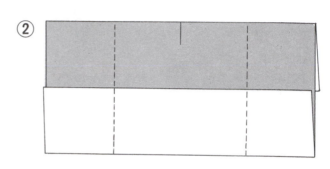

②

33. House

Use a five-inch square of paper.

1~2. Fold as indicated in the chart.
3. Flatten the two squares outward to form two triangles.
4. The front.
5. The back.

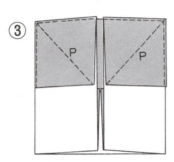

③ P   P

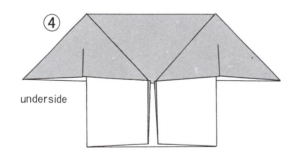

④ underside

⑤ upper side

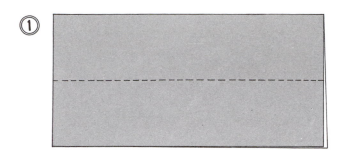

34. Overseas Cap

Use a five-inch square of paper.

1. Book fold the paper horizontally in half, then fold the lower edge of the top layer to the top fold.
2. Valley fold the top layer only in half.
3. The correct shape after the fold in step 2. Turn the model over.
4. Valley fold only the top two layers on the dotted lines.
5. Valley fold on the dotted lines.
6. Valley fold on the dotted lines in numerical order. Tuck the last flap behind the horizontal fold.
7. Tucking the flap in.
8. The finished cap.

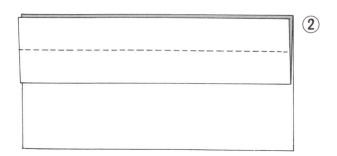

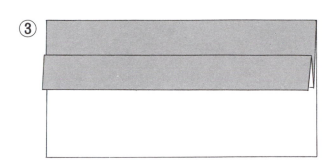

underside

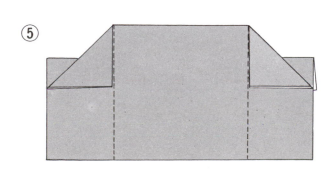

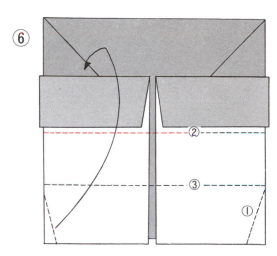

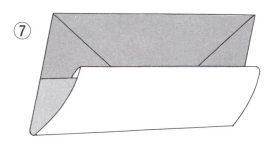

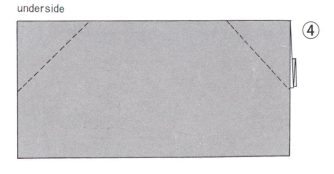

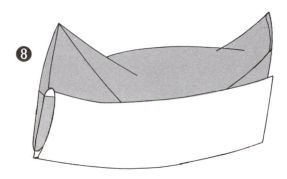

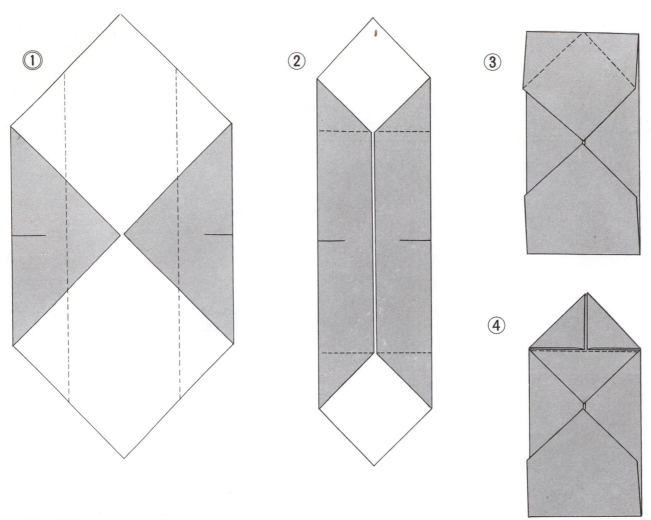

35. Winnowing Box

Use a six-inch square of paper.

1. Fold the points of the paper in as you see in the chart. Establish the center line. Valley fold on the dotted lines.
2. Valley fold on the dotted lines. The points should come to the center.
3. Valley fold all layers on the dotted lines.
4. Valley fold all layers on the dotted line.
5. This is the correct shape after the preceding folds.
6. Open the model out to the shape shown in the chart, and reassemble, peak folding on the dotted line and tucking the flaps in.
7. The completed winnowing box.

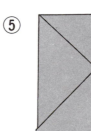

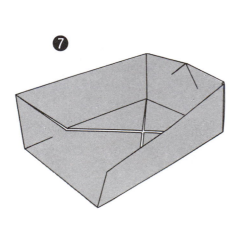

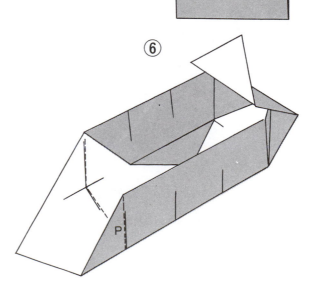

 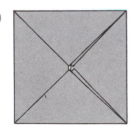 ⑥

⑦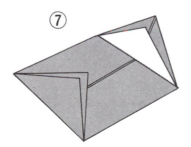

⑧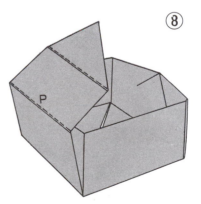

36. Box

(The type used to measure rice in Japan)

1~5. Fold as for the winnowing box (35) through step 5.

6. Repeat the same folds on the bottom of the figure for step 6.

7~8. Open the figure out as you see in these two steps, and peak and valley fold on the indicated dotted lines. Put the right and left points back inside.

9. The finished box.

❾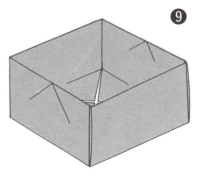

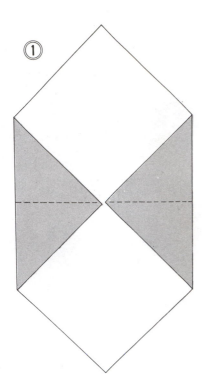

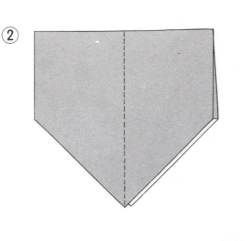

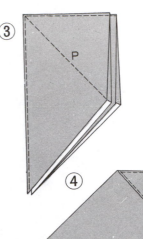

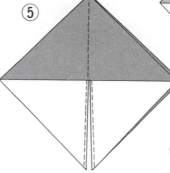

37. Snail

Use a five-inch sheet of pale brown paper with a white underside.

1. Fold the two points of the paper into the center. Valley fold on the dotted line.
2. Valley fold on the dotted line.
3. Peak and valley fold on the indicated lines. Put your fingers in the upper right hand fold, and press so that you form a square like the one in step 4.
4. Turn the model over and repeat the fold.
5. Valley fold on the dotted lines. This is equivalent to putting your fingers between the flaps on the right and left and flattening the figure out to form a solid square.
6. Valley fold on the dotted lines. Turn the model over, and repeat the folds.
7. Valley fold on the indicated lines. Once again, this is equivalent to flattening the figure from the sides, by putting your fingers in the right and left flaps.
8. Peak and valley fold as indicated, and reverse fold to form the head and tail.
9. Cut as indicated. Peak and valley fold, and crimp inward to form the head. Gently valley fold on the dotted lines on the back to give the shell a round appearance.
10. The completed snail. For a photograph of the snail model see the frontispiece.

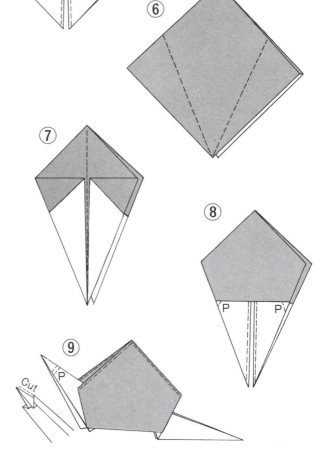

All-corner Fold

38. Lotus Blossom

Use an eight-inch square of strong red paper.

1. Prepare the sheet by folding the corners into the center as seen in the chart. Valley fold on the dotted lines.
2. Valley fold on the dotted lines.
3. The proper shape after the preceding folds. Turn the model over.
4. Valley fold on the dotted lines.
5. Hold the figure with your left hand, as you see in the chart, and fold the points from the underside to the top with the fingers of your right hand.
6. The process of bringing the petals around from bottom to top.
7. The completed blossom.

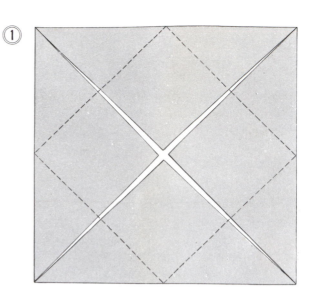

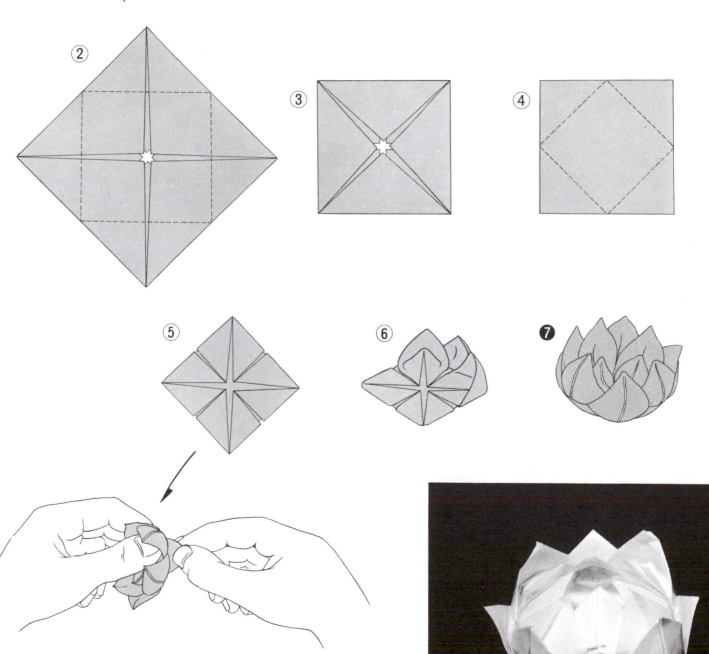

39. Pinwheel

Use a five-inch sheet of red paper.

1. Prepare the paper by folding the points into the center, as you see in the chart. Turn the model over.
2. Valley fold on the dotted lines.
3. Valley fold on the dotted lines.
4. Peak fold on the dotted lines.
5. Pull points A and B out to the positions indicated by the dotted lines.
6. Turn the model over.
7. Pull points C and D out to the positions indicated by the dotted lines.
8. The finished model. Attach the wheel to a stick with a straight pin, and it will whirl in the wind.

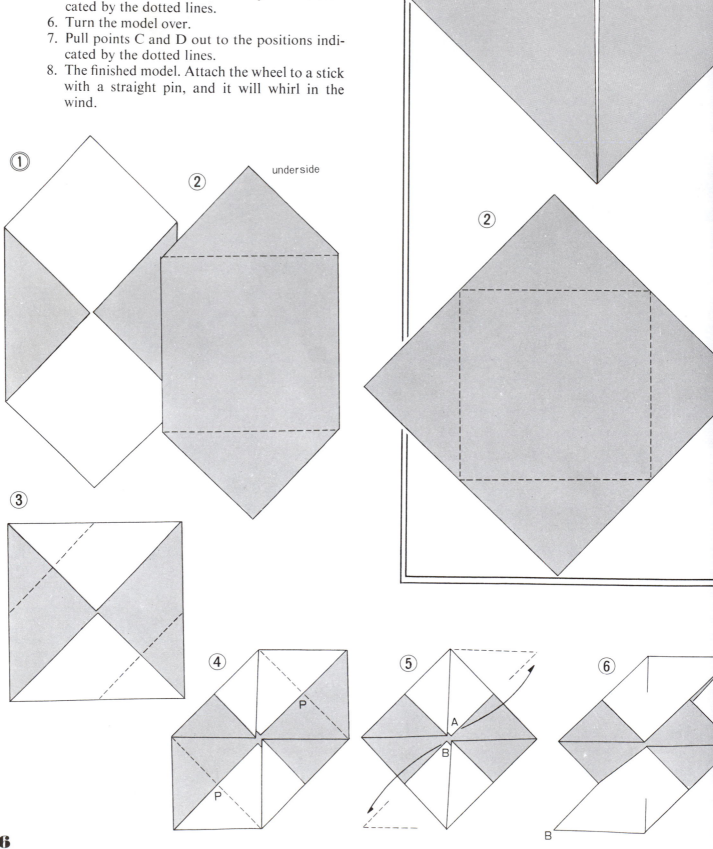

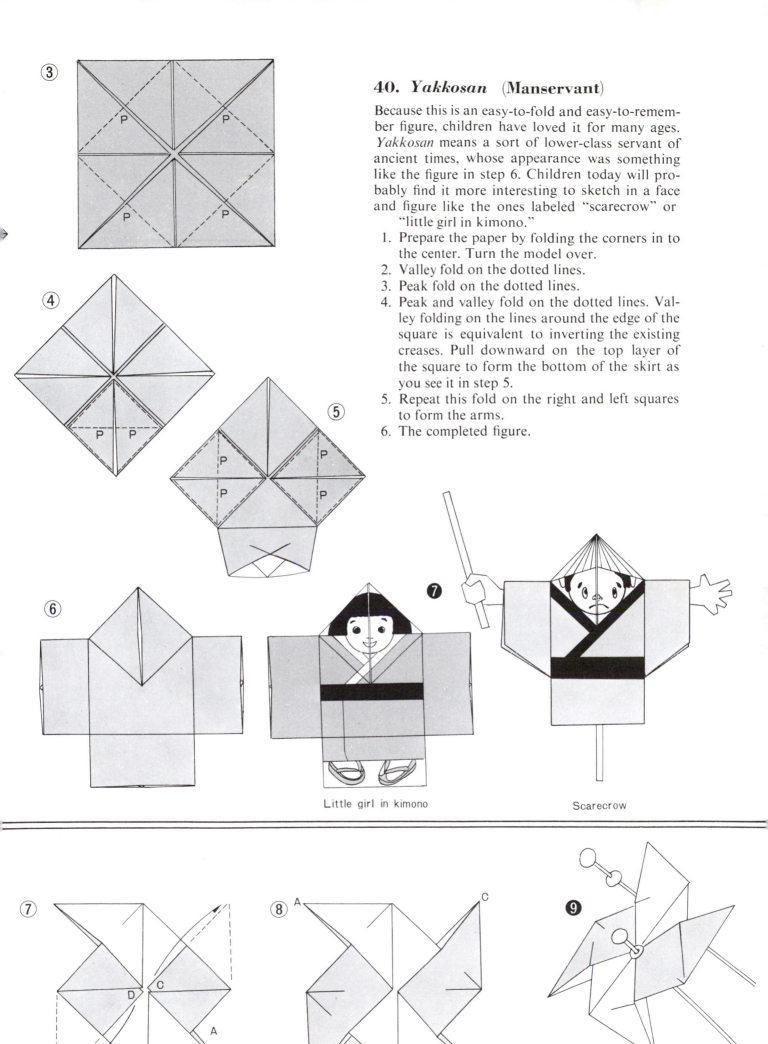

40. *Yakkosan* (Manservant)

Because this is an easy-to-fold and easy-to-remember figure, children have loved it for many ages. *Yakkosan* means a sort of lower-class servant of ancient times, whose appearance was something like the figure in step 6. Children today will probably find it more interesting to sketch in a face and figure like the ones labeled "scarecrow" or "little girl in kimono."

1. Prepare the paper by folding the corners in to the center. Turn the model over.
2. Valley fold on the dotted lines.
3. Peak fold on the dotted lines.
4. Peak and valley fold on the dotted lines. Valley folding on the lines around the edge of the square is equivalent to inverting the existing creases. Pull downward on the top layer of the square to form the bottom of the skirt as you see it in step 5.
5. Repeat this fold on the right and left squares to form the arms.
6. The completed figure.

Little girl in kimono

Scarecrow

57

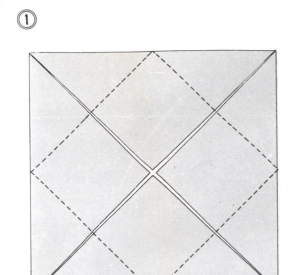

①

②

③ underside

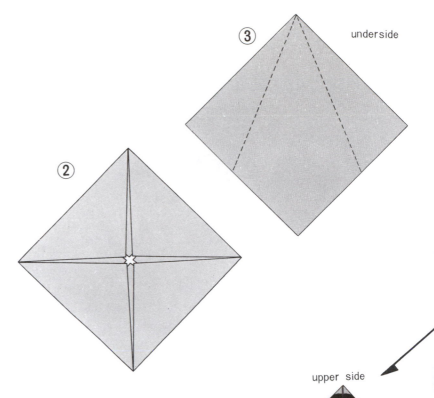

upper side

Ⓐ

41. Picture Forms

By using this folding method, you can create forms that suggest various picture contents. The model in the upper right corner is an example of a very old picture form. The four pictures at the bottom represent more modernized versions. The three-flower model at the bottom of the page is the reverse of the model showing the ship Santa Maria. If you fold the three-flower model into the shape in A you can make a single-flower model. Use a six-inch square of paper.

1. Prepare the paper by folding the corners in to the center. Valley fold on the dotted lines.
2. Turn the model over.
3. Valley fold on the dotted lines. Open the top flaps only out to form a square at the top of the figure as you see in step 4.
4. Valley fold on the dotted line. Let the point in the rear spring naturally upward to form the pointed top of step 5.
5. Peak fold on the dotted line.
   The picture of the little girl will fit into the model in step 4. Invert the same model, and turn it over. The woman with the basket will fit into it. Fold the model into the shape in C for space to draw the Santa Maria. Open the model completely out to the shape for the three flowers.

Ⓐ

④

⑤

P

⑥

underside

Ⓑ

⑤

Ⓒ

59

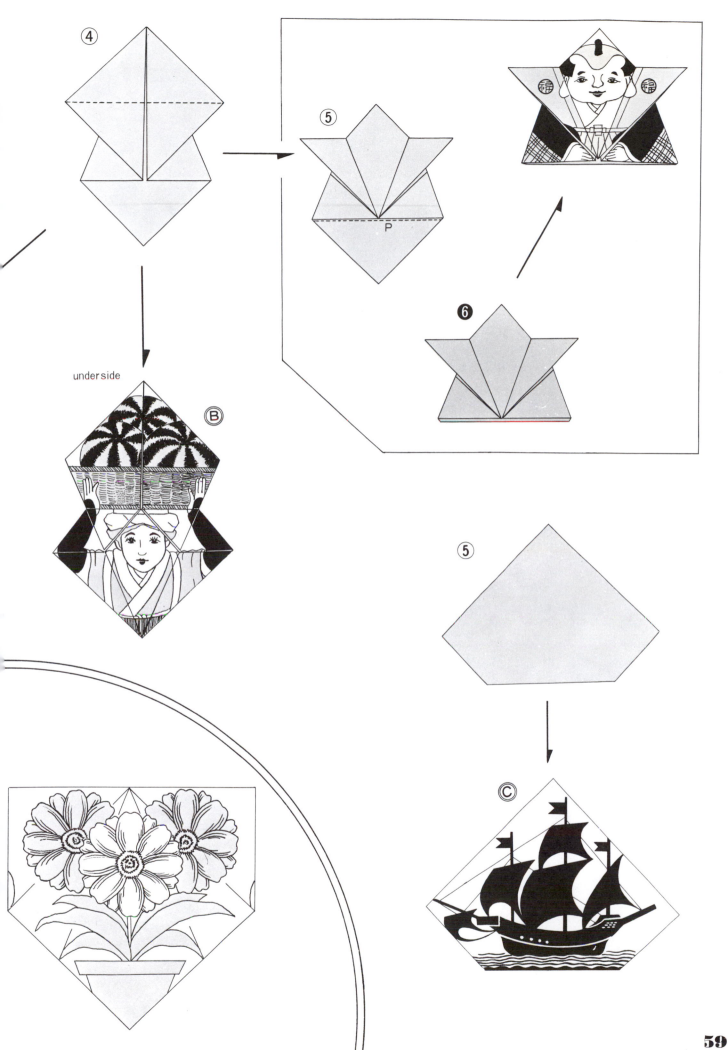

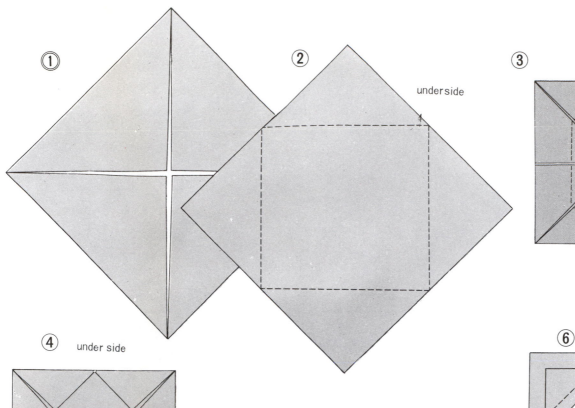

① ② ③ underside

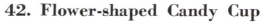

④ under side

⑤ upper side

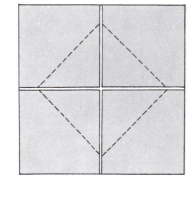

42. Flower-shaped Candy Cup

Use a six-inch square of paper.

1. Prepare the paper by folding the corners in to the center. Turn the model over.
2. Valley fold on the dotted lines.
3. Valley fold the points of the top flaps on the dotted lines.
4. The model should now look like this. Turn it over.
5. Valley fold the points of the flaps, as you see in the chart, towards the edges of the model but not to them.
6. Valley fold on the dotted lines.
7. Peak and valley fold as indicated.
8. Hold the model as shown, and with the fingertips of your right hand pinch the lower area of the corners firmly together, one by one, to form the cup.
9. The finished cup.

⑥ upper side

⑦ upper side

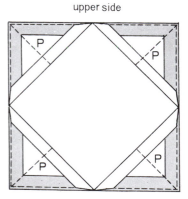

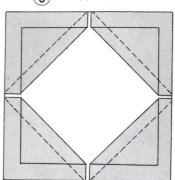

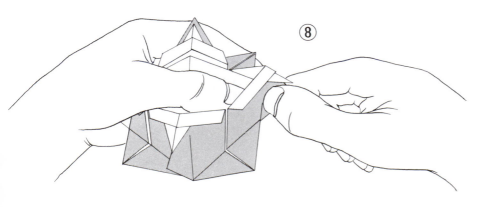

⑧

❾

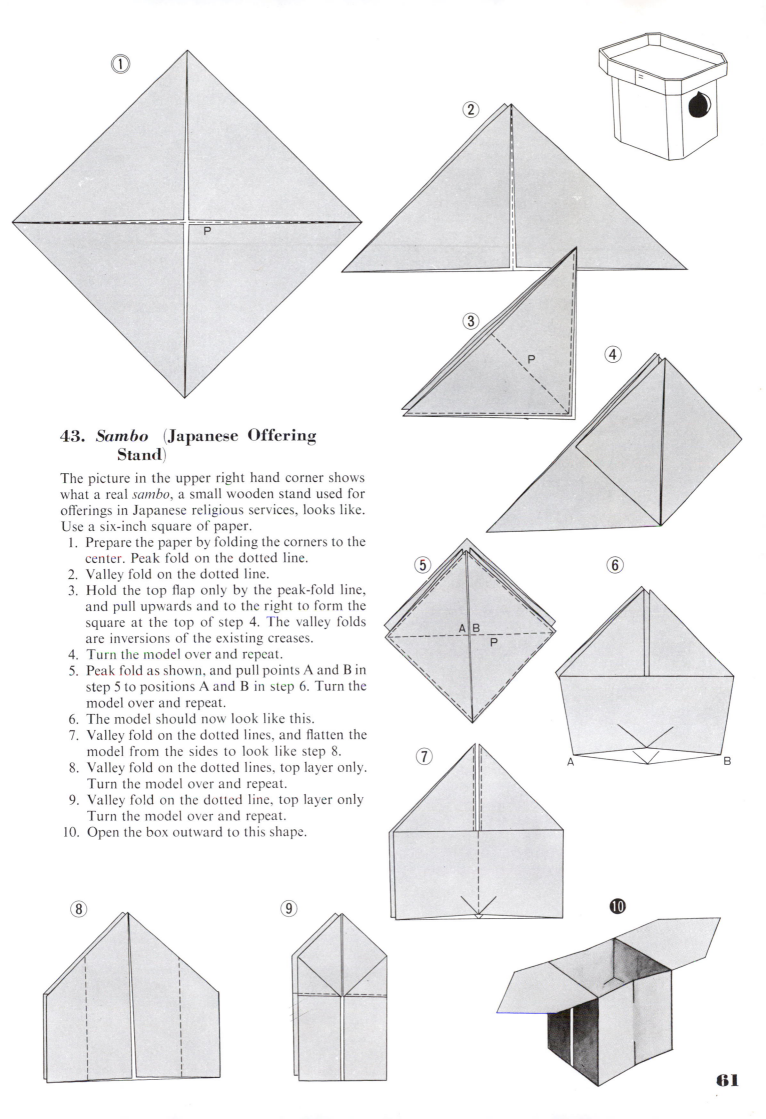

43. *Sambo* (Japanese Offering Stand)

The picture in the upper right hand corner shows what a real *sambo*, a small wooden stand used for offerings in Japanese religious services, looks like. Use a six-inch square of paper.

1. Prepare the paper by folding the corners to the center. Peak fold on the dotted line.
2. Valley fold on the dotted line.
3. Hold the top flap only by the peak-fold line, and pull upwards and to the right to form the square at the top of step 4. The valley folds are inversions of the existing creases.
4. Turn the model over and repeat.
5. Peak fold as shown, and pull points A and B in step 5 to positions A and B in step 6. Turn the model over and repeat.
6. The model should now look like this.
7. Valley fold on the dotted lines, and flatten the model from the sides to look like step 8.
8. Valley fold on the dotted lines, top layer only. Turn the model over and repeat.
9. Valley fold on the dotted line, top layer only Turn the model over and repeat.
10. Open the box outward to this shape.

61

44. *Sambo* on Legs

Use a six-inch square of paper.

1~6. Fold as for the *sambo* (43) through step 6.
7. Peak and valley fold on the dotted lines to open and flatten the top layer only as you see in step 8. Turn the model over and repeat.
8. Valley fold on the dotted line, and flatten the model from the sides to form step 9.
9. Valley fold on the dotted line, top layer only. Turn the model over and repeat.
10. Valley fold on the dotted lines, top layer only. Turn the model over and repeat.
11. Valley fold on the dotted lines, top layer only. Turn the model over and repeat.
12. Open the box out for the finished model.

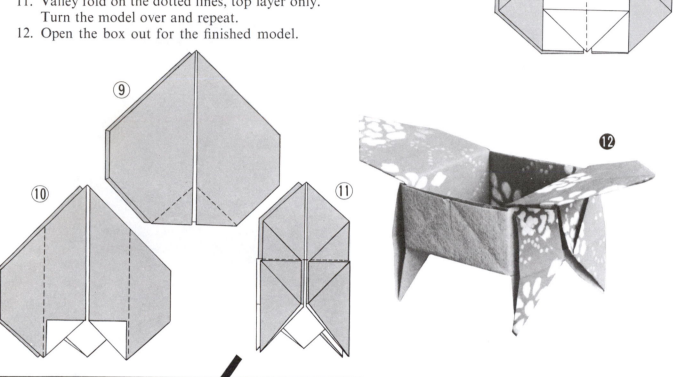

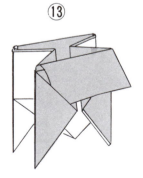

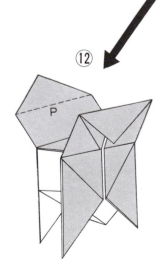

45. Cake Dish

1~11. Fold as for a *sambo* on legs (44) through step 11.
12. Peak fold both flaps on the dotted lines.
13. Tuck the folded flaps into the triangular pockets on the ends of the model.
14. The finished model.

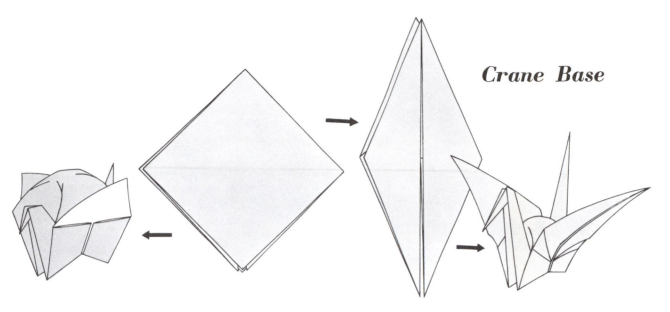

Crane Base

The crane base and the basic folds and forms you see that follow from it are the most important basic folds in origami because practically all animal and bird figures use them. If the Japanese people hadn't invented this basic fold, origami itself would doubtless never have come into being. Practice this fold until you have mastered it. You will then be ready to proceed to enjoy the more difficult origami folding techniques.

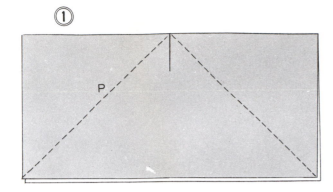

46. Crane Base (I)

Use a six-inch square of paper.

1. Book fold the sheet in half horizontally. Peak and valley fold on the dotted lines (two layers).
2. Peak and valley fold on the dotted lines. The valley folds are inversions of existing creases.
3. Pull at the places and in the directions the arrows indicate to form the square shown in step 4.
4. Valley fold on the dotted lines in numerical order, top two layers only in the case of fold 1.
5. The model should look like this.
6. Pull the bottom point up to the position indicated by the dotted lines. All indicated folds are inversions of existing creases.
7. Invert the folds made in step 5 as indicated. Pull the bottom point to the position shown by the dotted lines above the figure.
8. Reverse fold the remaining flaps at the bottom inside for the completed crane base.

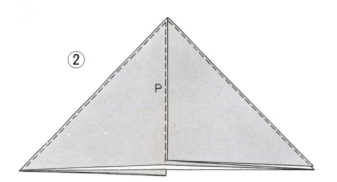

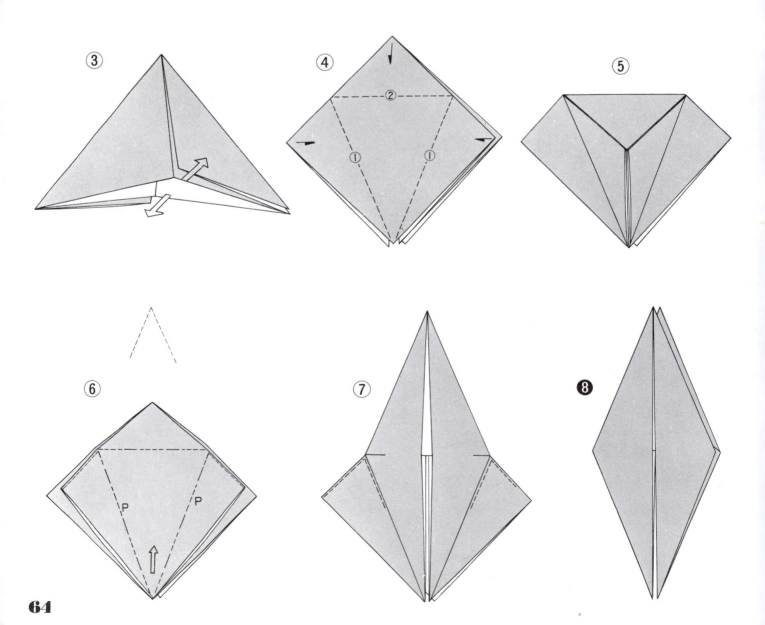

64

47. Crane Base (II)

Use a six-inch square of paper.

1. Prepare the paper by folding it diagonally in half. Valley fold on the dotted line.
2. Valley and peak fold on the dotted lines, and bring the top layer point at the far right down to the bottom point to form the square you see in step 3.
3. Turn the model over and repeat.
4. Valley fold the top layer only on the dotted line.
5. Valley fold the upper layers only on the dotted line.
6. Peak fold the bottom layers around to the rear on the dotted line.
7. Valley fold all layers on the dotted line.
8. The model should look like this. Open it out again to the position in step 7.
9. Take the top layer only of the top point in your fingers, and pull it up into the position in the chart. Turn the model over and repeat.
10. The finished crane base.

Note: Both crane bases are the same figures folded different ways.

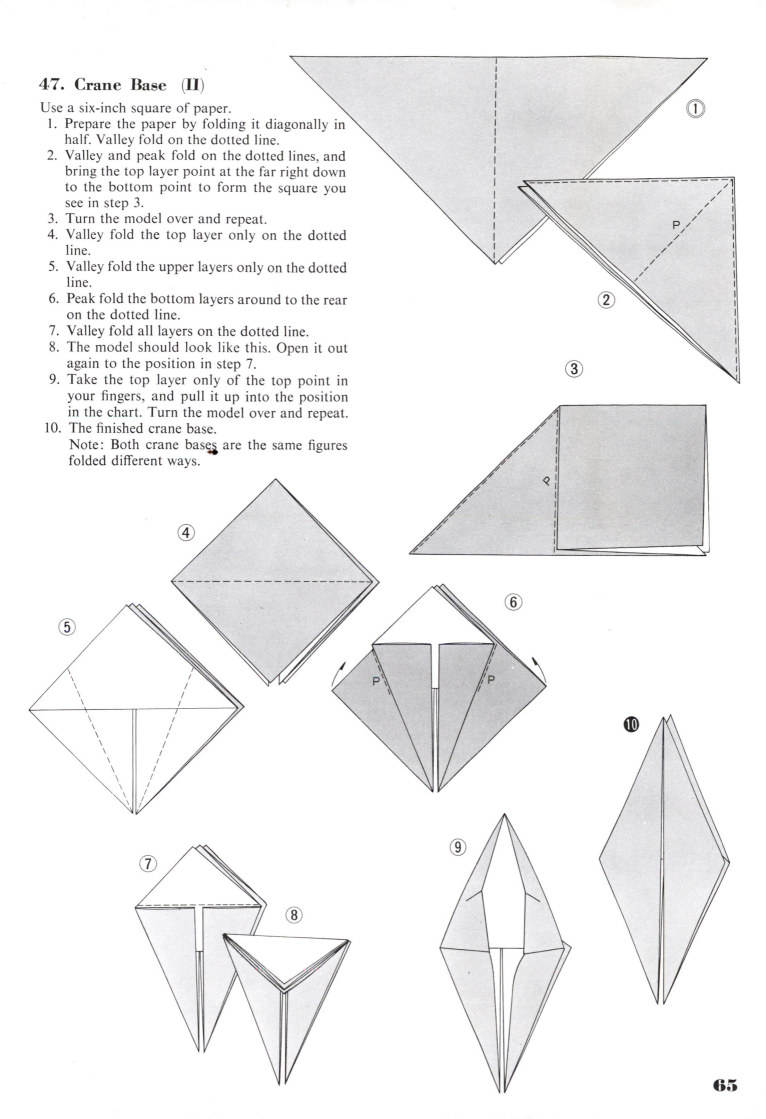

65

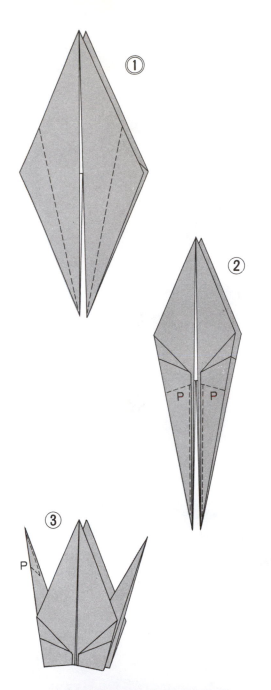

① ②

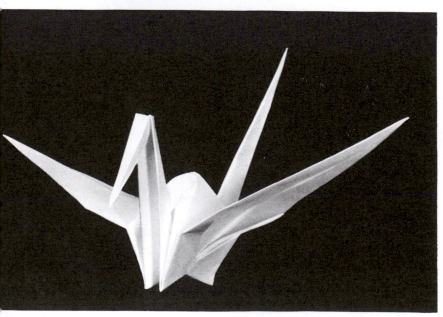

③

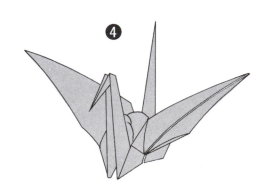

❹

48. Crane

Use a six-inch square of paper.

1. Begin with the crane base. Valley fold on the dotted lines, top layer only. Turn the model over and repeat.
2. Reverse fold the tail and neck sections outside in.
3. Reverse fold the neck section outside in to form the head.
4. Bend the wings into proper position for the completed crane.

Folds from the Various Stages of the Crane Base

1. Origami from the Square Base

We call step 4 in folding the crane the square base. From that form we can make the following origami:

    49. Small Star-shaped Box
    50. Morning Glory
    51. Cake Box

2. Origami from the Crane Base

The basic form (A) we are calling the crane base is acutally rhombic in shape, but since it is not a regular rhombus as is the paper shape we use in section two of this book, we are calling it "crane."

Folding methods using this base fall into five categories, A-E in the chart.

Folds from the Various Stages of the Crane Base

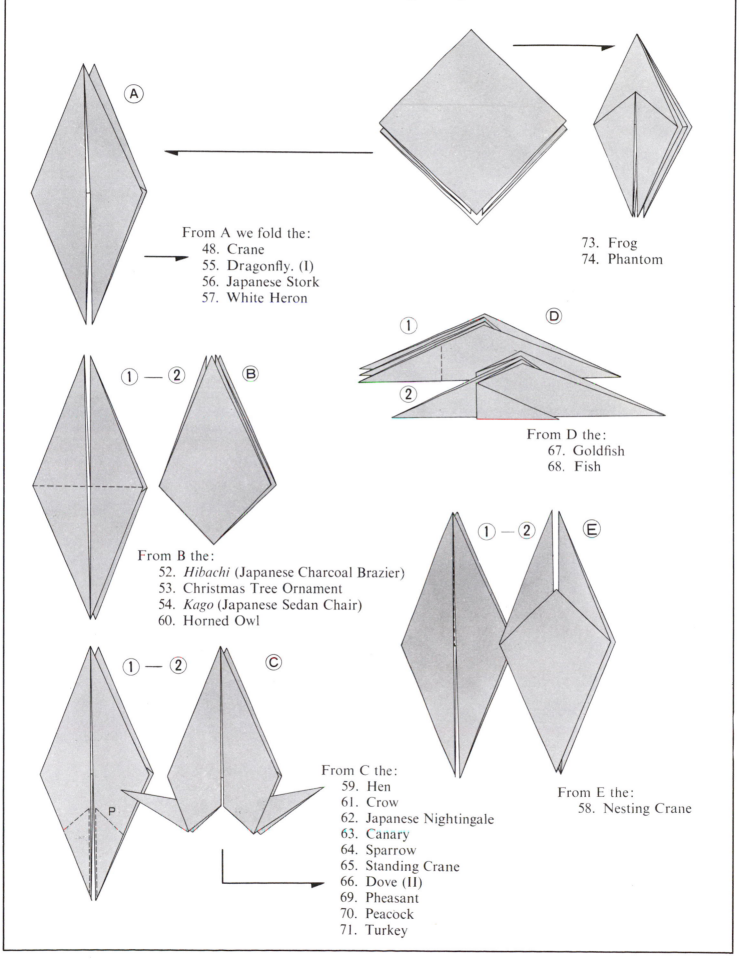

(A)

From A we fold the:
48. Crane
55. Dragonfly. (I)
56. Japanese Stork
57. White Heron

73. Frog
74. Phantom

① — ② (B)

From B the:
52. *Hibachi* (Japanese Charcoal Brazier)
53. Christmas Tree Ornament
54. *Kago* (Japanese Sedan Chair)
60. Horned Owl

① (D)
②

From D the:
67. Goldfish
68. Fish

① — ② (E)

From E the:
58. Nesting Crane

① — ② (C)

P

From C the:
59. Hen
61. Crow
62. Japanese Nightingale
63. Canary
64. Sparrow
65. Standing Crane
66. Dove (II)
69. Pheasant
70. Peacock
71. Turkey

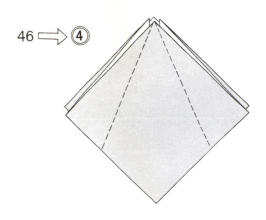

46 ⟹ ④

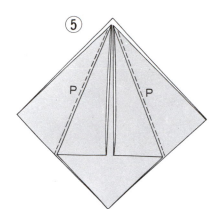

⑤

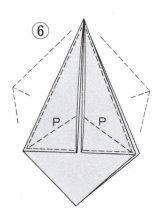

⑥

⑦

49. Star-shaped Box

Use a five-inch square of paper.

1~4. Begin with step 4 of the crane base. Valley fold on the dotted lines, top flap only.

5. Peak fold the remaining flap on the dotted lines.

6. Peak and valley fold on the dotted lines, and squash the top flaps out to the position indicated by the dotted lines outside the figure.

7. Turn the figure over and repeat. Valley fold on the dotted lines, top flaps only. Turn the model over and repeat.

8. Valley fold on the dotted lines, the top flaps only. Turn the model over and repeat.

9. Valley fold on the dotted line. Turn the model over and repeat.

10. Peak and valley fold on the dotted lines. The peak fold is a new crease. The valley folds are inversions of existing creases, and the entire process is equivalent to pushing the bottom point upward to form a flat bottom for the box.

11. Fold the two remaining flaps to form the star-shaped box.

⑧

⑨

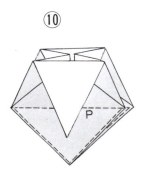

⑩

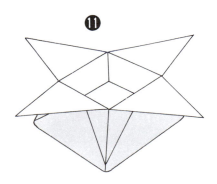

⑪

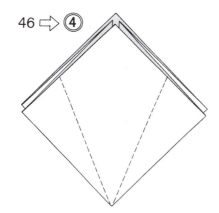

46 ⇨ ④

50. Morning Glory

Use a five-inch sheet of blue, red, or purple paper with a lighter underside. The darker side goes inside.

1~4. Start with step 4 of the crane base. Valley fold on the dotted lines, top flaps only.
5. The figure should look like this. Turn it over, and repeat the first fold.
6. Pull points A and B out and down as you see in the chart.
7. The process of pulling the flaps out and down.
8. Valley fold on the dotted lines.
9. Cut on the indicated line.
10. Flatten the figure to its original position.
11. Valley fold the top flap only on the dotted line.
12. The finished flower.

⑤

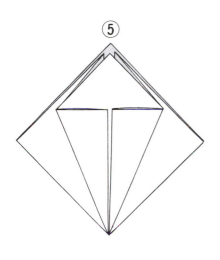

⑥

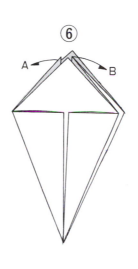

A ⟵   ⟶ B

⑦

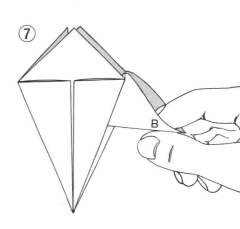

B

⑧

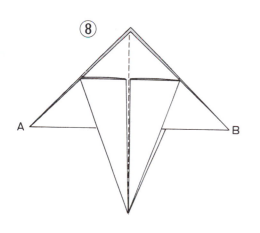

A   B

⑪

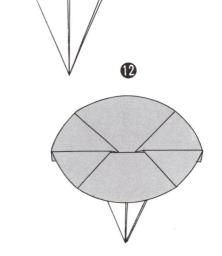

⑩

⑨

Cut

⑫

69

④

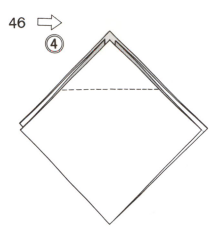

51. Cake Box

Use a five-inch sheet of colored paper with the colored side inside.

  1~4. Begin with step 4 of the crane base. Valley fold the top flap only on the dotted line. Turn the model over and repeat.

  5. Valley fold the top flap only on the dotted line. Turn the model over and repeat.

  6. Flatten the model from the sides by valley folding on the dotted lines.

  7. Valley fold the top flap only on the dotted lines in numerical order.

  8. The model should look like this. Turn it over and repeat.

  9. Valley fold on the dotted lines in numerical order. Turn the model over and repeat.

  10. Tuck the bottom flaps under the existing folds, and push the bottom point upward to form a flat box bottom. This will be easier if you peak fold on the dotted line, then turn the model over and peak fold again on the same line.

  11. The finished box.

⑤

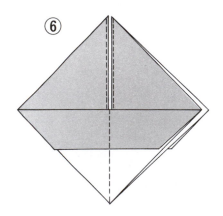

⑥

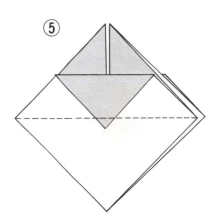

⑦

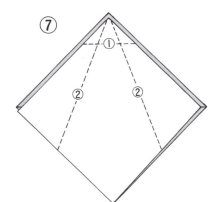

⑧

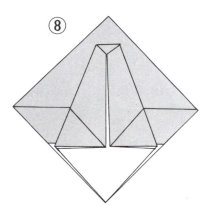

⑨

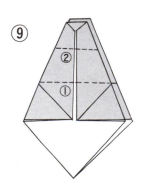

⑩

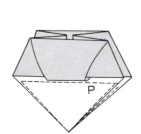

⓫

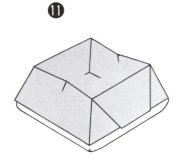

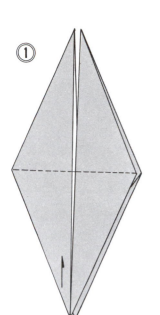

①

②

52. *Hibachi* (Japanese Charcoal Brazier)

Use a six-inch square of paper.

1. Begin with the completed crane base. Valley fold the top flap only on the dotted line. Turn the model over and repeat.
2. Valley fold on the dotted line, top flap only. The top point should meet the bottom point. Turn the model over and repeat.
3. Flatten the model from the sides by valley folding on the dotted lines.
4. Valley fold on the dotted lines, the top flap only. Turn the model over and repeat.
5. Peak fold the top flaps only on the dotted line.
6. Continue around the model peak folding all of the top flaps on the line indicated in step 5.
7. Push the bottom point upward to form the bottom of the brazier. Leave the four pointed legs as a stand.
8. The finished *hibachi*.

③

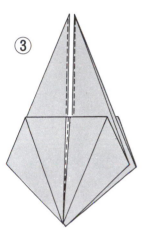

④

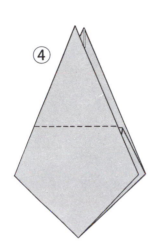

⑤

⑥

⑦

❽

71

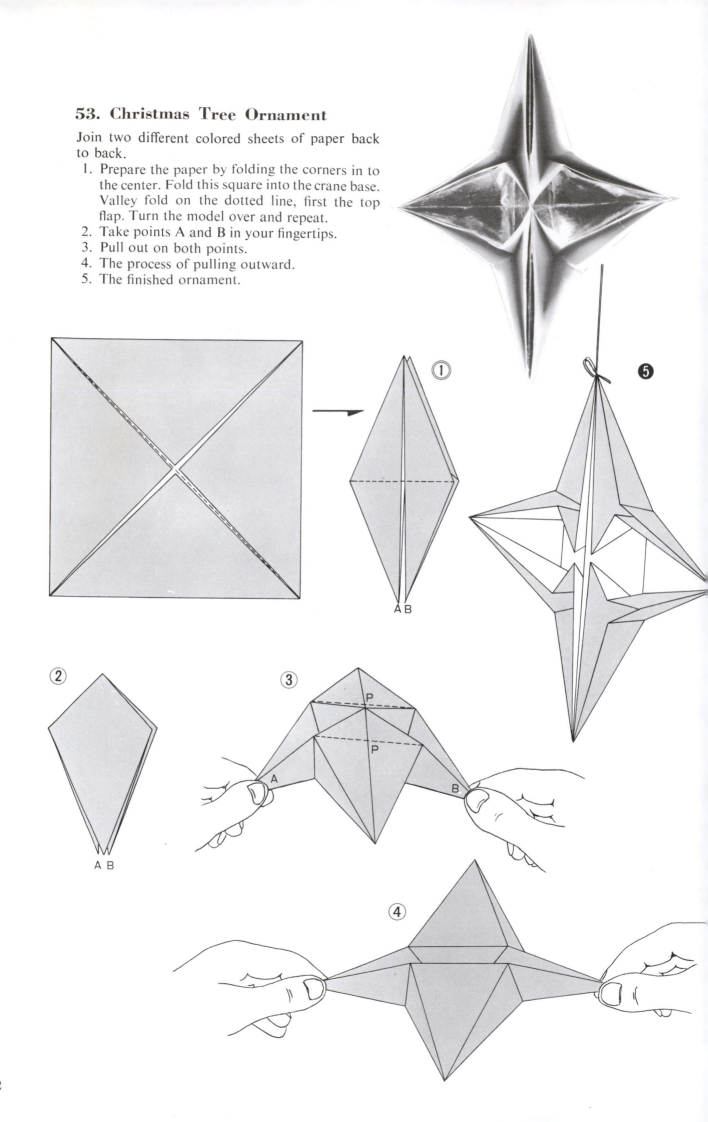

53. Christmas Tree Ornament

Join two different colored sheets of paper back to back.

1. Prepare the paper by folding the corners in to the center. Fold this square into the crane base. Valley fold on the dotted line, first the top flap. Turn the model over and repeat.
2. Take points A and B in your fingertips.
3. Pull out on both points.
4. The process of pulling outward.
5. The finished ornament.

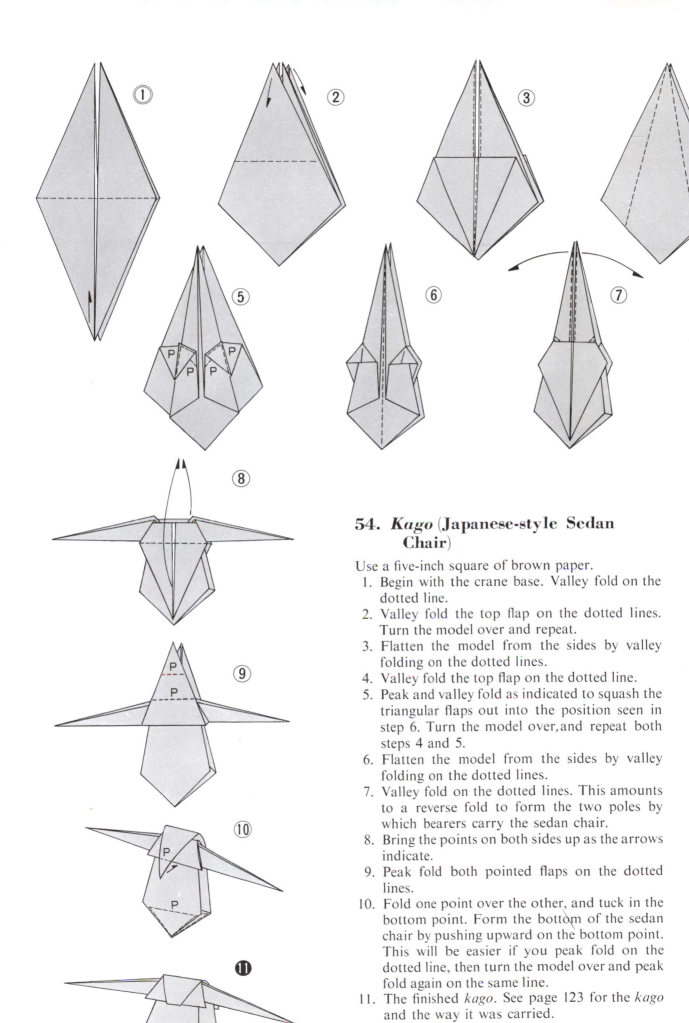

54. *Kago* (Japanese-style Sedan Chair)

Use a five-inch square of brown paper.

1. Begin with the crane base. Valley fold on the dotted line.
2. Valley fold the top flap on the dotted lines. Turn the model over and repeat.
3. Flatten the model from the sides by valley folding on the dotted lines.
4. Valley fold the top flap on the dotted line.
5. Peak and valley fold as indicated to squash the triangular flaps out into the position seen in step 6. Turn the model over, and repeat both steps 4 and 5.
6. Flatten the model from the sides by valley folding on the dotted lines.
7. Valley fold on the dotted lines. This amounts to a reverse fold to form the two poles by which bearers carry the sedan chair.
8. Bring the points on both sides up as the arrows indicate.
9. Peak fold both pointed flaps on the dotted lines.
10. Fold one point over the other, and tuck in the bottom point. Form the bottom of the sedan chair by pushing upward on the bottom point. This will be easier if you peak fold on the dotted line, then turn the model over and peak fold again on the same line.
11. The finished *kago*. See page 123 for the *kago* and the way it was carried.

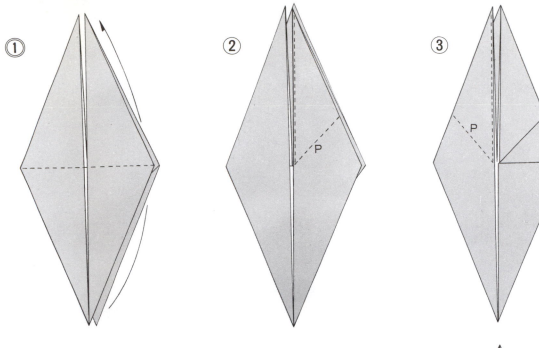

55. Dragonfly

Use a six-inch square of blue paper.

1. Begin with the crane base. Fold the bottom under flap up to the top point as the arrow indicates.
2. Peak and valley fold as indicated to reverse fold the top right point out to the position in step 3. The valley fold in this case is only a flattening out of the existing crease.
3. Repeat this process with the top left point.
4~5. Valley fold the extreme tips of the left and right points. Valley fold along the dotted lines in the lower point. Be careful to line the outer edges with the center line as you fold. If you do, the secondary folds will fall in place naturally.
6. Turn the model over and fold on the dotted lines. Once again, the important thing is to be sure to line the outer edges of the point with the center line.
7. Peak fold on the dotted line.
8. Cut the wings where indicated. Valley fold on the dotted lines, and reverse fold the head section inside out.
9. Valley fold the wings on the dotted line. Reverse fold the head section inside out.
10. Make three more inside-out reverse folds in the head section as shown. This will make the characteristic bulging eyes of a dragonfly.
11. The completed model.

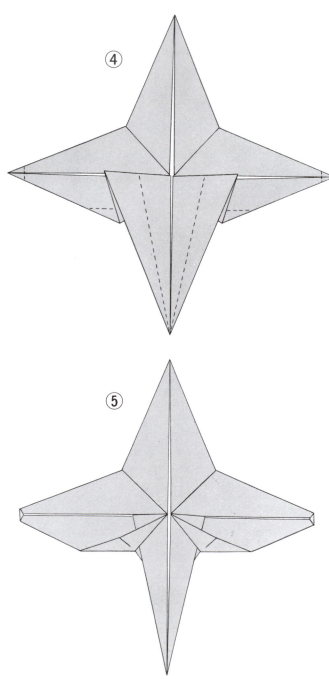

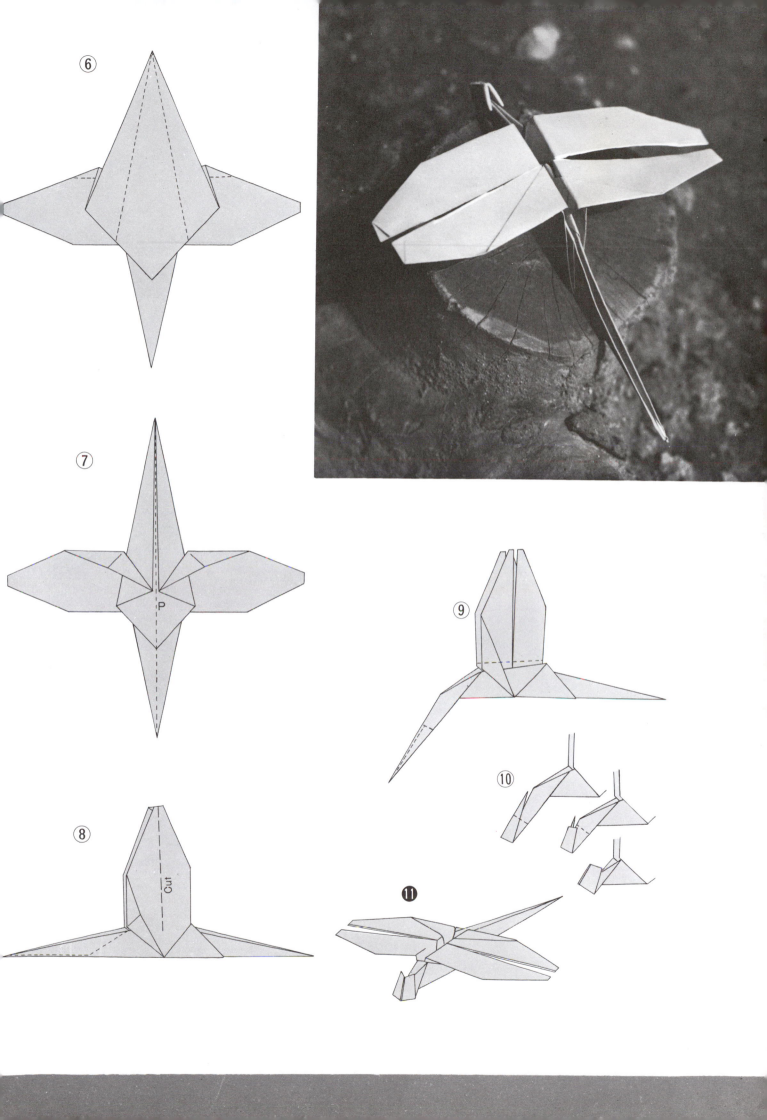

⑥

⑦

P

⑧

Cut

⑨

⑩

⑪

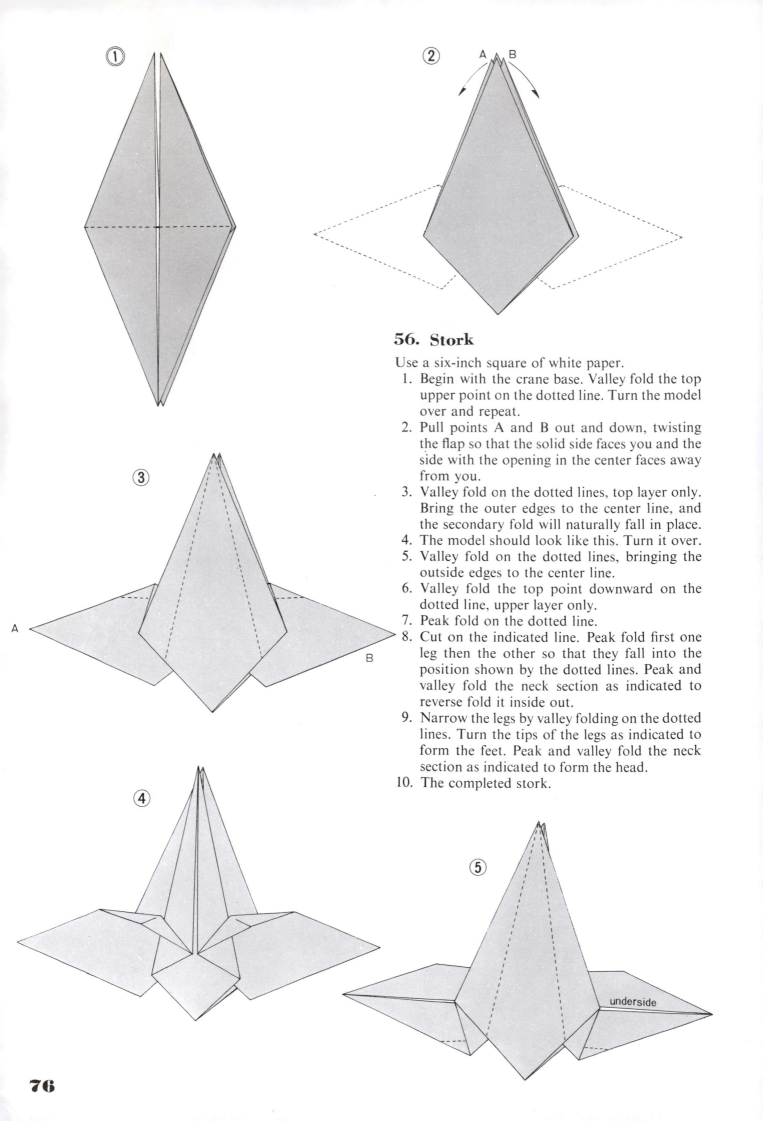

56. Stork

Use a six-inch square of white paper.

1. Begin with the crane base. Valley fold the top upper point on the dotted line. Turn the model over and repeat.
2. Pull points A and B out and down, twisting the flap so that the solid side faces you and the side with the opening in the center faces away from you.
3. Valley fold on the dotted lines, top layer only. Bring the outer edges to the center line, and the secondary fold will naturally fall in place.
4. The model should look like this. Turn it over.
5. Valley fold on the dotted lines, bringing the outside edges to the center line.
6. Valley fold the top point downward on the dotted line, upper layer only.
7. Peak fold on the dotted line.
8. Cut on the indicated line. Peak fold first one leg then the other so that they fall into the position shown by the dotted lines. Peak and valley fold the neck section as indicated to reverse fold it inside out.
9. Narrow the legs by valley folding on the dotted lines. Turn the tips of the legs as indicated to form the feet. Peak and valley fold the neck section as indicated to form the head.
10. The completed stork.

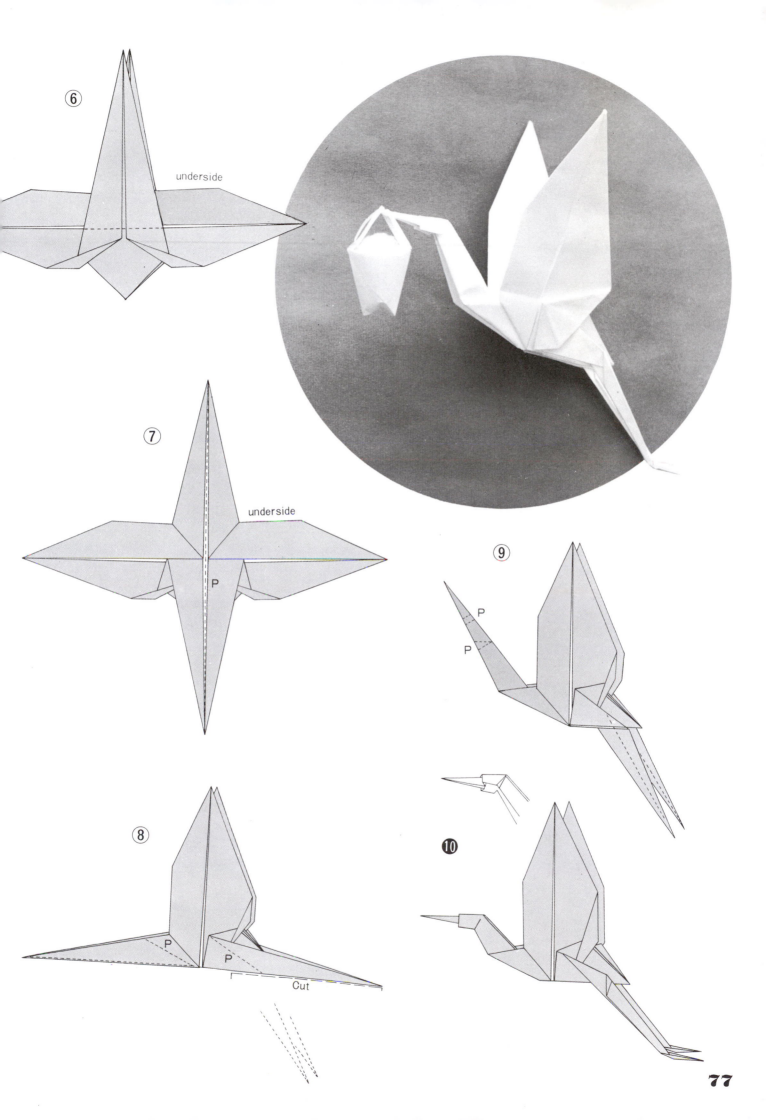

⑥

underside

⑦

underside

P

⑨

P

P

⑧

P

P

Cut

⑩

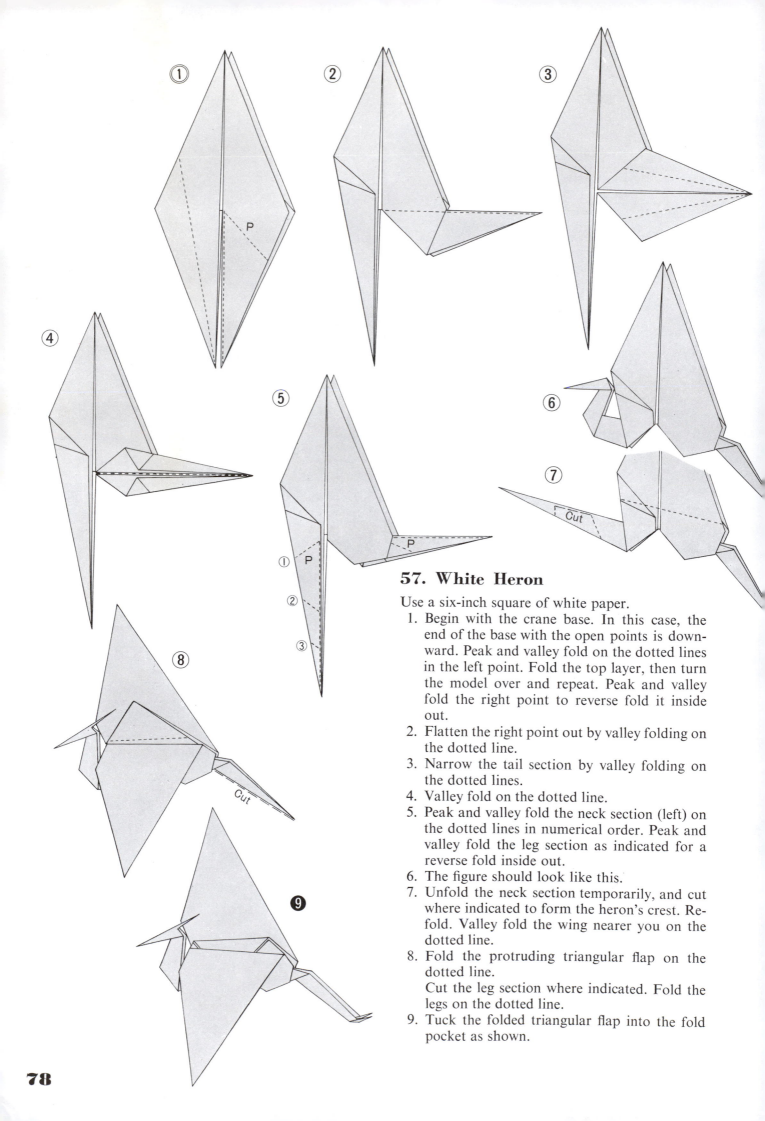

57. White Heron

Use a six-inch square of white paper.

1. Begin with the crane base. In this case, the end of the base with the open points is downward. Peak and valley fold on the dotted lines in the left point. Fold the top layer, then turn the model over and repeat. Peak and valley fold the right point to reverse fold it inside out.
2. Flatten the right point out by valley folding on the dotted line.
3. Narrow the tail section by valley folding on the dotted lines.
4. Valley fold on the dotted line.
5. Peak and valley fold the neck section (left) on the dotted lines in numerical order. Peak and valley fold the leg section as indicated for a reverse fold inside out.
6. The figure should look like this.
7. Unfold the neck section temporarily, and cut where indicated to form the heron's crest. Refold. Valley fold the wing nearer you on the dotted line.
8. Fold the protruding triangular flap on the dotted line.
   Cut the leg section where indicated. Fold the legs on the dotted line.
9. Tuck the folded triangular flap into the fold pocket as shown.

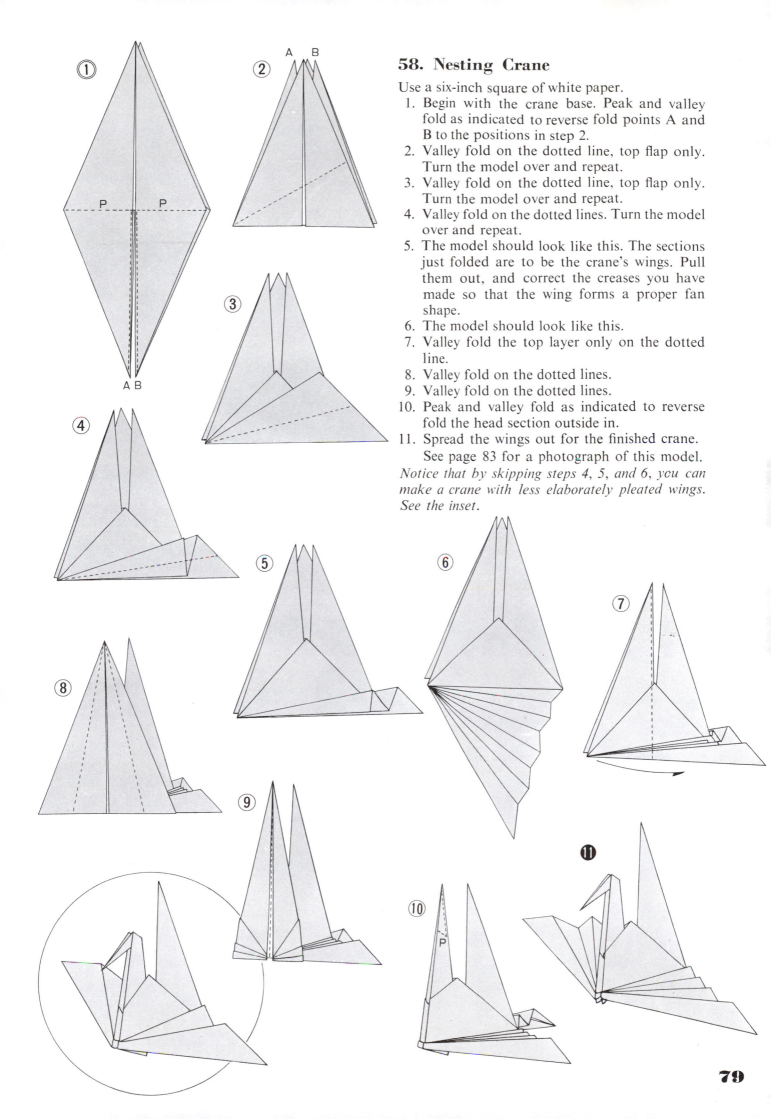

58. Nesting Crane

Use a six-inch square of white paper.

1. Begin with the crane base. Peak and valley fold as indicated to reverse fold points A and B to the positions in step 2.
2. Valley fold on the dotted line, top flap only. Turn the model over and repeat.
3. Valley fold on the dotted line, top flap only. Turn the model over and repeat.
4. Valley fold on the dotted lines. Turn the model over and repeat.
5. The model should look like this. The sections just folded are to be the crane's wings. Pull them out, and correct the creases you have made so that the wing forms a proper fan shape.
6. The model should look like this.
7. Valley fold the top layer only on the dotted line.
8. Valley fold on the dotted lines.
9. Valley fold on the dotted lines.
10. Peak and valley fold as indicated to reverse fold the head section outside in.
11. Spread the wings out for the finished crane.
   See page 83 for a photograph of this model.

Notice that by skipping steps 4, 5, and 6, you can make a crane with less elaborately pleated wings. See the inset.

79

59. Hen

Use a six-inch square of yellow paper.

1. Begin with the crane base, open points down. Peak and valley fold as indicated to reverse fold both points upward inside out.
2. Valley fold on the dotted line down the center.
3. Valley fold as indicated to reverse both the neck and tail sections inside out.
4. Valley fold the head section as shown for a reverse fold inside out. Peak and valley fold the legs for a reverse fold outside in.
5. Peak and valley fold the head, tail and legs.
6. The completed hen, on the right in the photograph.

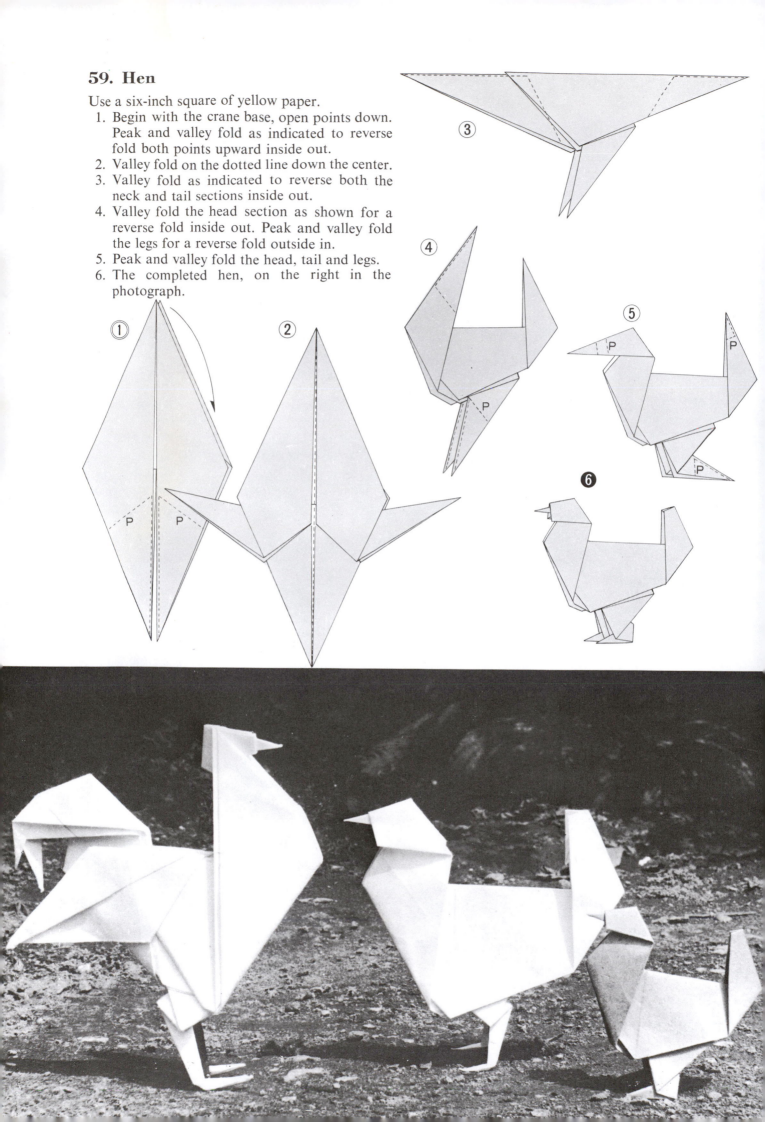

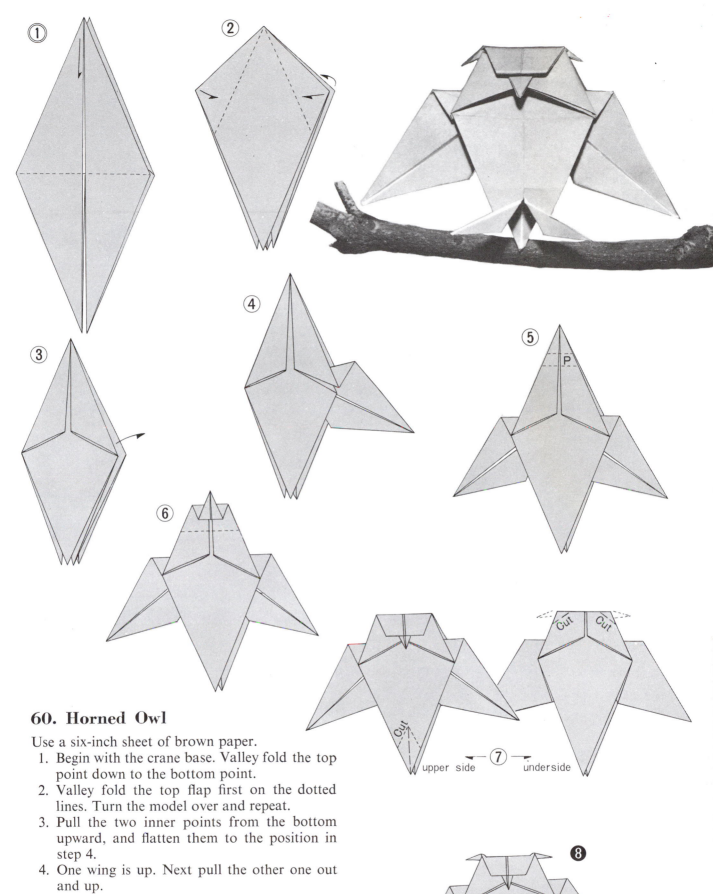

60. Horned Owl

Use a six-inch sheet of brown paper.

1. Begin with the crane base. Valley fold the top point down to the bottom point.
2. Valley fold the top flap first on the dotted lines. Turn the model over and repeat.
3. Pull the two inner points from the bottom upward, and flatten them to the position in step 4.
4. One wing is up. Next pull the other one out and up.
5. Peak and valley fold as indicated.
6. Valley fold on the dotted line.
7. Cut and valley fold (top layer only) as indicated on the front of the model for the tail. Turn the model over, and cut and fold the ear-shaped feathers out. (top layer only).
8. The completed horned owl.

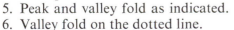
upper side   underside

81

61. Crow

Use a sixteen-inch square of black paper.
1. Begin with the crane base. Peak and valley fold as shown for a reverse fold outside in.
2. Valley fold the top layer up on the dotted line.
3. Valley fold on the dotted lines.
4. Valley fold on the dotted line. Be sure you bring the top section of the flap down to the bottom section.
5. The model should look like this. Valley fold on the dotted line.
6. Peak and valley fold the head for a reverse fold outside in.
7. Peak and valley fold the feet as seen for a crimp inward.
8. The completed crow.

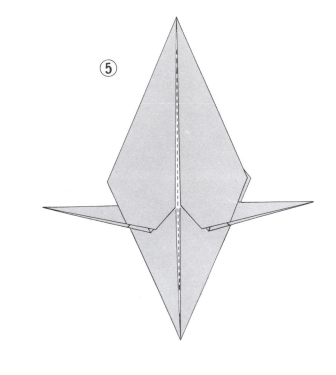

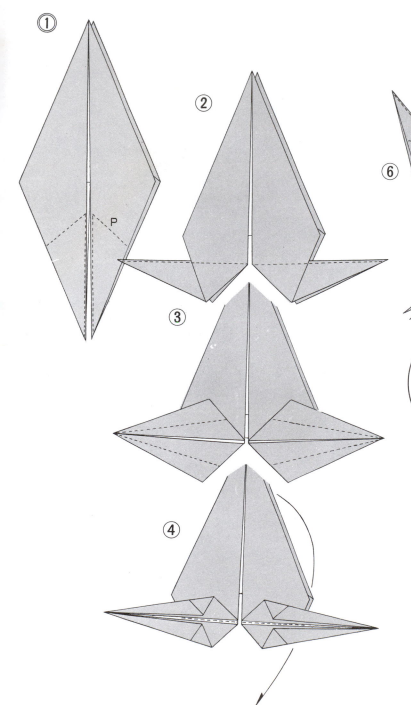

Note: Folding the legs of birds
When we are folding bird figures it is particularly important to fold the legs narrow enough to suggest the real thing. The folding methods in the crow are representative examples of how we fold bird legs. Since the methods used in 63. Canary, 66. Dove, 71. Turkey, 64. Sparrow, 69. Pheasant, 62. Nightingale, and 70. Peacock are the same as those for the crow, we will omit steps 3 and 4 in all of those charts.

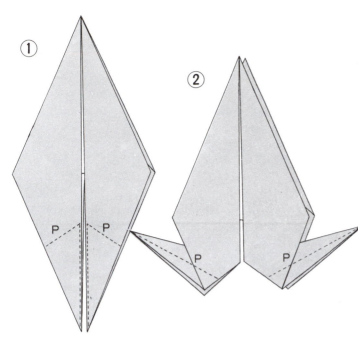

62. Japanese Nightingale

Use a six-inch sheet of olive paper.

1. Begin with the crane base.
2. Peak and valley fold on the dotted lines for a reverse fold inside out.
3. and 4. are the same as in the crow (61).
5. Valley fold the top layer only on the dotted line. Be sure you bring the inner point downward as you see in step 6.
6. The figure should look like this. Turn it over.
7. Valley fold on the dotted lines in numerical order.
8. Valley fold on the dotted lines.
9. Valley fold on the dotted line.
10. Cut top flap where indicated. Turn the model over and repeat. Valley fold first one wing then the other on the dotted line.
11. Peak and valley fold the legs and crimp them inward.
12. The finished nightingale.

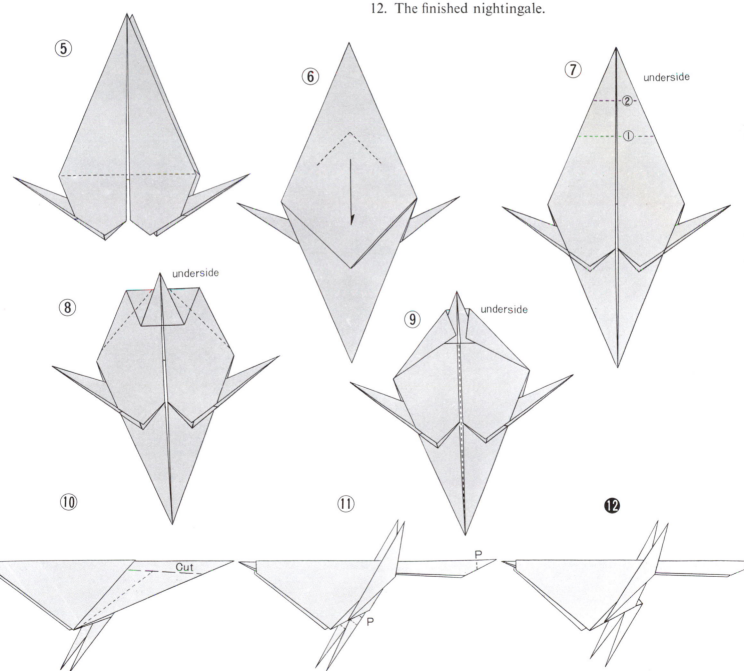

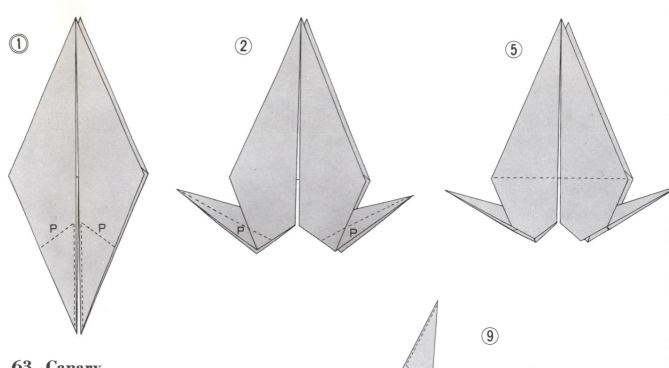

63. Canary

Use a six-inch square of yellow paper.
1. Begin with the crane base. Peak and valley fold as indicated for a reverse fold inside out.
2. Peak fold on the dotted lines, top flap only. Turn the model over and repeat.
3. and 4. are the same as for the crow (61).
5. Valley fold on the dotted line.
6. Peak fold on the dotted line.
7. Valley fold on the dotted line in the head section for a reverse fold inside out. Cut where indicated. Valley and peak fold on the wing section as shown.
8. Pull the wing into place, and flatten the creases at the base.
9. Valley fold on the head section for a reverse fold inside out.
10. Valley and peak fold on both the legs and the beak, and crimp inward. Peak and valley fold the tail for a reverse fold inward.
11. The canary.

64. Sparrow

Use a six-inch square of brown paper.
1~9. Begin with step 9 of the canary (63). Peak and valley fold the head section for a reverse fold outside in.
10. Peak and valley fold the head for a reverse fold outside in.
11. Peak and valley fold the head for a reverse fold outside in.
12. Valley fold the head for a reverse fold inside out.
13. Peak and valley fold the beak and legs, and crimp them inward. Peak and valley fold the tail inward.
14. The finished sparrow.

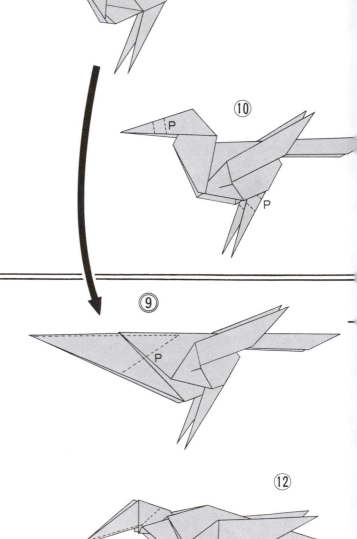

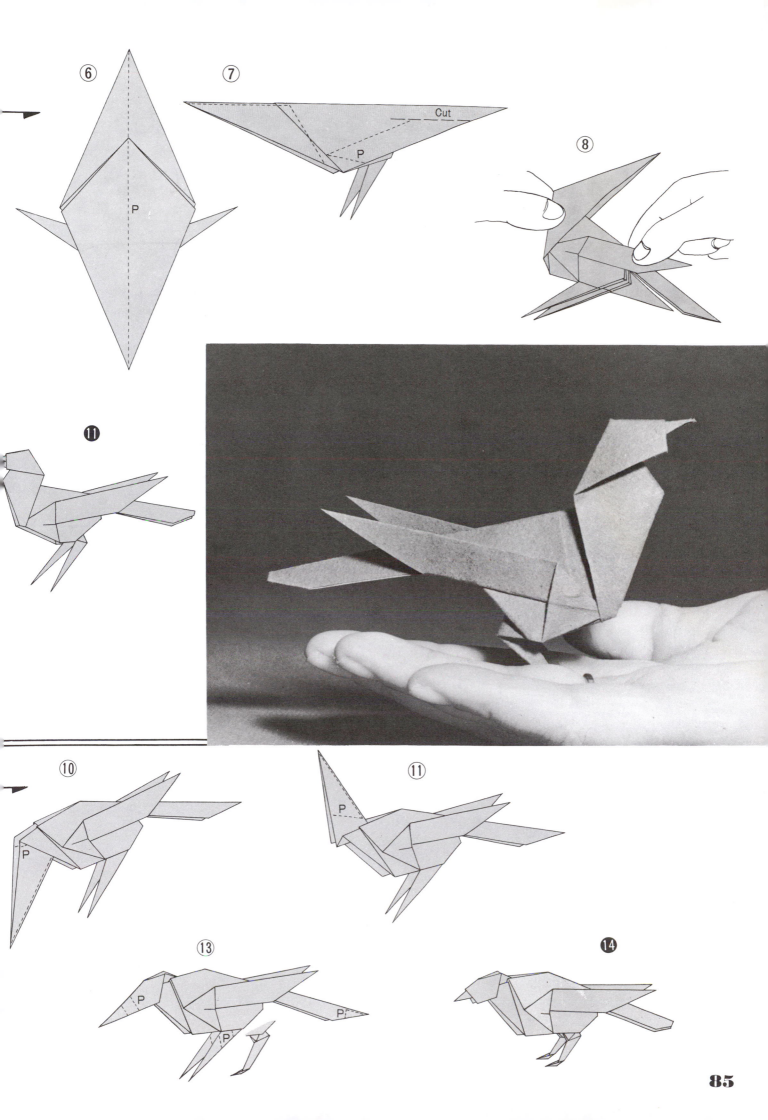

⑥

⑦

Cut

P

P

⑧

⑪

⑩

P

⑪

P

⑬

P

P

P

⑭

85

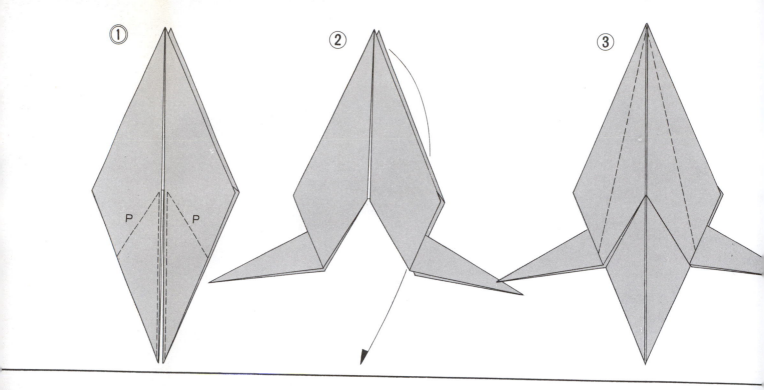

65. Standing Crane

The lovely crane has a long neck, long slender legs, and black pin feathers that look something like a **tail** when his wings are folded. This origami model reproduces these characteristics exactly. Use a six-inch square of white paper.

1. Begin with the crane base. Peak and valley fold as indicated for a reverse fold outside in.
2. Bring the under layer of the top point down as the arrow indicates.
3. Valley fold on the dotted lines, top flap only.
4. Open the two side flaps outward to the position you see in step 5.
5. Valley fold on the dotted lines in numerical order.
6. Valley fold the leg sections on the dotted lines.
7. Valley fold the entire model on the dotted line down the center.
8. Valley fold the neck section as indicated for a reverse fold inside out. Peak and valley fold the tail section for a reverse fold outside in.
9. Valley fold the head section for a reverse fold inside out. Peak and valley fold the tail for a reverse fold outside in. Peak fold through the leg and breast section on the dotted line. Valley fold the legs where indicated.
10. Valley fold the feet on the dotted line. Peak and valley fold the tail as indicated so that it falls on the outside of the wings and is pleated to suggest feathers.
11. The finished crane.

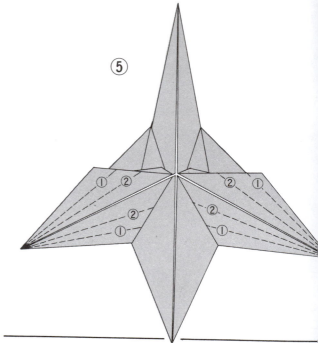

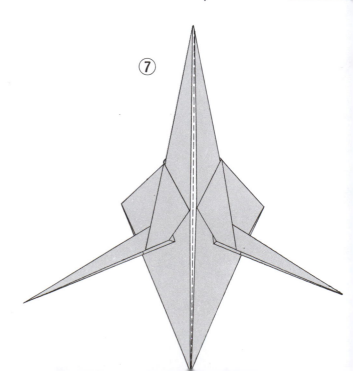

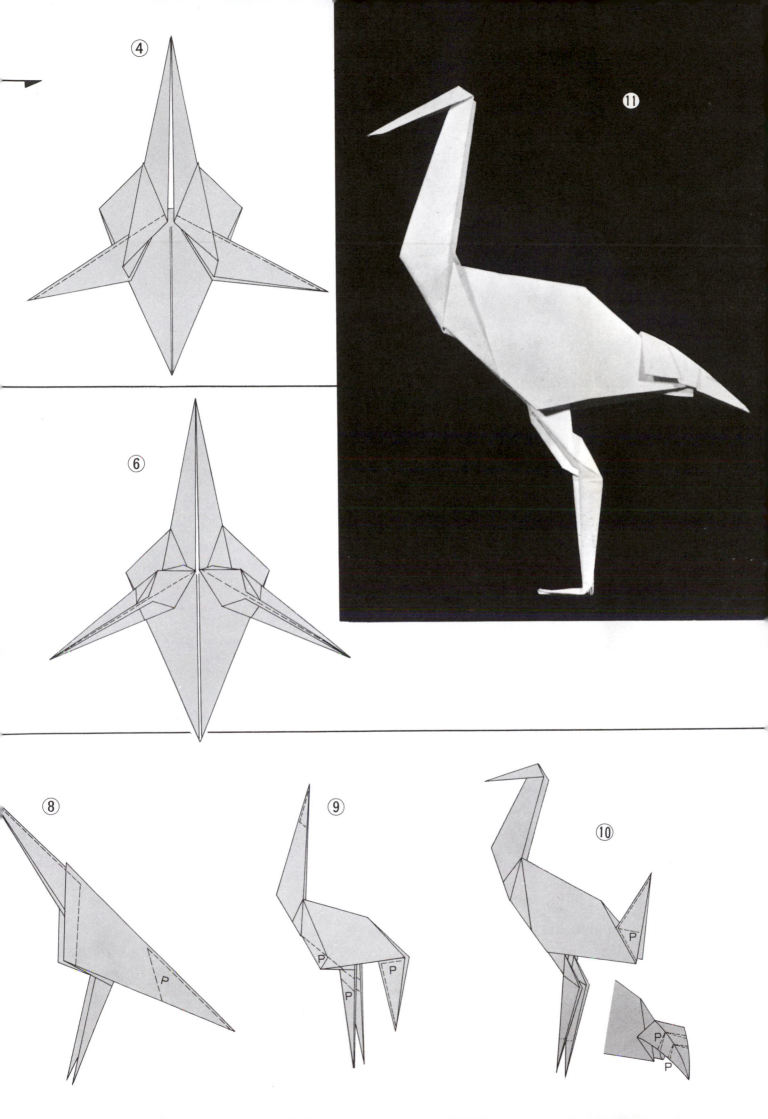

④

⑥

⑪

⑧

⑨

P

P

P

⑩

P

P

P

66. Dove (II)

Use a six-inch square of pale blue paper.

1. Begin with the crane base. Peak and valley fold for reverse folds inside out.
2. Peak fold the foot sections on the dotted lines, upper layer first. Turn the model over and repeat.
3. and 4. are just as for the crow (61).
5. Valley fold the top layer only on the dotted line.
6. Peak fold the top section of the inner point on the dotted line.
7. Valley fold the upper point downward on the dotted line.
8. Peak fold on the dotted line.
9. Valley fold the head section out for a reverse fold inside out.
10. Peak and valley fold the head section again for a reverse fold outside in. Peak and valley fold the tail tip in as indicated.
11. Peak and valley fold the head on the dotted lines, and crimp to form the beak. Cut the top layer only where indicated. Turn the model over and repeat. Peak and valley fold the tail as indicated for a reverse fold inside out. Peak and valley fold the legs, and crimp them inward.
12. Make the dove's tail by valley folding on the dotted lines and tucking the tail behind the wings.
13. The finished dove.

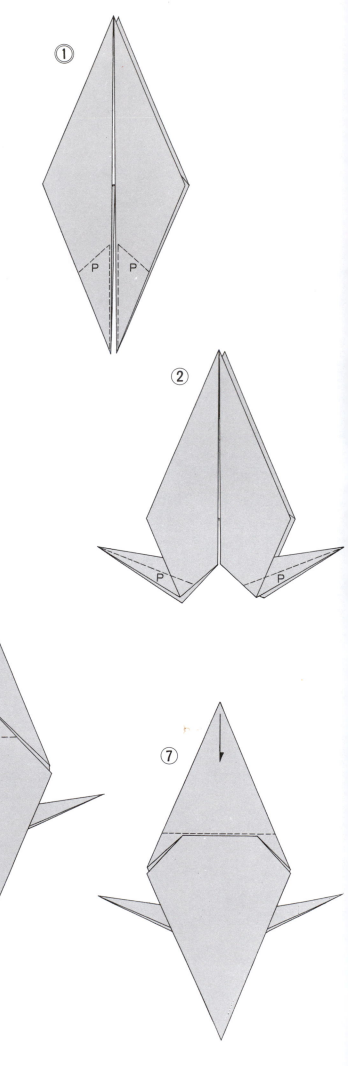

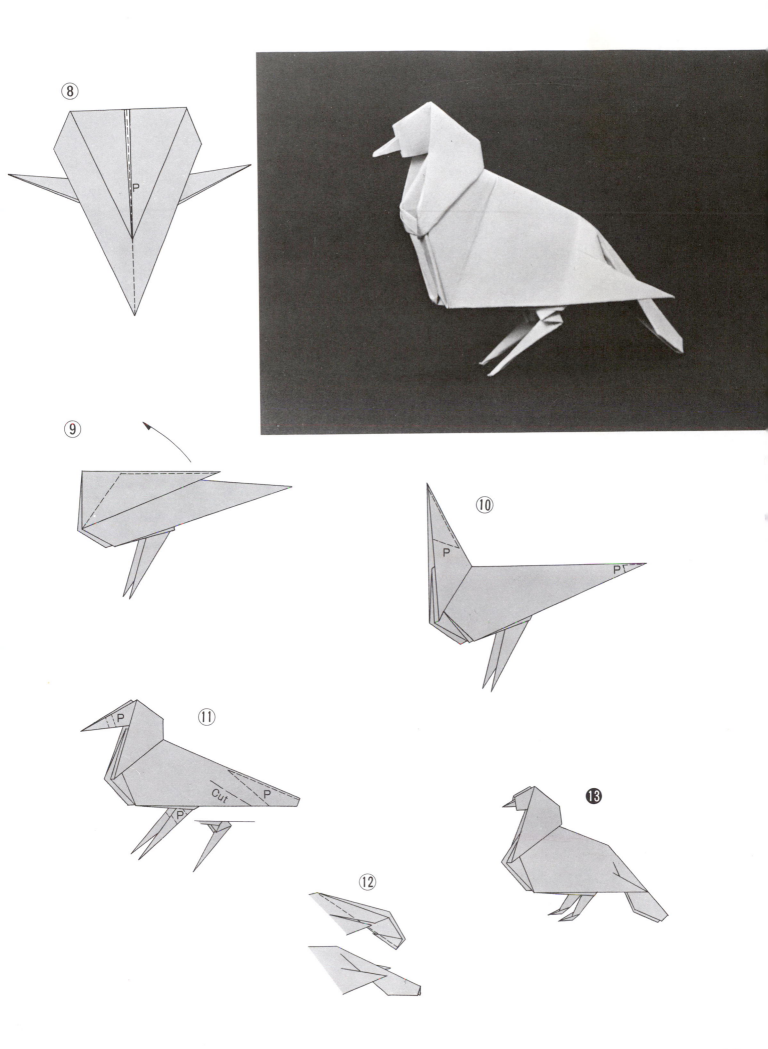

⑧

P

⑨

⑩

P

P

⑪

P

Cut

P

P

⑫

❸

89

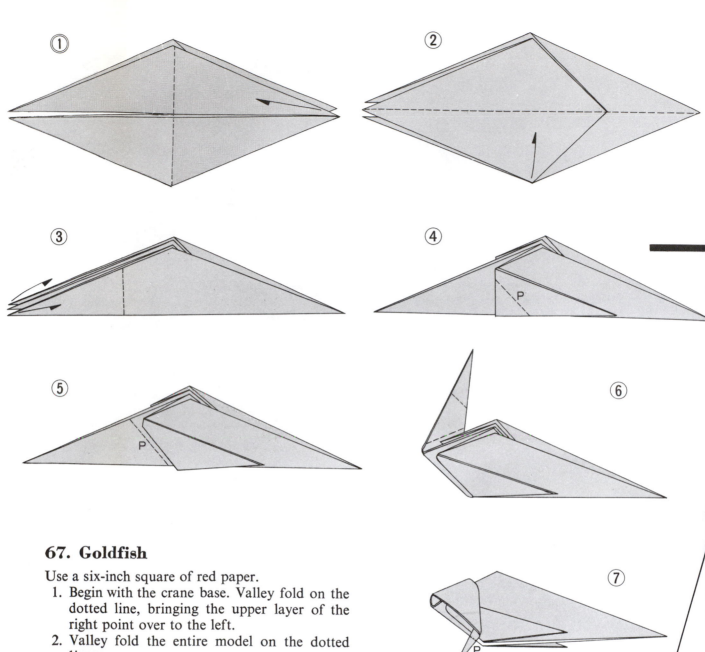

67. Goldfish

Use a six-inch square of red paper.

1. Begin with the crane base. Valley fold on the dotted line, bringing the upper layer of the right point over to the left.
2. Valley fold the entire model on the dotted line.
3. Valley fold the top flap only on the dotted line. Turn the model over and repeat.
4. Peak fold on the dotted line. Turn the model over and repeat.
5. Peak fold the remaining point as indicated. It will wrap around to the other side of the model.
6. Valley fold where shown, and wrap the point around to the front of the model.
7. Peak fold on the dotted line, and tuck the remaining flap up into the pocket.
8. Cut on the indicated line.
9. Flatten out the two front fins by peak and valley folding as shown. This technique involves a degree of squashing the paper. Peak and valley fold the tail sections one at a time.
10. Open the tail sections by valley folding on the dotted line.
11. The front and back of the finished goldfish.

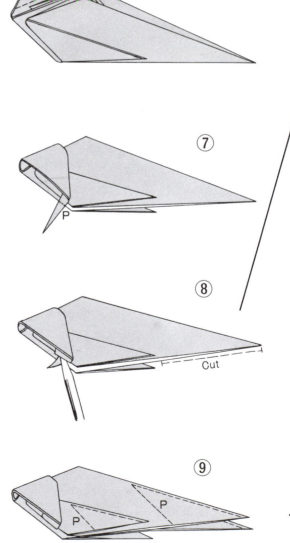

68. Fish

Use a six-inch square of black paper.

1~4. Begin with step 4 of the goldfish (67).

5,6, and 7 are folded as for the goldfish.

8. Peak and valley fold the tail as indicated for a reverse fold outside in.

9. Cut and peak fold the tail as indicated.

10. The front and back of the finished fish.

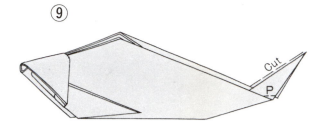

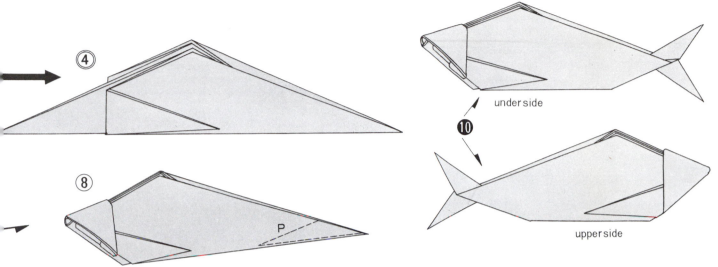

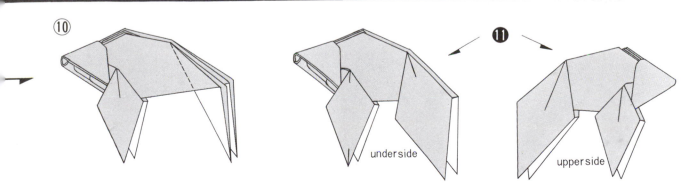

69. Pheasant

Use a six-inch square of green paper.

1. Begin with the crane base. Peak and valley fold as shown for a reverse fold inside out.
2. Valley fold the top layer only on the dotted lines.
3. Open the two bottom points by valley folding on the dotted line.
4. Valley fold on the dotted lines.
5. Valley fold on the dotted lines.
6. Valley fold on the dotted line, leaving the bottom point unfolded.
7. Peak fold on the dotted line.
8. Peak and valley fold for a reverse fold outside in.
9. Peak and valley fold for a reverse fold outside in.
10. Repeat the same process.
11. Peak and valley fold the beak and legs, and crimp inward.
12. The finished pheasant.

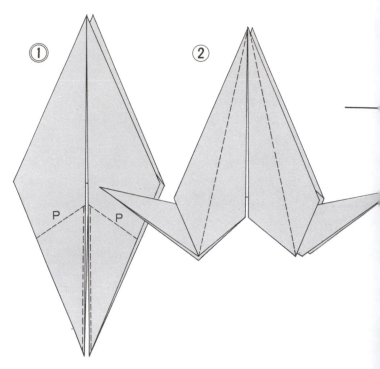

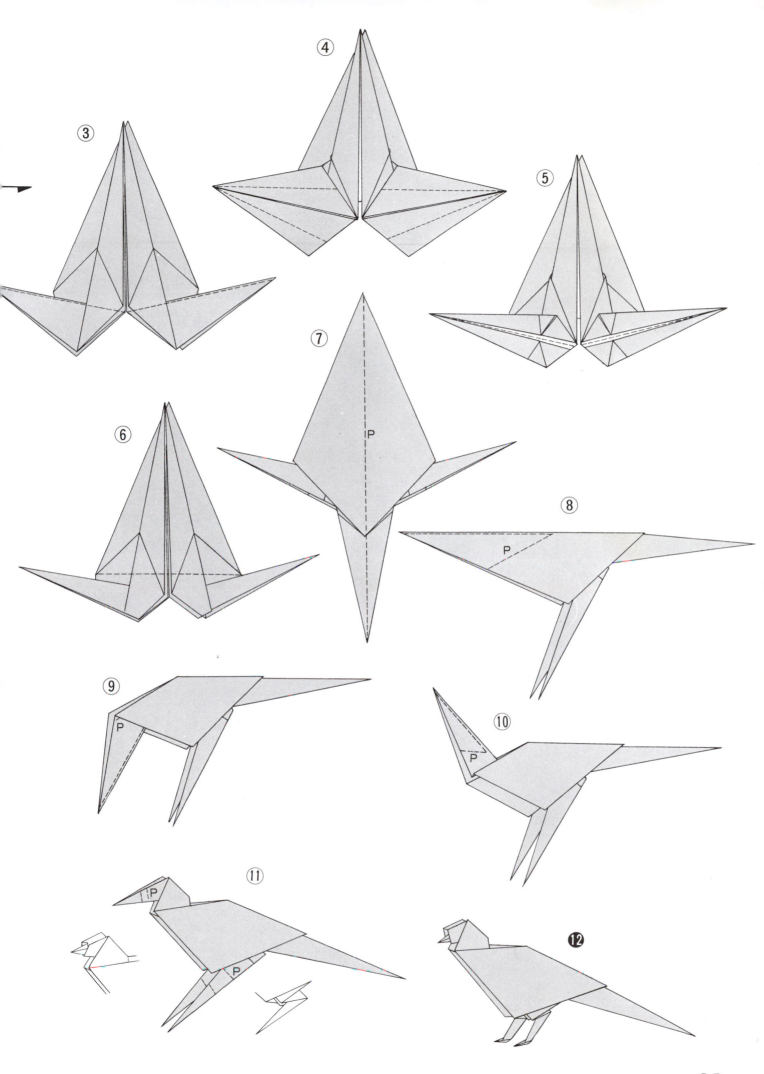

93

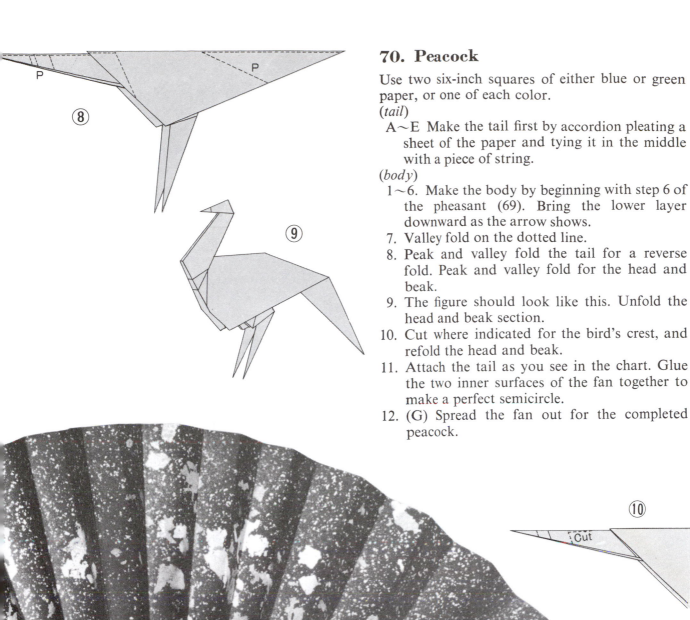

⑧

⑨

⑩

Cut

70. Peacock

Use two six-inch squares of either blue or green paper, or one of each color.

(tail)

A~E Make the tail first by accordion pleating a sheet of the paper and tying it in the middle with a piece of string.

(body)

1~6. Make the body by beginning with step 6 of the pheasant (69). Bring the lower layer downward as the arrow shows.

7. Valley fold on the dotted line.

8. Peak and valley fold the tail for a reverse fold. Peak and valley fold for the head and beak.

9. The figure should look like this. Unfold the head and beak section.

10. Cut where indicated for the bird's crest, and refold the head and beak.

11. Attach the tail as you see in the chart. Glue the two inner surfaces of the fan together to make a perfect semicircle.

12. (G) Spread the fan out for the completed peacock.

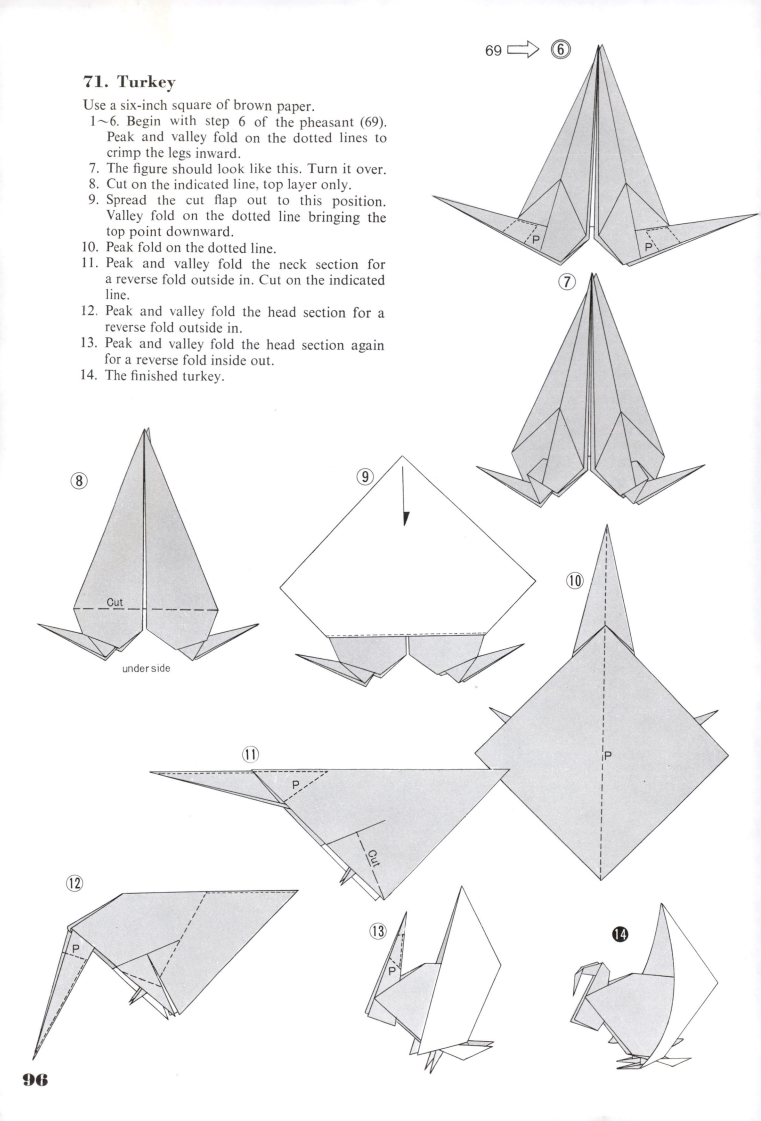

71. Turkey

Use a six-inch square of brown paper.

1~6. Begin with step 6 of the pheasant (69). Peak and valley fold on the dotted lines to crimp the legs inward.

7. The figure should look like this. Turn it over.

8. Cut on the indicated line, top layer only.

9. Spread the cut flap out to this position. Valley fold on the dotted line bringing the top point downward.

10. Peak fold on the dotted line.

11. Peak and valley fold the neck section for a reverse fold outside in. Cut on the indicated line.

12. Peak and valley fold the head section for a reverse fold outside in.

13. Peak and valley fold the head section again for a reverse fold inside out.

14. The finished turkey.

69 ⟹ ⑥

⑦

⑧ under side

Cut

⑨

⑩ P

⑪ P Cut

⑫ P

⑬ P

❶❹

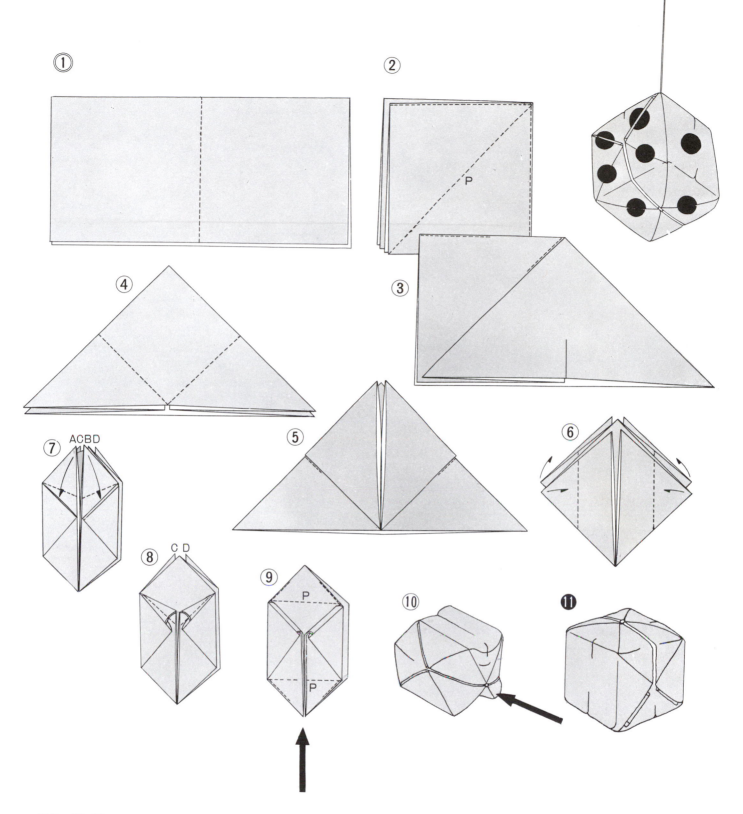

72. Balloon

The balloon base is an origami that Japanese children learn in kindergarten. With it we can make a number of interesting folds.
Use a six-inch square of paper.

1. Prepare the paper by book folding it in half. Valley fold on the dotted line.
2. Open the square into a triangle by peak and valley folding as indicated.
3. Repeat step 2 on the underside.
4. Valley fold the top folds on the dotted lines, bringing the bottom edges up to the center line.
5. Turn the model over and repeat.
6. Valley fold the right and left points into the center line. Turn the model over and repeat.
7. Valley fold points A and B down into the pockets shown.
8. Repeat with points C and D.
9. Peak and valley fold as shown to flatten out the top and bottom of the cube shape.
10. Blow air into the indicated hole.
11. The finished balloon.

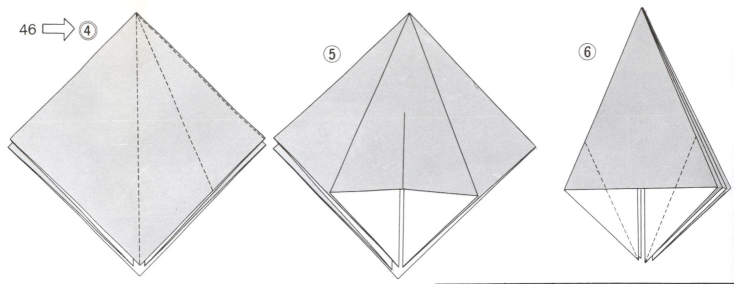

46 ⇨ ④

⑤

⑥

⑪

⑫

73. Frog

Use a six-inch square of either pale brown or green paper.

1~5. Begin with step 4 of the crane base. Valley fold on the dotted lines. This is equivalent to taking the top right fold, centering it on the middle of the figure, and squashing it flat.

6. Continue this process around the entire model for a figure like this one. Fold on the dotted lines, top fold only.

7. Bring the topmost under layer up in the direction the arrow indicates. This will be easier if you first crease the whole model on the dotted line.

8. The model should look like this. Continue this process all around the model for a figure like that in step 9.

9. Valley fold on the dotted lines to flatten the figure from the sides.

10. Valley fold on the dotted lines.

11. The figure should look like this. Continue this folding process all around the model for a figure like that in step 12.

12. Flatten the model open from the sides by valley folding on the dotted line.

13. The figure should look like this. Notice that there is an opening between the two sides of the bottom point in all layers.

14. Peak and reverse fold the top two points as shown to form the hind legs. Peak and reverse fold the bottom points as shown to form the forelegs.

15. Blow air into the hole shown to fill the frog's body out.

16. The finished frog.

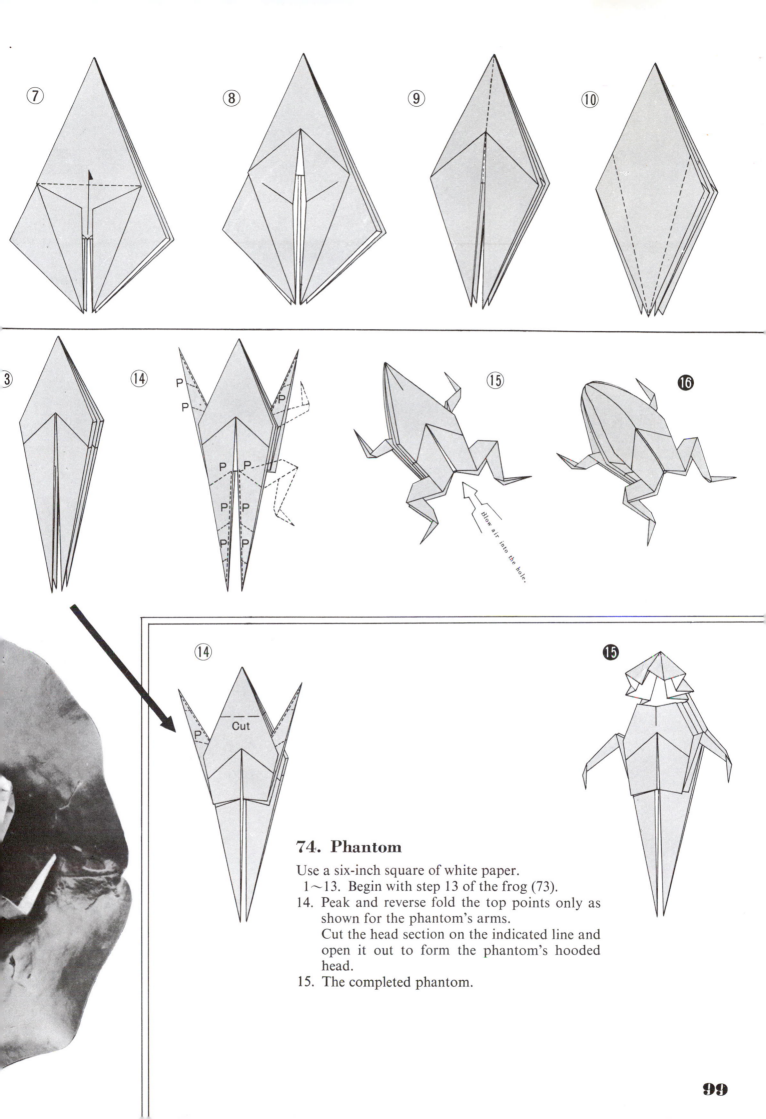

⑦ ⑧ ⑨ ⑩

⑬ ⑭ ⑮ ⑯

P P
P P P
P P
P P

blow air into the hole.

⑭ Cut
P

⑮

74. Phantom

Use a six-inch square of white paper.

1~13. Begin with step 13 of the frog (73).

14. Peak and reverse fold the top points only as shown for the phantom's arms.
    Cut the head section on the indicated line and open it out to form the phantom's hooded head.

15. The completed phantom.

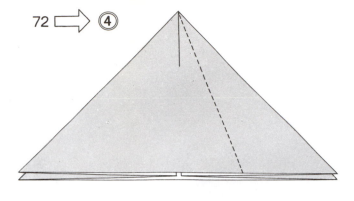

75. Lily

Use a six-inch square of white paper.

1~4. Begin with step 4 of the balloon. Valley fold on the dotted line.
5. Raise and flatten the fold out by valley folding on the dotted lines.
6. The figure should look like this. Continue this fold all around the model for a figure like that in step 7.
7. Valley fold on the dotted lines, top flap only.
8. The figure should look like this.
9. Open the folds you just made, and pull the bottom point upward as the arrow indicates.
10. Bring the same point back down by valley folding on the dotted line.
11. The figure should look like this. Continue this folding process all around the model for a figure like that in step 12.
12. Valley fold on the dotted line for a figure like that in step 13.
13. The figure should look like this. Continue this folding process all around the model for a figure like that in step 14.
14. Valley fold on the dotted line, one petal at a time.
15. Wrap the petals around a pencil to curl them.
16. The finished lily.

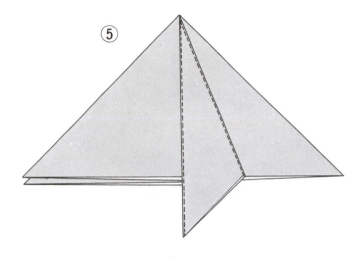
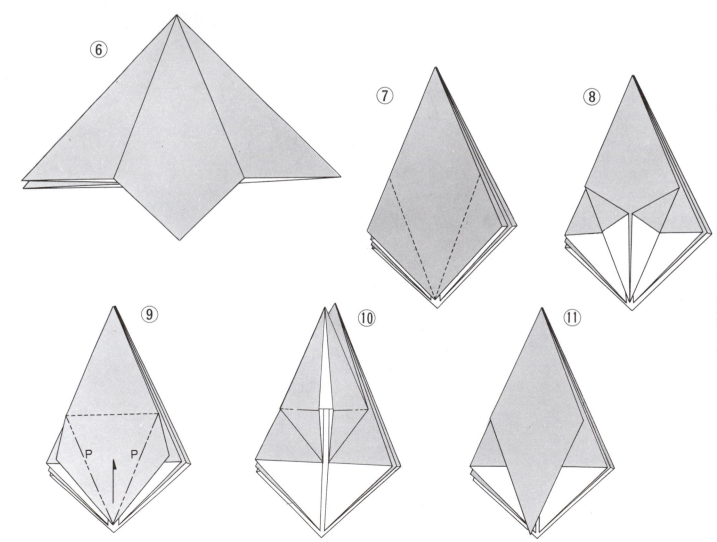

⑫

⑬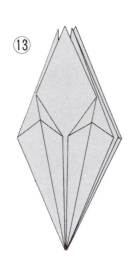

⑭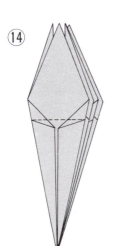

⑮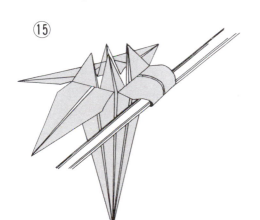

⑯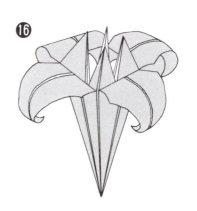

RECTANGULAR PAPER

Use any size paper with a length-width ratio of 7 to 5.

76. Paper Cracker

Use a rectangular piece of strong paper about the size of half a newspaper page.

1. Prepare the paper by folding the four corners in as shown. Valley fold on the dotted line.
2. Valley fold on the dotted line.
3. Peak and valley fold on the dotted lines for the position in step 4.
4. Turn the model over and repeat.
5. Flatten the model from the sides by valley folding on the dotted line.
6. Fold in half for the finished cracker. Grip the lower section in your fingers as you see in the diagram. If you snap it downward fast and hard, the side section will pop out with a sharp sound.

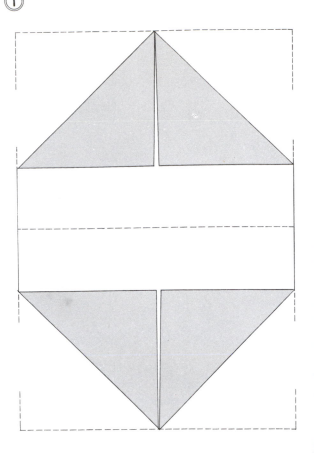

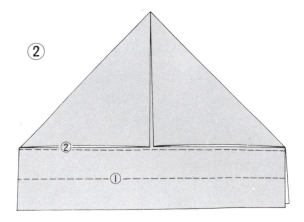

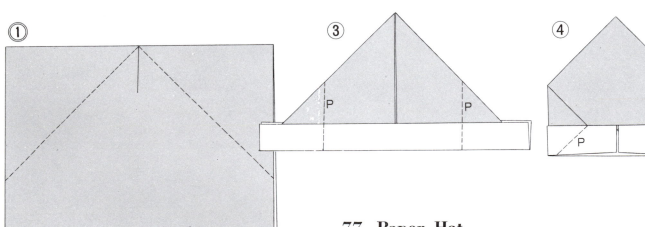

77. Paper Hat

Use a rectangle of paper about the size of a sheet of newspaper.

1. Prepare the paper by folding it in half as shown. Valley fold on the dotted lines.
2. Valley fold the top layer of the flap on the dotted lines in numerical order. Turn the model over and repeat.
3. Peak fold on the dotted lines so that it will fit your head.
4. Peak fold on the dotted lines.
5. Peak fold the protruding flaps into the pocket.
6. The finished hat.

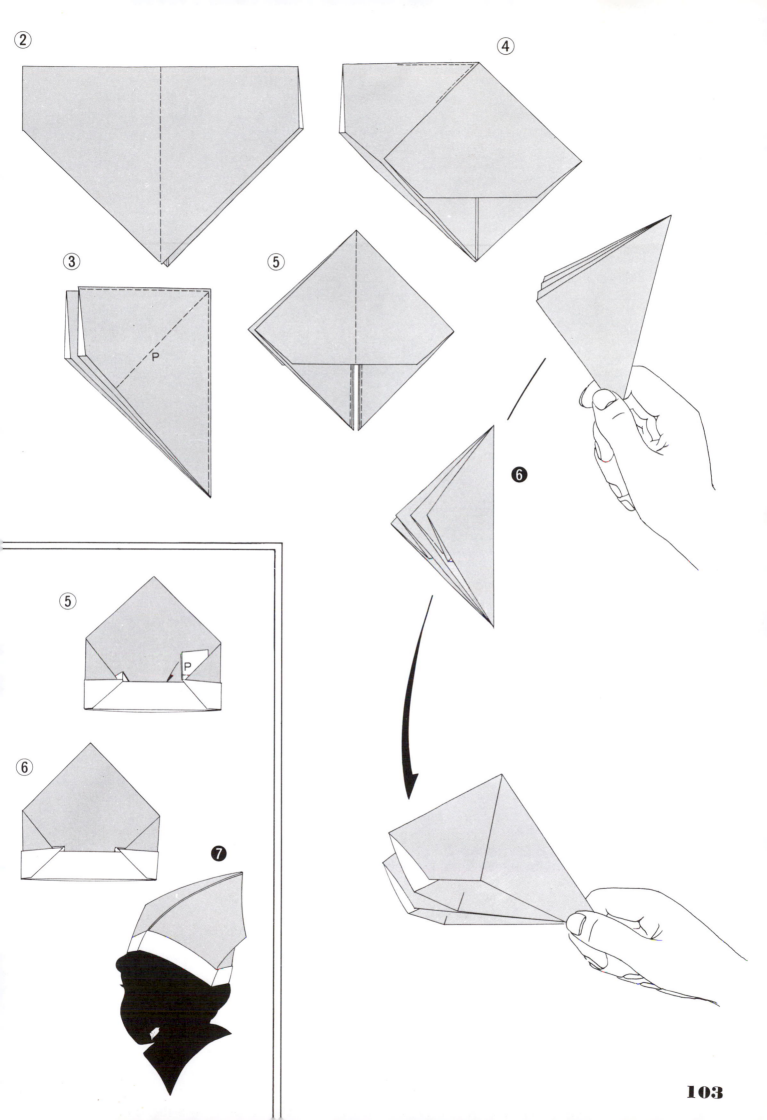

② ④ ③ P ⑤ ❻

⑤ P ⑥ ❼

78. Wastepaper Basket

Use a large rectangle of paper.

1~2. Fold as for the paper hat (77) to step 2, but do not turn the model over or repeat. The model should look like this. Turn it over.

3. Valley fold on the dotted lines so that the outer edges meet on the center line.

4. Narrow the bottom of the flap slightly as the chart shows. Valley fold it on the dotted lines in numerical order tucking it into the pocket.

5. Valley and peak crease on the dotted line. Crease vertically in half, both valley and peak.

6. Take the tip of the model in your fingertips at the center of each side, and pull outward till you form a square-top box shape. Fold the pointed bottom in half in the direction in the chart, and you will have a temporary-use wastepaper basket.

7. The finished wastepaper basket.

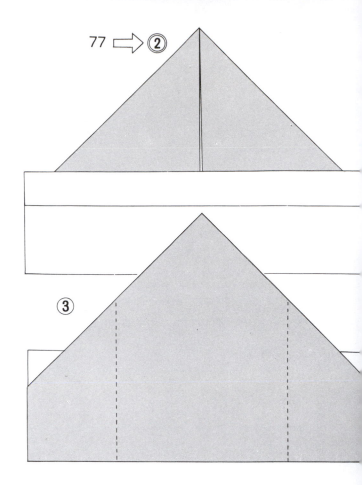

79. Folding Box (I)

Use a sheet of standard typewriter paper.

1. Establish a middle line, and valley fold the outer edges in to that line.

2. Peak fold the figure in half on the dotted line.

3. Peak fold on the dotted lines.

4. Valley fold on the dotted line.

5. From two additional creases by folding on the dotted lines.

6. Open the figure out to the position shown. Open the upper flap to the position in step 7 by peak and valley folding on the dotted lines.

7. Repeat the process with the remaining flap.

8. Valley fold the top flap on the dotted lines. Turn the model over and repeat.

9. Valley fold on the dotted lines in numerical order. Turn the model over and repeat.

10. The figure should look like this.

11. Open the figure out for the box. You can also flatten it out as the chart shows.

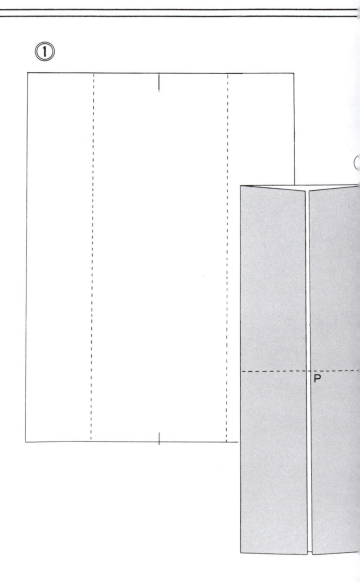

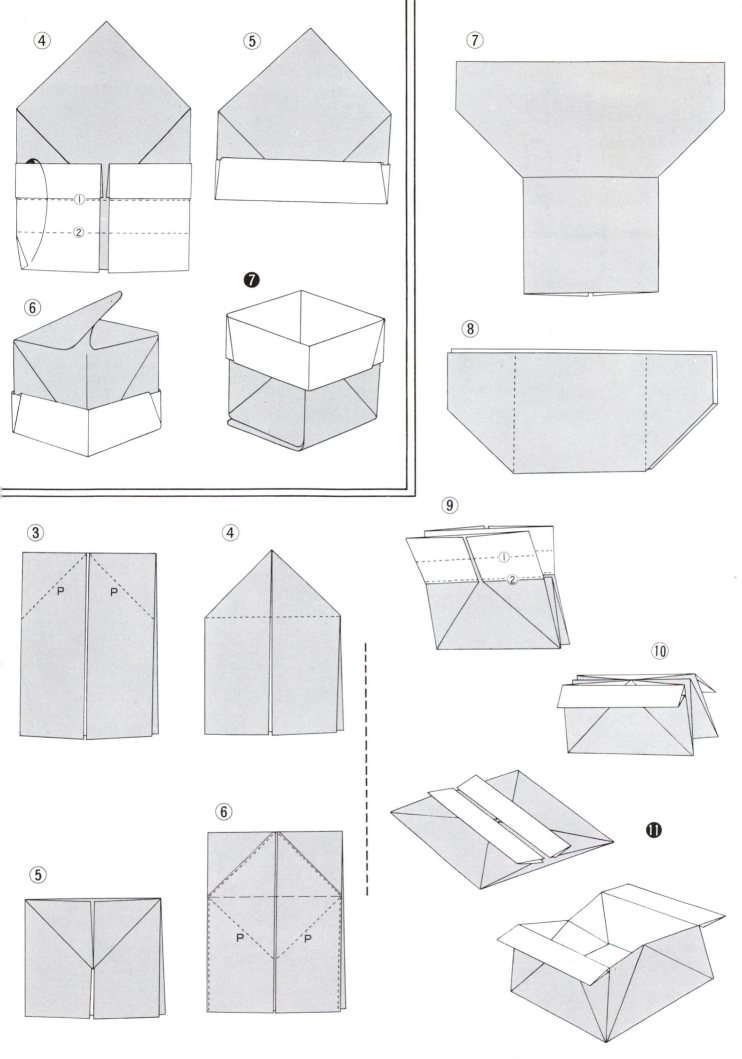

④

⑤

⑦

⑥

❼

⑧

⑨

⑩

❶❶

③

④

⑤

⑥

P P

P P

① ②

① ②

105

80. Folding Box (II)

Use a sheet of standard typewrighting paper.

1. Establish both center lines indicated in the chart. Valley fold the outer edges in to the horizontal center line.
2. Valley fold on the dotted lines.
3. Valley fold on the dotted lines.
4. Valley fold on the dotted lines.
5. Valley fold on the dotted lines, left side to right.
6. Valley fold the top layer only on the dotted lines.
7. Repeat from step 2.
8. Pull as shown in the chart.
9. The completed box.

①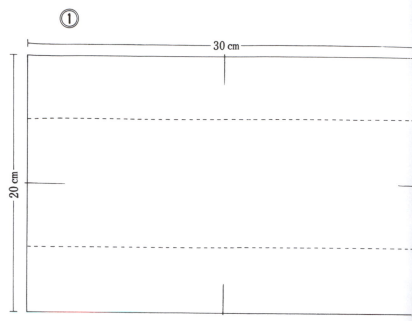

②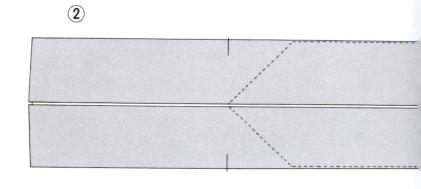

③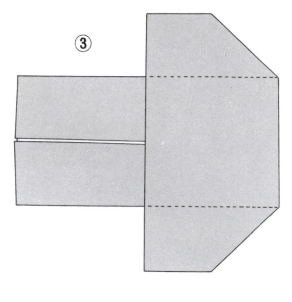

④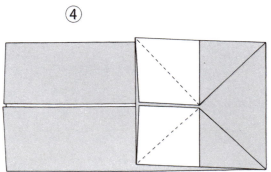

⑤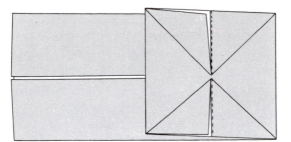

⑥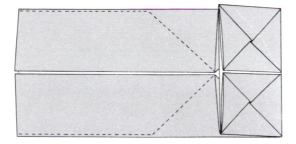

⑦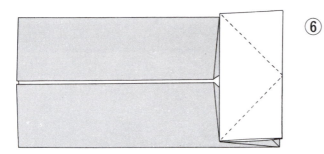

⑧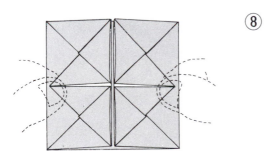

❾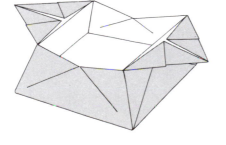

81. Kimono

Use a sheet of standard typewriter paper.

1. Peak and valley fold on the dotted lines, so that the paper is folded into thirds.
2. Peak fold only the top layer on the dotted lines.

①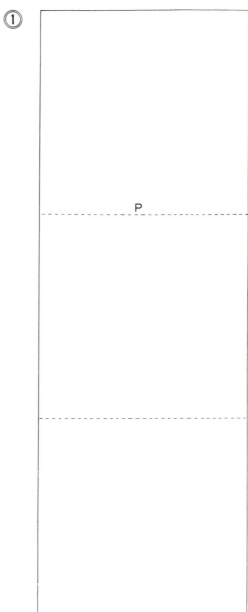

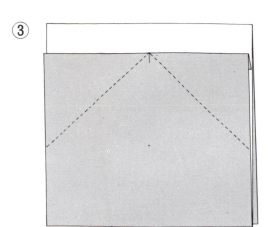

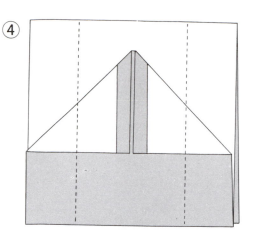

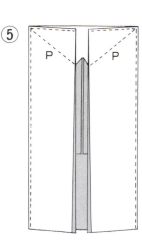

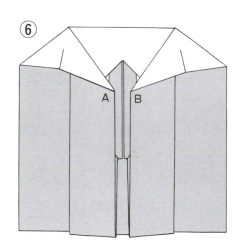

3. Valley fold the top layer only on the dotted lines. The outer edges should fall along the paper's center line.

4. Valley fold the remaining three layers on the dotted lines. The outer edges should be somewhat apart as you see them in step 5.

5. Flatten the sides out to the position in step 6 by peak and valley folding on the dotted lines.

6. Insert points A and B under what is to be the kimono collar. See step 7 for an idea of how this should look.

7. Peak fold on the dotted lines.

8. The figure should look like this. Turn it over.

9. Valley fold the top flap upward on the dotted line, and insert it as the arrow shows.

10. The underside of the completed figure.

11. The front of the completed figure.

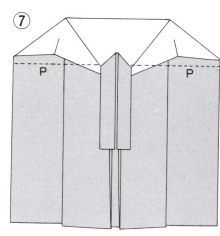

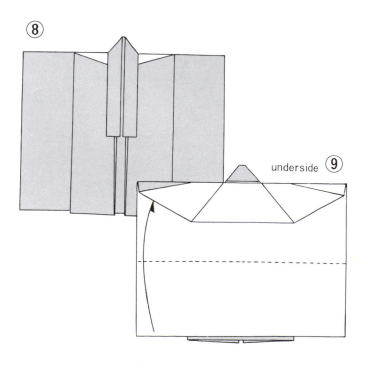

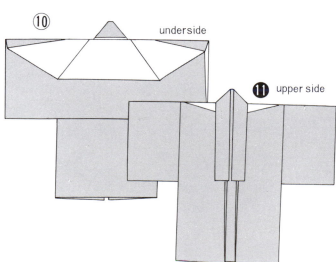

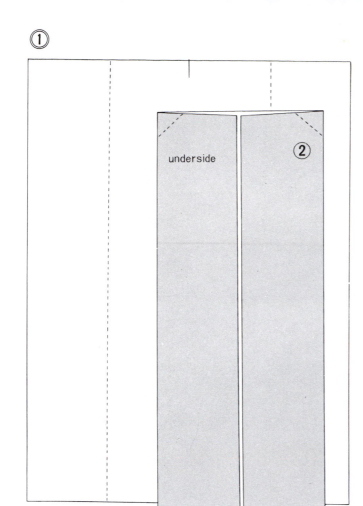

①

②

underside

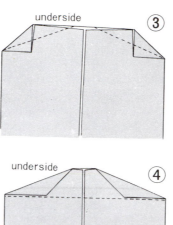

③ underside

④ underside

⑤ underside

P   P

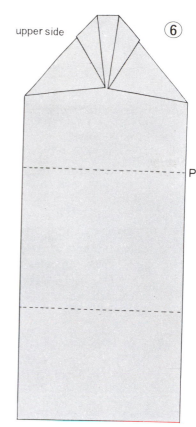

⑥ upper side

P

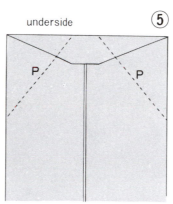

⑦

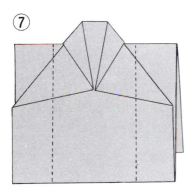

⑧

P   P

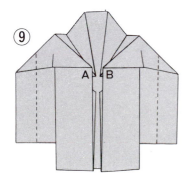

⑨

A B

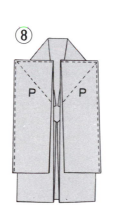

⑩

82. Jacket

Use an ordinary sheet of typing paper.

1. Valley fold the outer edges in to the center line.
2. Turn the model over, and valley fold the right and left upper corners.
3. Valley fold on the dotted lines.
4. Valley fold on the dotted line.
5. Peak fold on the dotted line.
6. Turn the model over, and peak and valley fold on the dotted lines.
7. Valley fold on the dotted lines.
8. Peak and valley fold as shown to open the side flaps out to the position in step 9.
9. Slip points A and B under the collar. Valley fold on the dotted line, and tuck the edges of the sleeves under the sides of the jacket.
10. The finished jacket.

COMPOUND FIGURES (Square Paper)

In the following figures we will have to use two sheets of paper for the necessary number of pointed ends. If you will look at the completed figure of the horse (84) you can see that seven pointed ends are needed for the neck, the ears, the four legs, and the tail. With one sheet of paper in the crane base we can get points for the neck, the wings, and the tail, four points in all. With the basic frog fold (step 14 in the frog) we can get five points, one for the head and one for each of the four legs. With neither of them can we get a total of three pointed ends. If you observe the compound method used in the horse you will see that section A gives the head, the ears (actually only one pointed end cut in two), and the two forelegs for a total of four. The rear section B gives the body, the two rear legs, and the tail, or four points. If we glue these two section together we have the needed seven points because the point that is the end of the rear section is actually hidden within the front section.

From forms FF we fold the following animal shapes:

84. Horse	100. Lion
85. Deer	101. Tiger
86. Reindeer	102. Squirrel
87. Rabbit	103. Spitz
88. Pegasus	104. Seal (II)
89. Pointer	107. Wolf
90. Cat	From forms FG the:
91. Japanese Monkey	105. Bear
92. Dachshund	106. Fisherman Bear
93. Fox	108. Elephant
94. Seated Fox	109. Polar Bear
95. Badger	110. Rhinoceros
96. Kangaroo	111. Pig
97. Camel	112. Cow
98. Goat	113. Water Buffalo
99. Kid	

In addition to the above, we use different combinations for the Rooster (83) (See charts.)

83. Rooster

Front Section

Use crane bases made from six-inch squares of red paper.

1. Crease the paper on the dotted lines. When you have made the second crease leave the figure folded as you see in step 2.
2. Fold the entire figure into the shape in step 3.
3. Valley fold on the dotted lines for a reverse fold inside out.
4. Valley fold the right flap on the dotted lines, and crimp the entire wing section inward. Peak fold one layer of the top flap only into the position in step 5.
5. Peak and valley fold the beak into position. Peak and valley fold the comb into position.

Rear Section

1.~2. Fold as for the horse (84) to step 2. Narrow the legs by valley folding on the dotted lines, one layer at a time.
3. Valley fold the two top flaps on the dotted line, front flap forward, rear flap to the rear.
4. Valley fold the entire model in half on the dotted line.
5. Valley fold the tail for a reverse fold inside out. Peak and valley fold the front of the body section in on the dotted lines.
6. Peak fold the legs into position.

▶ Join the two sections for the completed rooster. Do not forget to valley fold the feet into the shape in step 6. See photograph on page 80.

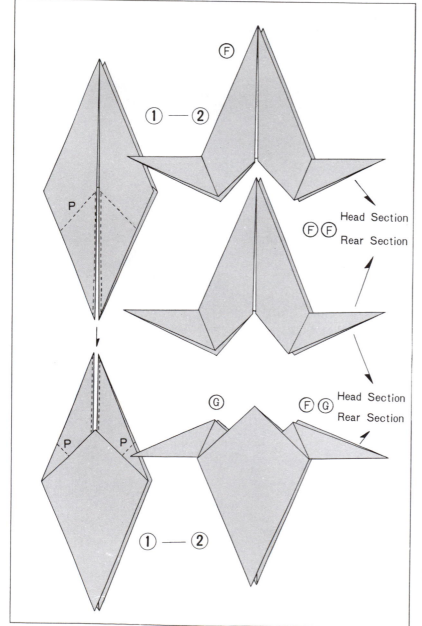

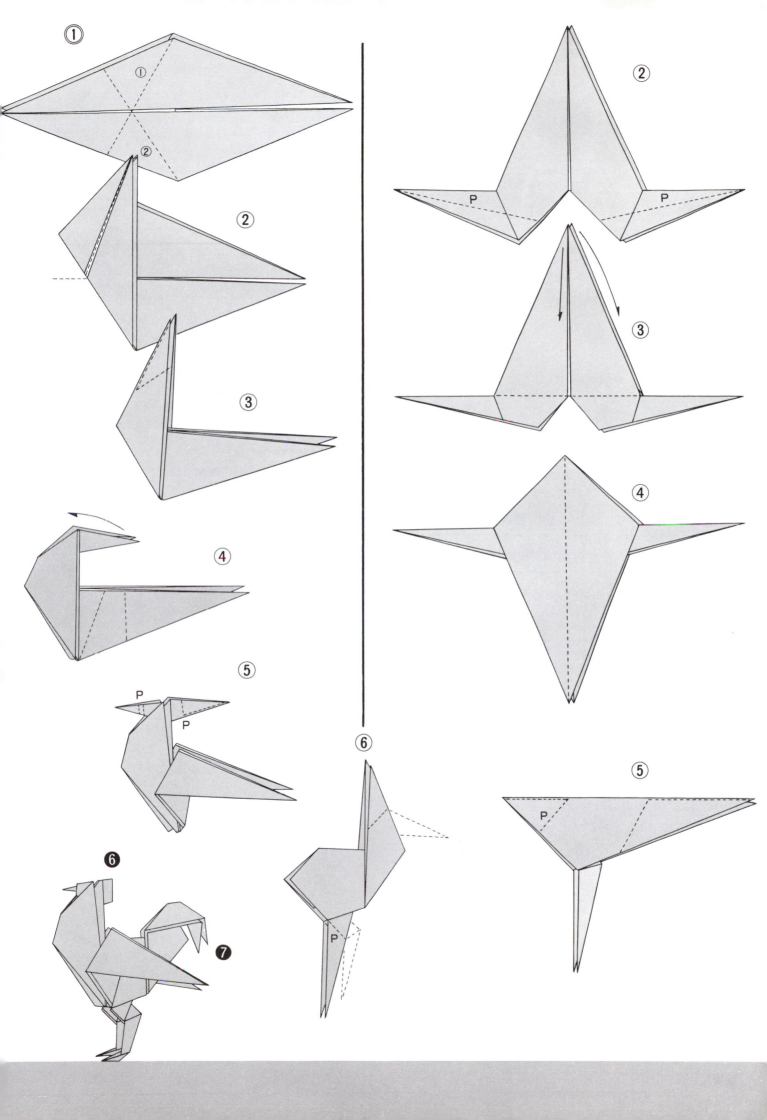

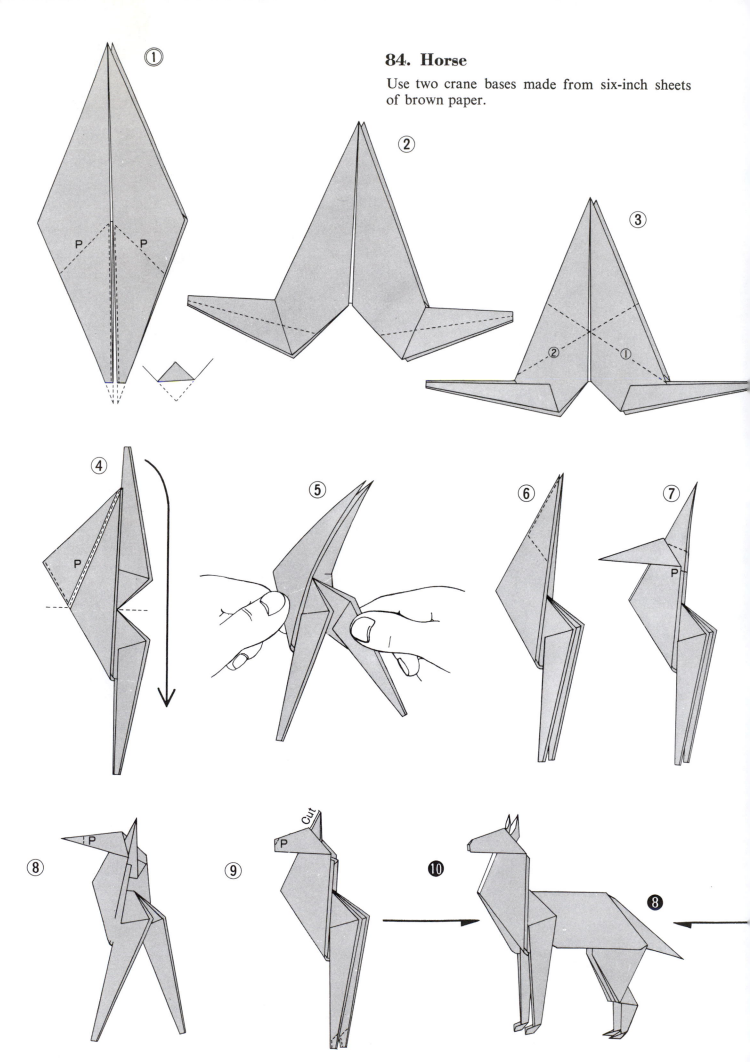

84. Horse

Use two crane bases made from six-inch sheets of brown paper.

Head Section

1. First turn the tips of the bottom points in as shown. Peak and valley fold each point as indicated for a reverse fold inside out.
2. Narrow the legs by valley folding the top flap on the dotted line. Turn the model over and repeat.
3. Valley fold on the dotted lines in numerical order. After you have creased line 1, open it out again and crease line 2, leaving it folded.
4. Peak and valley fold the triangle on the left where indicated. At the same time bring the top leg down as the arrow indicates, and valley fold the model in the middle.
5. This is how step 4 should progress.
6. Valley fold on the dotted lines for a reverse fold inside out, one layer only.
7. Peak and valley fold as shown, and crimp the ears down.
8. Peak fold the end of the muzzle under.
9. Cut where indicated.

Rear Section

1. Peak and valley fold for a reverse fold inside out.
2. Valley fold on the dotted line, top flap only.
3. Valley fold bottom flap on the dotted line. Valley fold on right and left dotted lines.
4. Valley fold on the dotted line.
5. Peak and valley fold the tail for a reverse fold outside in. Peak and valley fold each leg as indicated.
6. Peak fold the belly area on each side, and valley fold the tail on the dotted line.
7. The finished rear section.

▶ Join the two, and glue them together for the finished horse. Insert the rear section behind the shoulders of the front section.

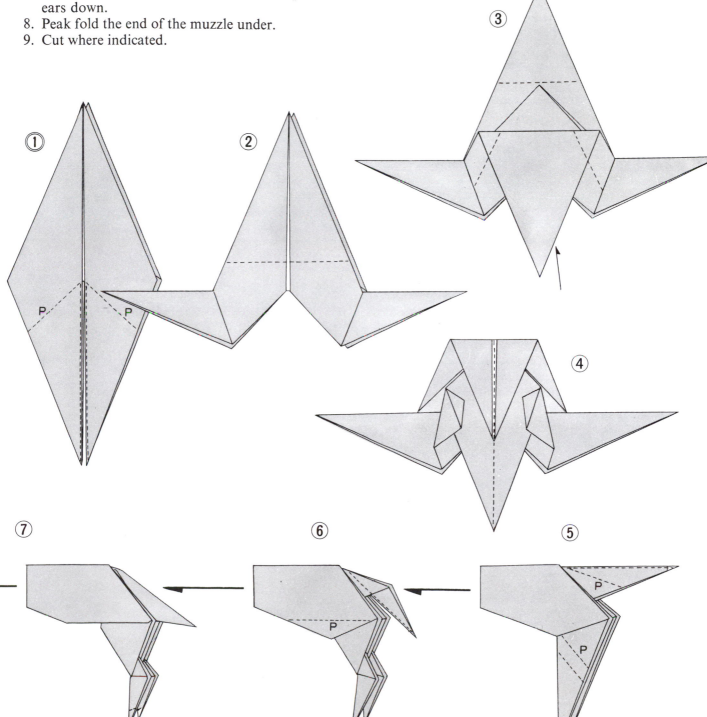

113

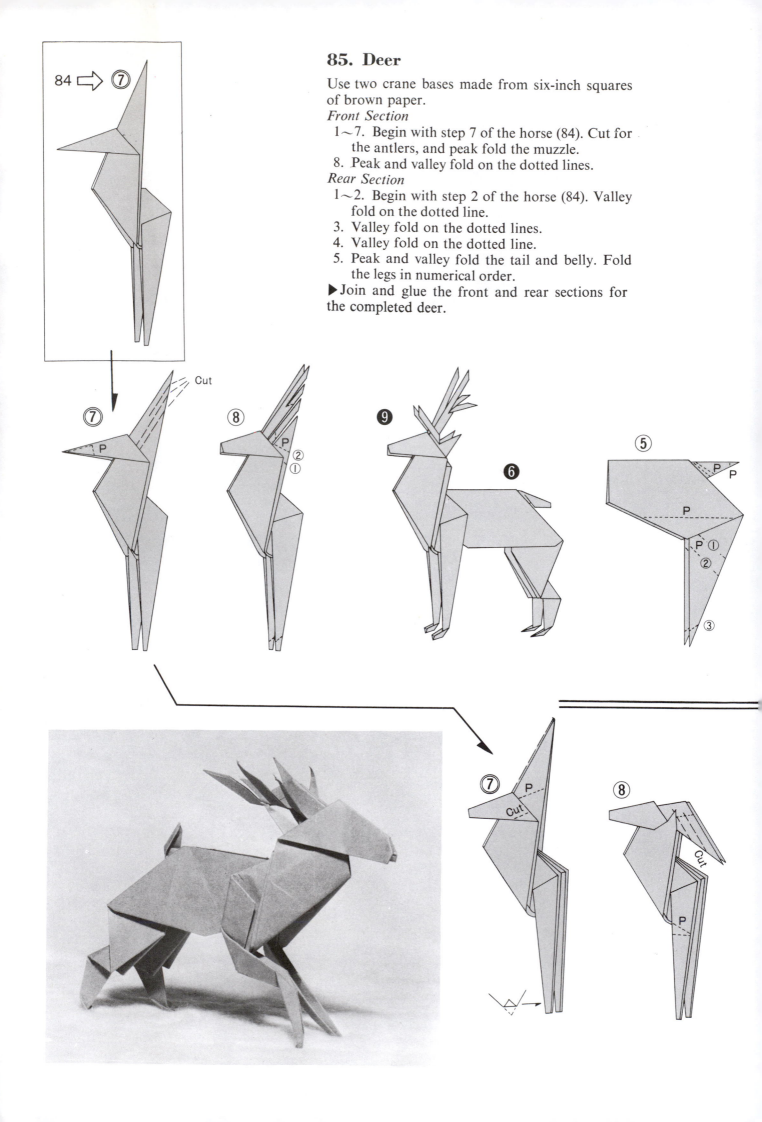

85. Deer

Use two crane bases made from six-inch squares of brown paper.

Front Section

1~7. Begin with step 7 of the horse (84). Cut for the antlers, and peak fold the muzzle.

8. Peak and valley fold on the dotted lines.

Rear Section

1~2. Begin with step 2 of the horse (84). Valley fold on the dotted line.

3. Valley fold on the dotted lines.

4. Valley fold on the dotted line.

5. Peak and valley fold the tail and belly. Fold the legs in numerical order.

▶ Join and glue the front and rear sections for the completed deer.

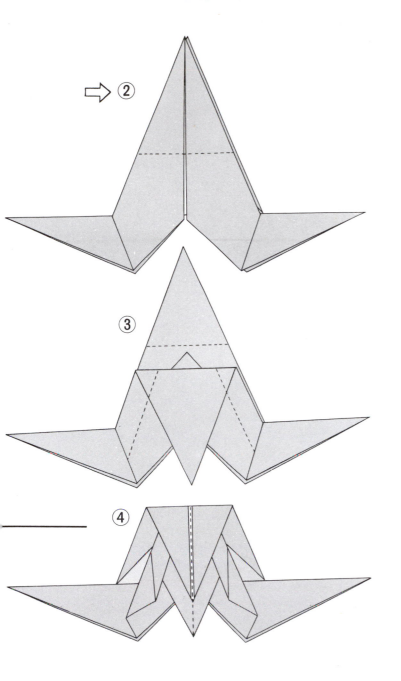

⇨ ②

③

④

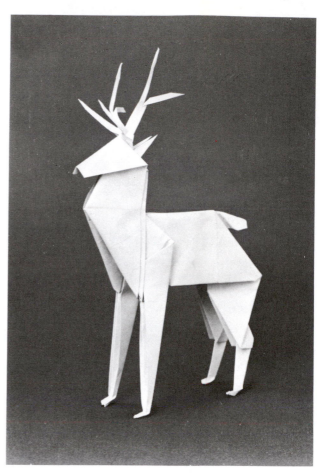

86. Reindeer

Use two crane bases made from six-inch squares of brown paper. The reindeer is folded just as the deer (85) except that you must be careful to cut the antlers and ears as indicated in the chart and to fold the tail and legs to suggest a running reindeer.

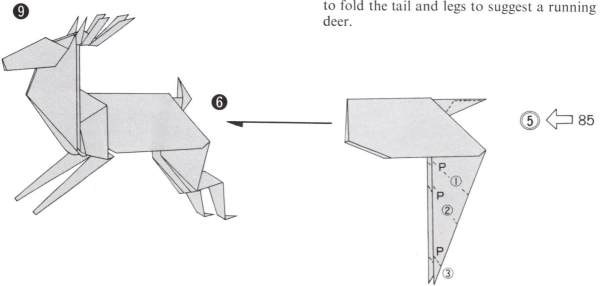

❾

❻

⑤ ⇦ 85

P ①
P ②
P ③

115

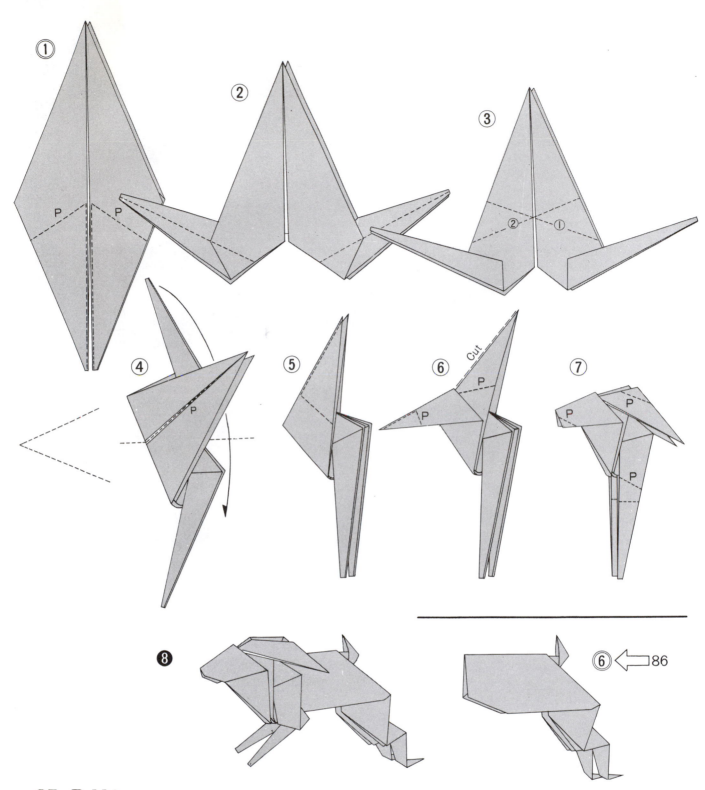

87. Rabbit

Use two crane bases made of six-inch squares of brown or white paper.

Front Section

1. Peak and valley fold on the dotted lines for reverse folds inside out.
2. Valley fold on the dotted lines, top flaps first. Turn the model over and repeat.
3. Valley fold on the dotted lines in numerical order. When you have made crease 1, unfold again and make crease 2; leave it folded.
4. Peak and valley fold the triangular flap as indicated. At the same time bring the uppermost point downward as the arrow indicates for a figure like that in step 5.
5. Valley fold the outer flap on the dotted lines for a reverse fold outside in.
6. Peak fold the rabbit's nose under. Cut the ears as indicated, and peak fold them back into the position in step 7. Peak and fold the nose and ears where indicated. Peak and valley fold the legs into the position in step 8.

Rear Section.

1∼6. Fold as for the reindeer (86) through step 6.

▶Join the two sections for the completed rabbit.

88. Pegasus, the Flying Horse

Use two crane bases made from six-inch squares of white paper.

Front Section

1. Cut on the indicated lines.
2. Peak fold the top flap only so that the ends go under and come out in the position shown in step 3.
3. Valley fold the tips of the right and left points in as shown. Fold the model in half on the dotted line.
4. Valley fold on the dotted lines on the left to reverse fold the neck section inside out. Valley fold the legs to narrow them, and valley fold the wings on the dotted line.

5. Valley fold the head section to reverse fold it inside out. Peak fold the wings on the dotted line.
6. Fold the muzzle. Invert the crease indicated by a dotted line on the wing. This will bring the wing around to form a trapezoidal shape like that in the finished model. Peak and valley fold the legs to reverse fold them into the prancing position seen in the finished model.

Rear Section

1~7. Fold as for the horse (84) to step 7. Peak and valley fold the legs and tail into position as shown.

▶Join the front and rear sections for the completed model.

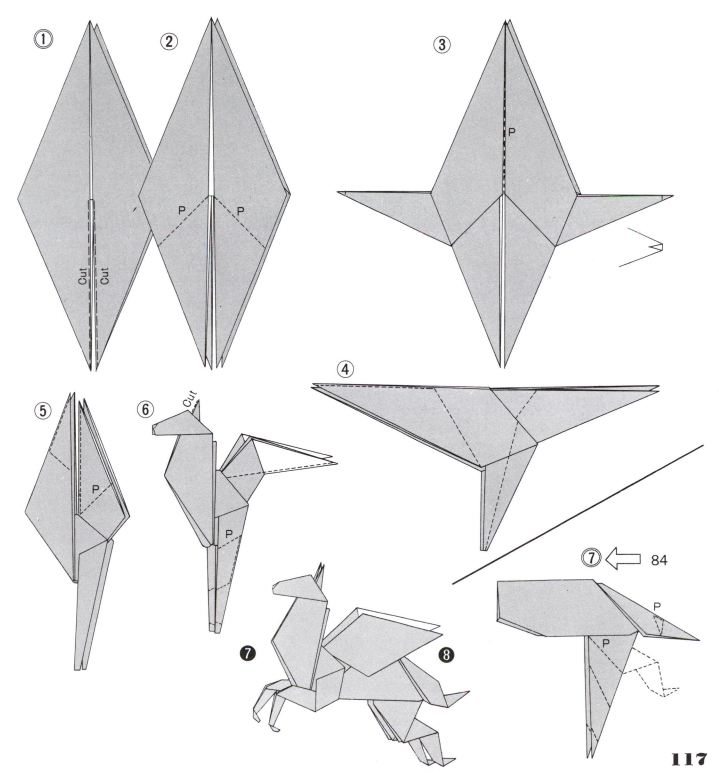

89. Pointer

Use two crane bases made from six-inch squares of brown or black paper.

Front Section

1~6. Fold as for the horse (84) through step 6.
7. Cut the ears as shown, and valley fold them down as shown.
8. Peak and valley fold the muzzle inward. Peak fold the ears as shown. Peak and valley fold the tips of the ears inward.
9. Fold the tips of the forelegs in as shown in the chart. Valley fold again on the dotted lines to form the front paws.

Rear Section

1~2. Fold as for the horse (84) through step 2. Valley fold on the dotted lines.
3. Narrow the lower point by valley folding on the dotted lines. Concentrate on lining the outer edges with the center line, and the secondary folds will naturally fall into place.
4. Valley fold on the dotted line.
5. Valley fold on the dotted line.
6. Peak and valley fold the tail section for a reverse fold outside in. Peak fold the belly section on the dotted line. Peak and valley fold the legs in the dotted lines in numerical order.
7. Valley fold the tail as shown, and fold the tips of the legs.

▶ Join the front and rear sections for the finished pointer.

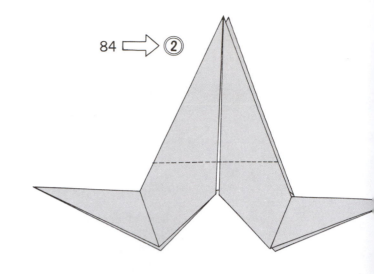

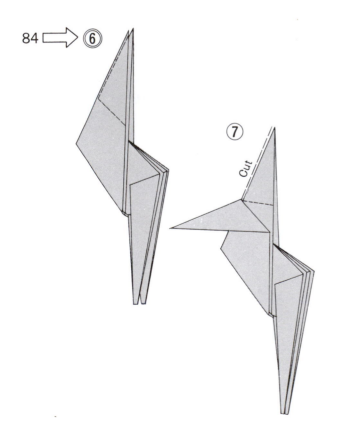

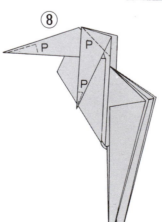

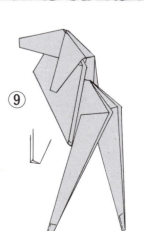

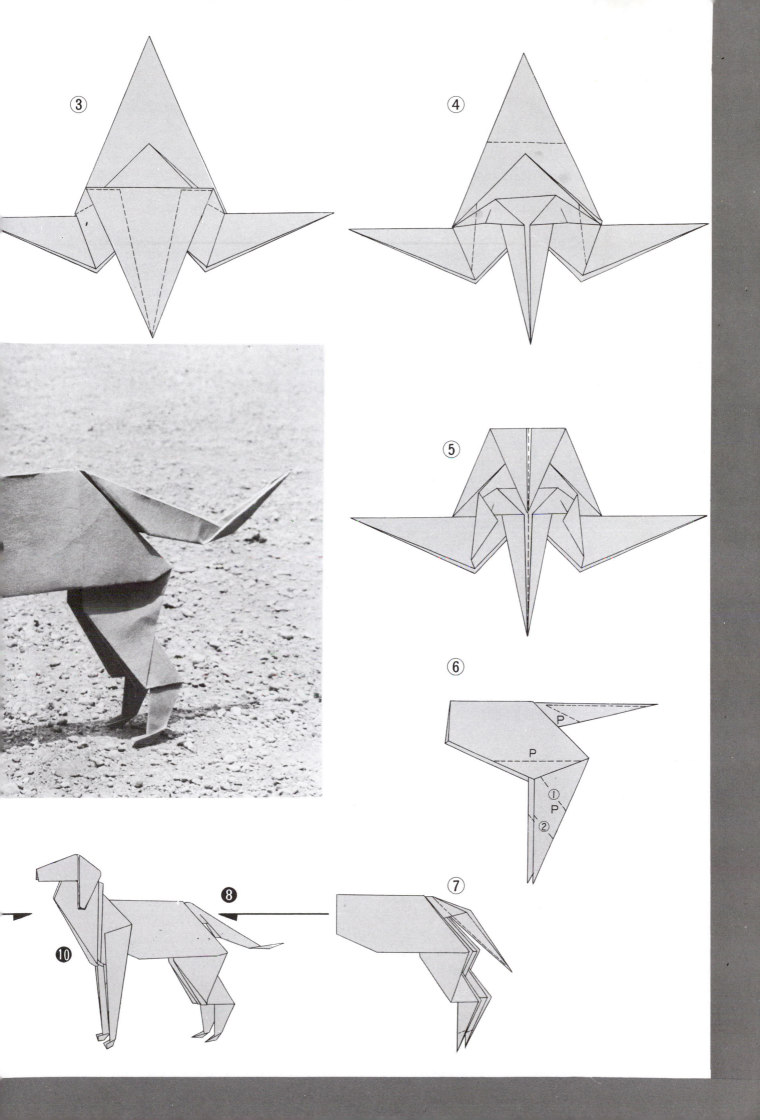

③

④

⑤

⑥
P
P
① P
②

⑦

❽

❿

90. Cat

Use two crane bases made from six-inch squares of any suitable color.

Front Section

1. Fold as for the rear section of the horse (84) to step 2.
2. Valley fold on the dotted line.
3. Peak and valley fold the triangular flap as indicated. At the same time, pull the uppermost point downward as the arrow indicates.
4. Peak and valley crease to invert the two layers of the projecting triangles.
5. Bring both layers of the upper points over to the front for a figure like that in step 6.
6. The figure should look like this. Turn it over.
7. Cut on the underside of the face section as indicated and fold the ears upward.
8. Peak fold the point on the dotted lines. Peak and valley fold the legs into shape.

Rear Section

1~6. Fold as for the pointer (89) to step 6. Peak and valley fold the tail for a reverse fold inward. Peak and valley fold the legs into shape.

▶Join the front and rear sections for the completed cat.

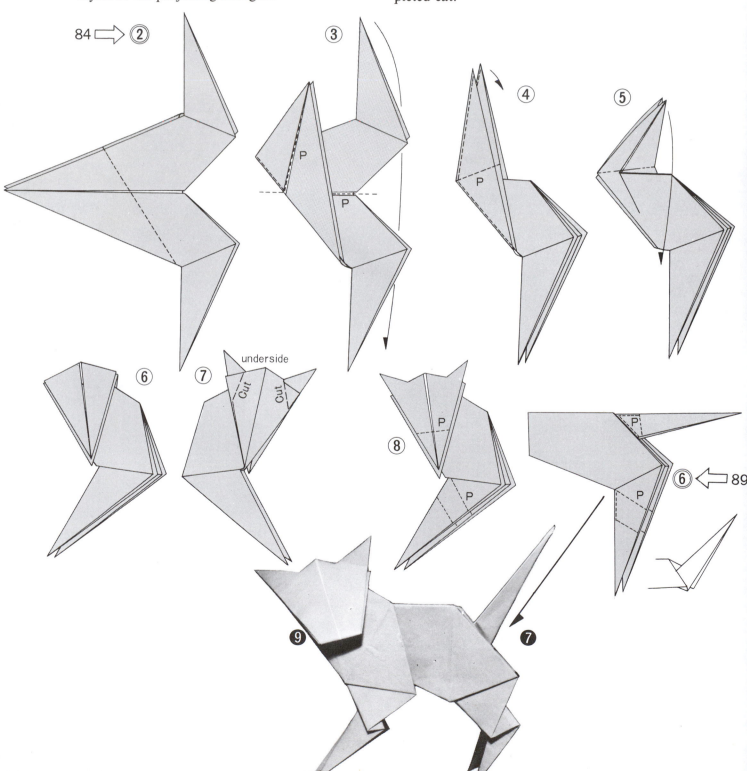

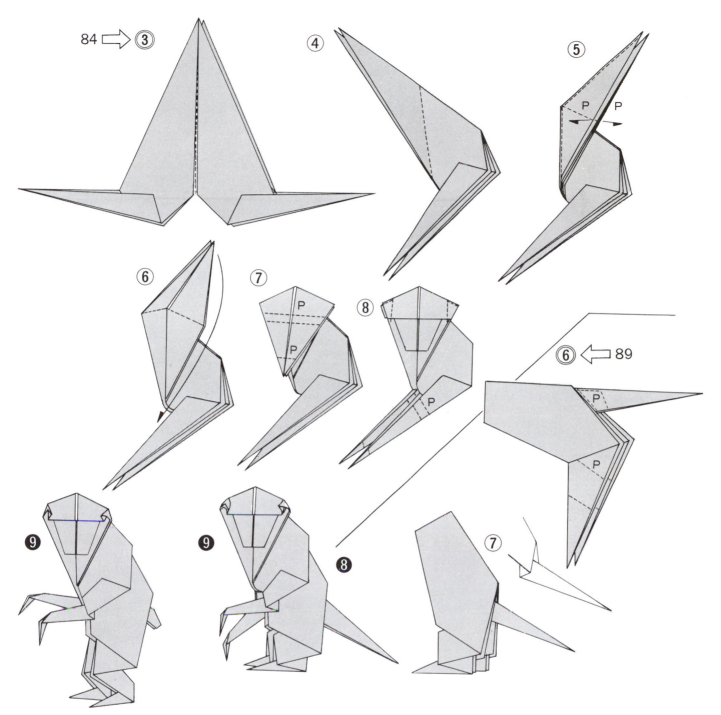

91. Monkey

Use two crane bases made from six-inch squares of light brown paper.

Note: Be careful to fold the tail short because a short tail is a characteristic of the Japanese monkey. When you have finished the model arrange the legs to make him look as if he were about to walk.

1~3. Fold as for the horse (84) to step 3. Valley fold the model in half on the dotted line.

4. Valley fold on the dotted line for a reverse fold inside out.

5. Peak and valley fold as indicated to bring the flap (both layers) over to the position you see in step 7.

6. The process of pulling the flaps over.

7. Peak and valley fold on the indicated dotted lines.

8. Valley fold on the dotted lines to squash fold the sides of the monkey's head into the position you see in step 9. Peak and valley fold the hands and arms as indicated.

Rear Section.

1~6. Fold as for the rear section of the pointer (89) to step 6. Peak and valley fold the tail, and crimp it inward. Peak and valley fold the legs as indicated, and crimp them inward.

7. The completed rear section. See photograph on page 123.

▶Join the two sections, and glue them together. If you are making a regular monkey, leave the tail long.

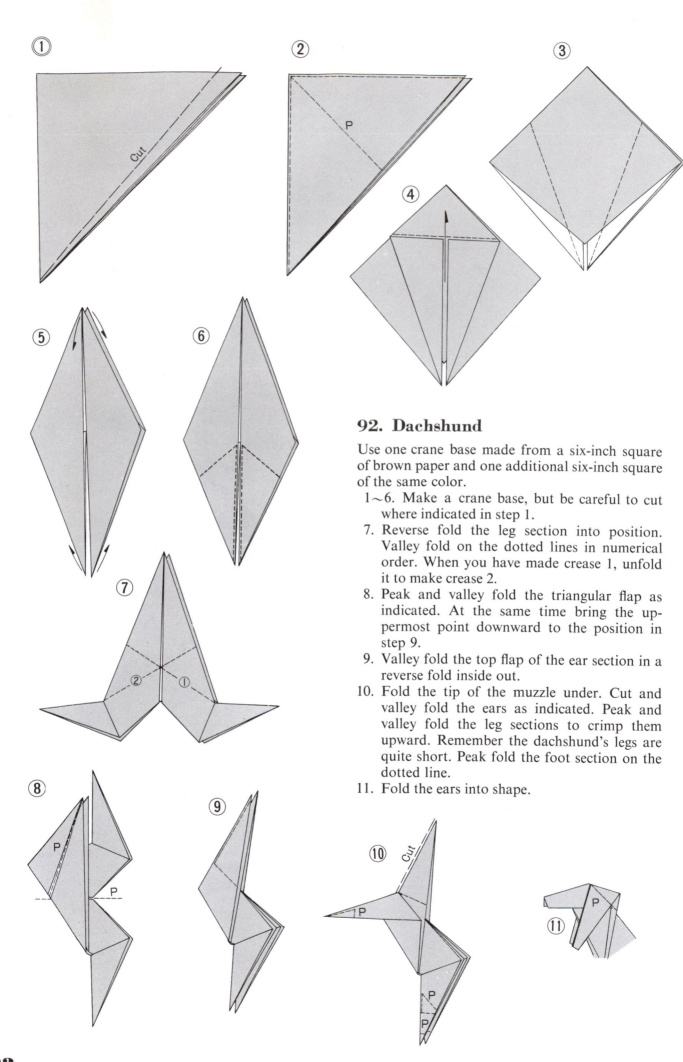

92. Dachshund

Use one crane base made from a six-inch square
of brown paper and one additional six-inch square
of the same color.

1~6. Make a crane base, but be careful to cut
where indicated in step 1.

7. Reverse fold the leg section into position.
Valley fold on the dotted lines in numerical
order. When you have made crease 1, unfold
it to make crease 2.

8. Peak and valley fold the triangular flap as
indicated. At the same time bring the uppermost point downward to the position in
step 9.

9. Valley fold the top flap of the ear section in a
reverse fold inside out.

10. Fold the tip of the muzzle under. Cut and
valley fold the ears as indicated. Peak and
valley fold the leg sections to crimp them
upward. Remember the dachshund's legs are
quite short. Peak fold the foot section on the
dotted line.

11. Fold the ears into shape.

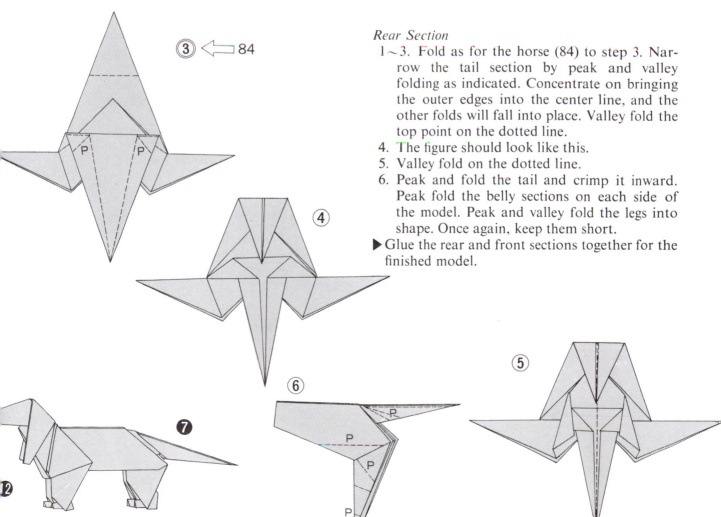

③ ⬅ 84

Rear Section

1~3. Fold as for the horse (84) to step 3. Narrow the tail section by peak and valley folding as indicated. Concentrate on bringing the outer edges into the center line, and the other folds will fall into place. Valley fold the top point on the dotted line.
4. The figure should look like this.
5. Valley fold on the dotted line.
6. Peak and fold the tail and crimp it inward. Peak fold the belly sections on each side of the model. Peak and valley fold the legs into shape. Once again, keep them short.
▶ Glue the rear and front sections together for the finished model.

123

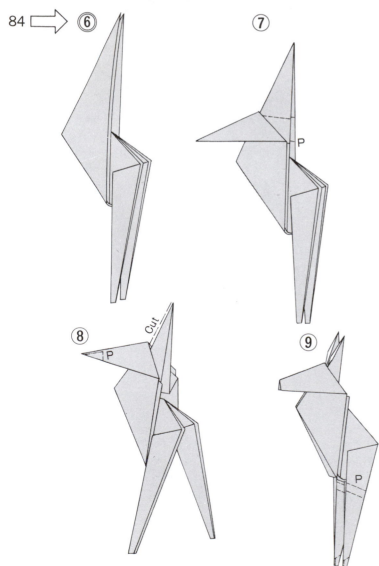

84 ⟹ ⑥　　　　　⑦

93. Fox

Use two crane bases made from six-inch squares of orange paper.

Front Section.

1~6. Fold as for the horse (84) to step 6.
7. Peak and valley fold the ear section, and crimp it down. Remember not to make the fox's ears too short.
8. Cut the ears as indicated, and spread them open a little. Fold the muzzle in as shown, but do not make it too blunt.
9. Peak and valley fold the legs as shown, and reverse fold the feet into position.

⑧

⑨

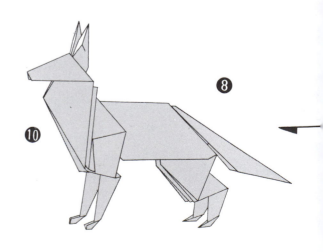

124

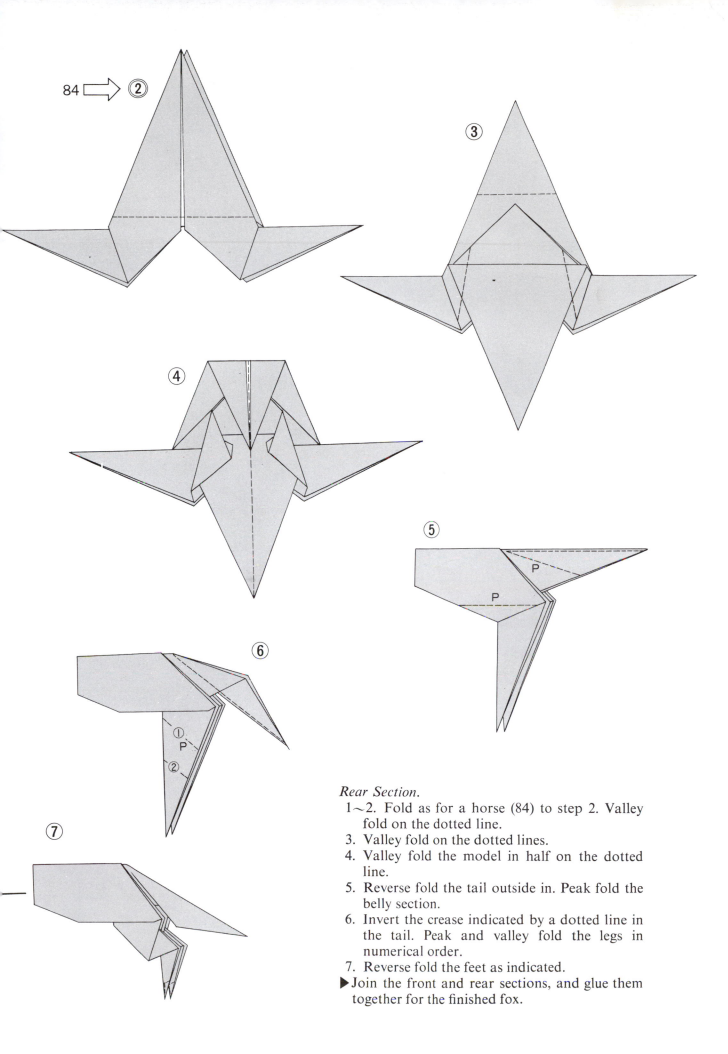

Rear Section.

1~2. Fold as for a horse (84) to step 2. Valley fold on the dotted line.

3. Valley fold on the dotted lines.

4. Valley fold the model in half on the dotted line.

5. Reverse fold the tail outside in. Peak fold the belly section.

6. Invert the crease indicated by a dotted line in the tail. Peak and valley fold the legs in numerical order.

7. Reverse fold the feet as indicated.

▶Join the front and rear sections, and glue them together for the finished fox.

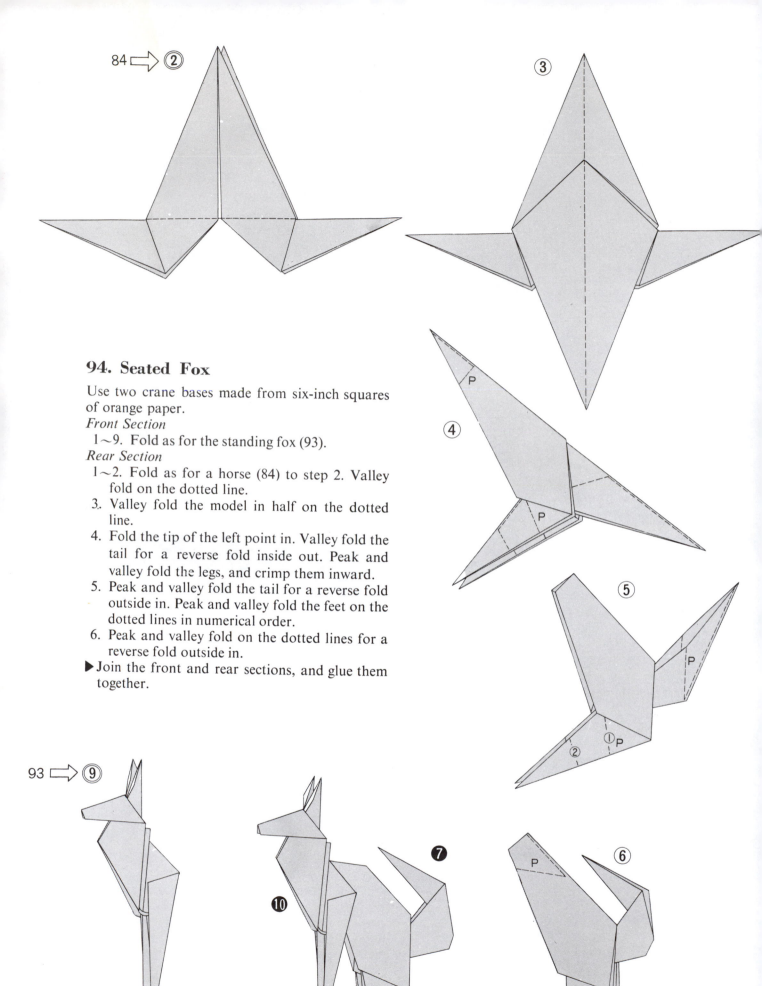

84 ⇨ ②

③

④

⑤

94. Seated Fox

Use two crane bases made from six-inch squares of orange paper.

Front Section

1~9. Fold as for the standing fox (93).

Rear Section

1~2. Fold as for a horse (84) to step 2. Valley fold on the dotted line.

3. Valley fold the model in half on the dotted line.

4. Fold the tip of the left point in. Valley fold the tail for a reverse fold inside out. Peak and valley fold the legs, and crimp them inward.

5. Peak and valley fold the tail for a reverse fold outside in. Peak and valley fold the feet on the dotted lines in numerical order.

6. Peak and valley fold on the dotted lines for a reverse fold outside in.

▶ Join the front and rear sections, and glue them together.

93 ⇨ ⑨

❼

❻

❿

126

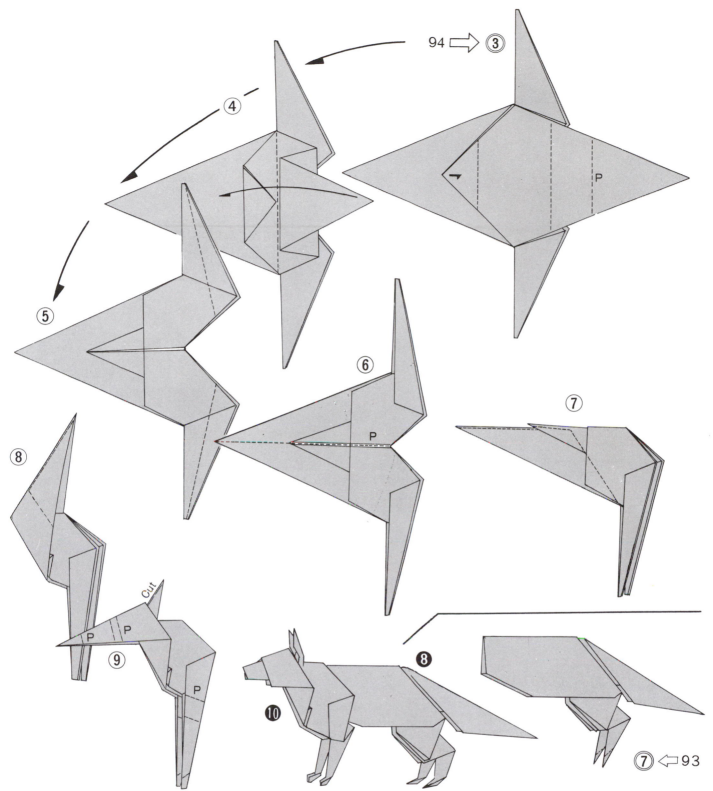

95. Badger

Use two crane bases made of six-inch sheets of light brown paper.

Front Section

1~3. Fold as for the rear section of the fox (93) to step 3. Peak and valley fold on the dotted lines.
4. Fold the model in half on the dotted line, bringing the right point to the left as the arrow indicates.
5. Narrow the leg sections by valley folding on the dotted lines. Turn the model over and repeat.
6. Valley fold the model in half on the dotted line.
7. Valley fold on the dotted lines for a reverse fold inside out.
8. Valley fold on the dotted lines for a reverse fold inside out.
9. Cut the ears as indicated. Peak and valley fold the head, and crimp it inward. Fold the end of the muzzle in. Peak and valley fold the legs as indicated.

Rear Section.

1~7. Fold as for the rear section of the fox (93).
Note: Be careful to make the legs shorter than for the fox to suit the badger's body.

▶Join the two sections, and glue them together.

127

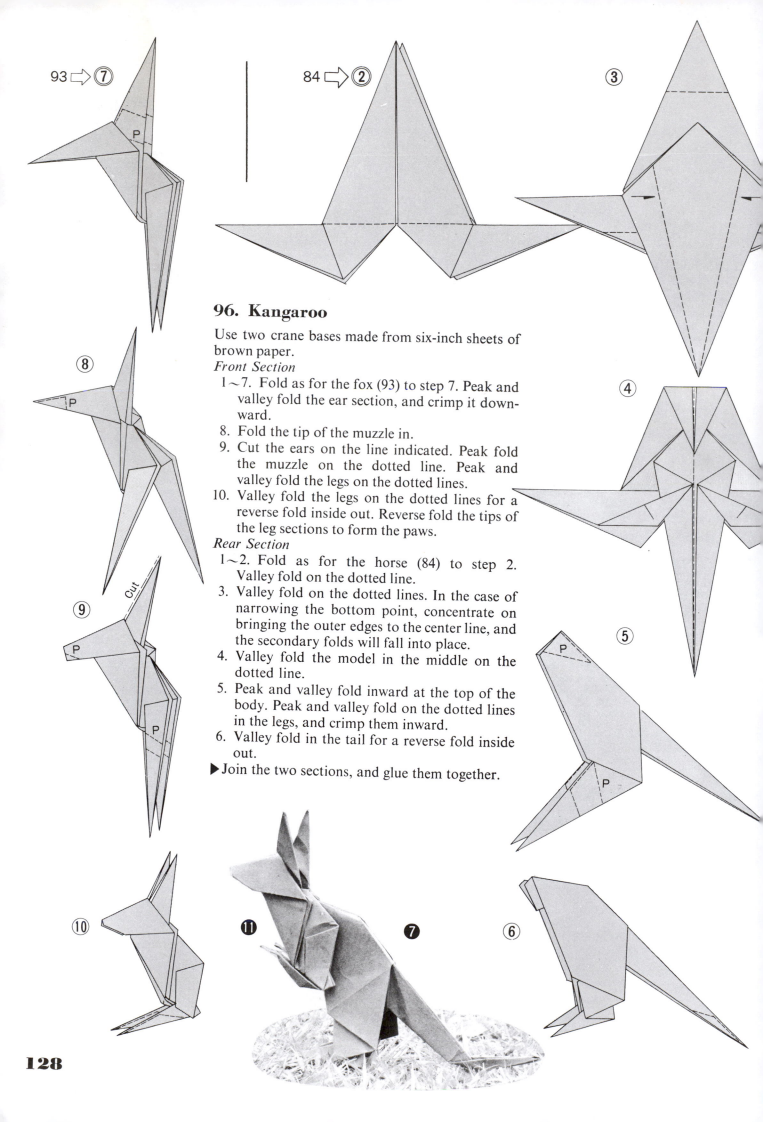

93 ⇨ ⑦

84 ⇨ ②

③

④

⑤

⑧

⑨

Cut

⑩

❶❶

❼

⑥

96. Kangaroo

Use two crane bases made from six-inch sheets of brown paper.

Front Section

1~7. Fold as for the fox (93) to step 7. Peak and valley fold the ear section, and crimp it downward.

8. Fold the tip of the muzzle in.

9. Cut the ears on the line indicated. Peak fold the muzzle on the dotted line. Peak and valley fold the legs on the dotted lines.

10. Valley fold the legs on the dotted lines for a reverse fold inside out. Reverse fold the tips of the leg sections to form the paws.

Rear Section

1~2. Fold as for the horse (84) to step 2. Valley fold on the dotted line.

3. Valley fold on the dotted lines. In the case of narrowing the bottom point, concentrate on bringing the outer edges to the center line, and the secondary folds will fall into place.

4. Valley fold the model in the middle on the dotted line.

5. Peak and valley fold inward at the top of the body. Peak and valley fold on the dotted lines in the legs, and crimp them inward.

6. Valley fold in the tail for a reverse fold inside out.

▶ Join the two sections, and glue them together.

128

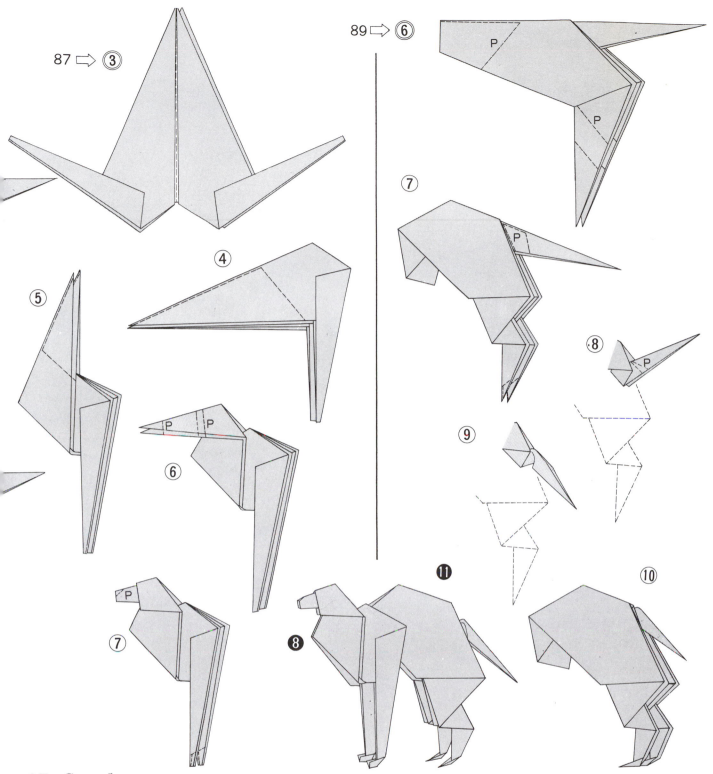

97. Camel

Use two crane bases made from six-inch squares of light brown paper.

Front Section

1~3. Fold as for the rabbit (87) to step 3. Valley fold the model in half on the dotted line.
4. Valley fold on the dotted lines for a reverse fold inside out.
5. Valley fold on the dotted lines for a reverse fold inside out.
6. Peak fold the end of the muzzle in. Peak and valley fold on the dotted lines, and crimp inward.
7. Round the end of the muzzle by peak folding. Valley fold the tips of the legs.

Rear Section

1~6. Fold as for the pointer rear section (89) to step 6.
   Peak and valley fold the trunk for a reverse fold outside in. Peak and valley fold the legs as indicated.
7. Peak and valley fold the tail, and push it inward into the position in step 8. Valley fold the tips of the legs as shown.
8. Peak and valley fold the tail again for a reverse fold inside out as seen in step 9.
9. The tail should look like this.
▶Join the two sections, and glue them together for the finished camel. See photograph on page 130.

129

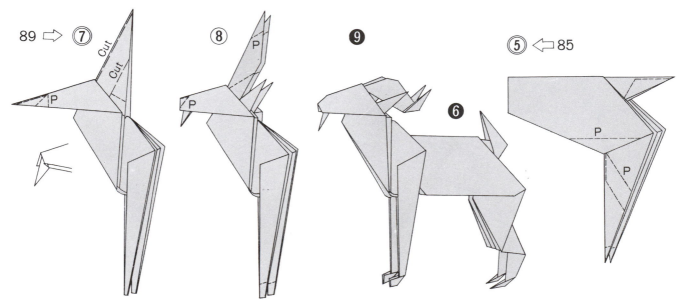

89 ⇨ ⑦   ⑧   ❾   ⑤ ⇦ 85

❻

98. Goat

Use two crane bases made from six-inch squares of cream paper.

Front Section

1~7. Fold as for the front section of the pointer (89) to step 7. Peak and valley fold the muzzle carefully as shown, and crimp it inward to leave the goat's beard jutting downward. Cut on the dotted lines, and valley fold the ears to crimp them inward.

8. Peak fold the muzzle as shown, and peak and valley fold the horns into the position in step 9. Valley fold the feet as indicated.

Rear Section.

1~5. Fold as for the rear section of the pointer (89) to step 5. Valley fold the tail as shown for a reverse fold inside out. Peak fold the belly. Peak and valley fold the legs into shape. Valley fold the feet as shown.

▶ Glue the two sections together for the finished goat.

99. Kid

Front Section

Use two crane bases made from six-inch squares of cream paper.

1~4. Fold as for the monkey (91) to step 4. Valley fold on the dotted line for a reverse fold inside out.

5. Valley fold on the dotted line for a reverse fold inside out.

6. Spread the head section into the position in step 7 by peak and valley folding as indicated.

7. Valley fold on the dotted line.

8. Cut on the indicated line, and valley fold as shown.

9. Valley fold on the dotted lines.

10. The figure should look like this. Return the top flap to its original position to make the head look as it does in step 11.

Rear Section

1~6. Fold as for the goat (98).

▶Glue the two sections together for the finished kid.

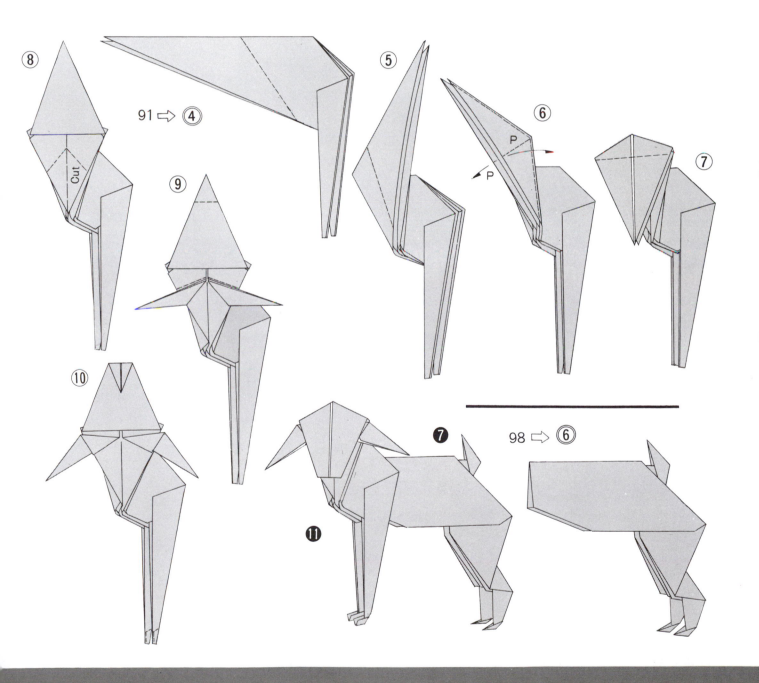

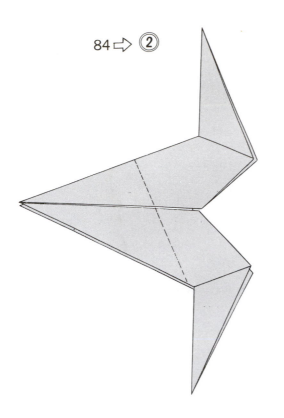

84 ⇨ ②

③

④

⑤

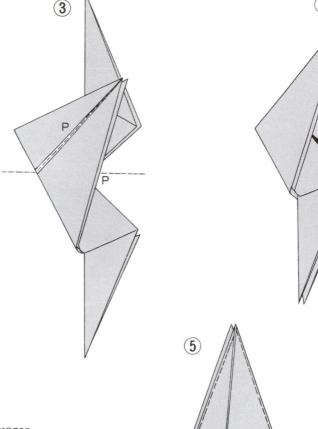

100. Lion

Use two crane bases made from six-inch squares of dark yellow paper.

1~2. Fold as for the horse to step 2. Valley fold on the dotted line.

3. Peak and valley fold into the position in step 4.

4. Open the figure out to the position in step 5.

5. Cut on the dotted lines, and open out the flaps that you cut.

6. Return the figure to the position in 6. Valley fold on the dotted lines for a reverse fold inside out. Be sure you fold far enough to expose the small inner point which will become the lion's ears.

7. Peak and valley fold the snout inward. Peak and valley fold the large flap as indicated.

8. Peak and valley fold the mane as indicated, and pull it into the position you see in step 9. Peak and valley fold the feet.

9. Cut the ears on the indicated line. Peak fold the tips of the feet for a reverse fold outside in to form the claws.

Rear Section

1~5. Fold as for the kangaroo (96) to step 5. Peak and valley fold the tail and legs as indicated.

6. Peak fold the belly. Valley fold to invert the crease in the tail.

7. Valley fold the tip of the tail for a reverse fold inside out. Valley fold the feet for the claws.

▶ Glue the two sections together for the completed lion.

⑥

⑦

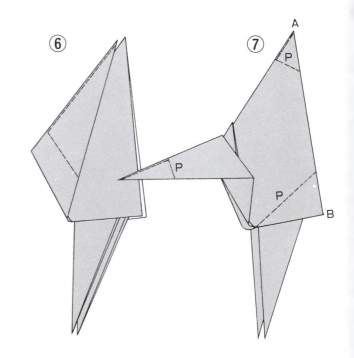

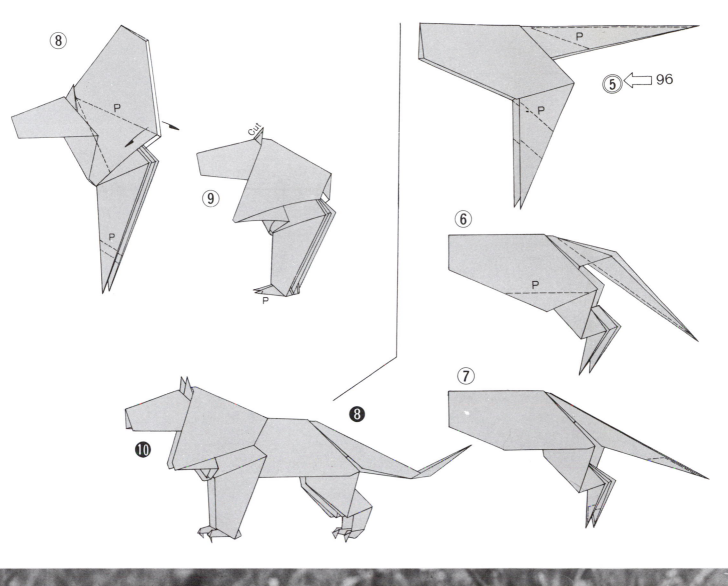

⑧

P

⑨ Cut

P

⑤ ⟵ 96

P

⑥

P

⑦

❽

❿

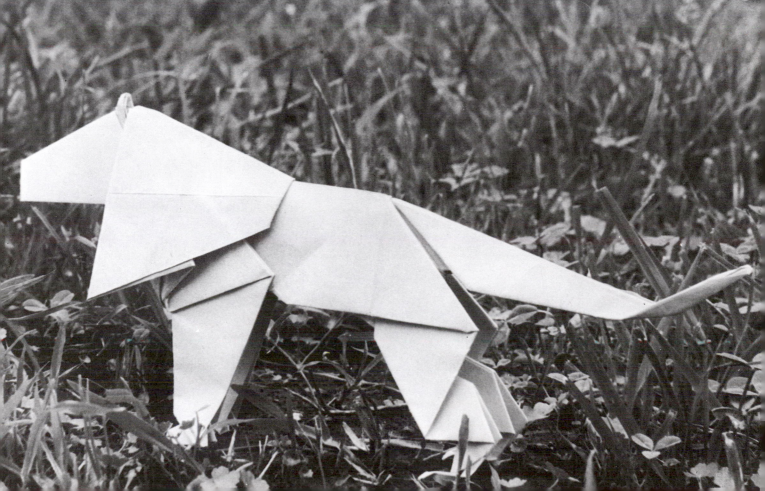

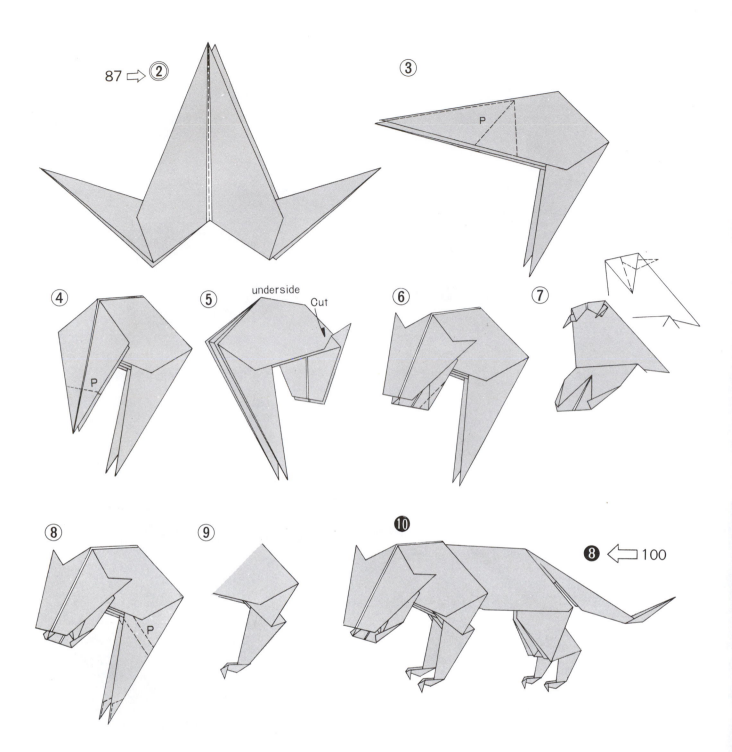

87 ⇨ ②

underside   Cut

❽ ⇦ 100

101. Tiger

Use two crane bases made of six-inch squares of yellow paper.

Front Section

1~2. Fold as for the rabbit (87) to step 2. Valley fold the figure in half on the dotted line.
3. Peak and valley fold as indicated to bring the head section into the position you see in step 4.
4. Peak fold each layer of the indicated flap separately. Turn the model over.
5. Cut on the indicated line on each side (top layer only) for the ears. Turn the model over.
6. Open the mouth. Valley fold on the dotted lines in the lower jaw. Cut on the indicated line in the upper jaw, and fold into the position you see in step 7.
8. Peak and valley fold the legs as indicated into the shape in step 9.

Rear Section

1~8. Fold as for the lion rear section.

▶ Glue the two sections together for the completed tiger.

102. Squirrel

Use two crane bases made from five-inch squares of light brown paper.

Front Section

1~3. Fold as for the rabbit (87) to step 3. Valley fold on the dotted lines in numerical order. Fold line 1, then unfold. Fold line 2, and leave it folded.

4. Fold the model in half on the dotted line, peak folding down the center of the top triangular section so that it falls into place as you see in step 5.

5. Valley fold the top layer only on the dotted lines for a reverse fold inside out to the position shown by the dotted lines.

6. Peak and valley fold the end of the snout under. Peak and valley fold the legs into the position in step 7.

7. Peak fold the muzzle under. Valley fold the legs as indicated for a reverse fold inside out.

8. Valley fold the ears, one layer at a time, on the dotted lines. Notice that the fold begins deep down in the neck section.

9. Peak fold on the dotted line, and open the pointed ears outward as the arrow shows to the shape in step 10.

Rear Section

1~3. Fold as for the fox rear section (93) to step 3. Peak fold the figure in half on the dotted line.

4. Valley fold the tail section on the dotted lines for a reverse fold inside out. Peak and valley fold the end of the trunk section in.

5. Peak and valley fold the legs inward into the position in step 6.

6. Round the top of the back section by peak and valley folding on the indicated lines. Peak and valley fold the feet into the position in step 7. Peak and valley fold the tail for a reverse fold outside in.

7. The finished rear section.

▶Join the two sections, and glue them together as shown for the finished squirrel.

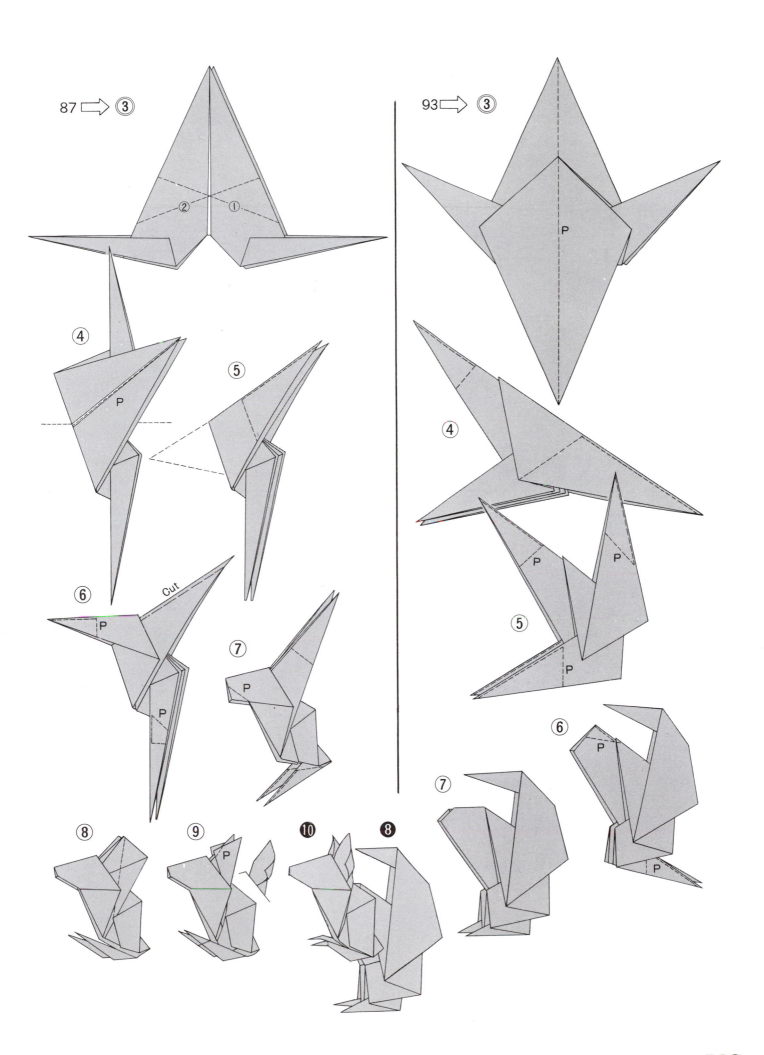

87 ⟹ ③

93 ⟹ ③

④

⑤

P

⑥

Cut

P

⑦

P

P

④

P

⑤

P

P

⑥

P

⑦

P

⑧

⑨

P

❿

❽

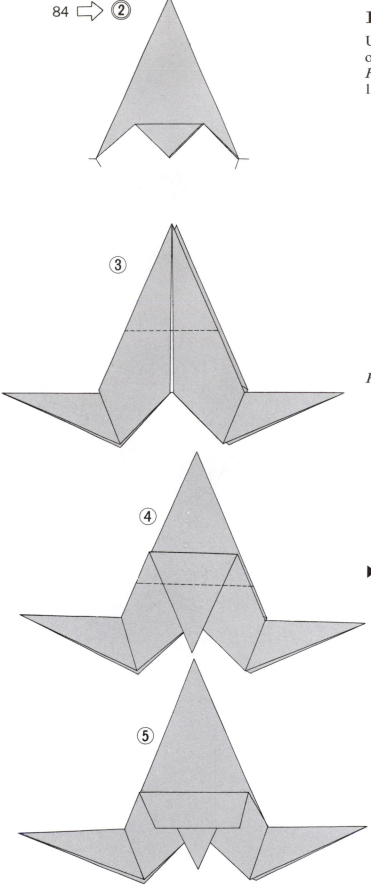

84 ⇨ ②

③

④

⑤

103. Spitz

Use two crane bases made from six-inch squares of white paper.

Front Section

1~2. Fold as for the horse (84) to step 2. Temporarily open the top point, and fold the innermost point in to hide it as you see in the chart.
3. Valley fold on the dotted line.
4. Valley fold the top layer only on the dotted line.
5. The figure should look like this. Turn the model over.
6. Valley fold the top layer only in numerical order.
7. Valley fold the top layer only on the dotted lines.
8. Valley fold the model in half on the dotted line.
9. Cut the ears as indicated. Peak and valley fold the legs, and crimp them into position. Valley fold the feet into shape.

Rear Section

1~3. Fold as for the rear section of the fox (93) to step 3. Valley fold on the dotted lines in numerical order.
4. Peak fold the belly section under. Valley fold the tail for a reverse fold inside out.
5. Peak and valley fold the tail for a reverse fold outside in. Peak and valley fold the legs into the position shown by the dotted lines.
6. Valley fold the tip of the tail for a reverse fold inside out.
7. Valley fold the feet into position.

▶ Join the two sections, and glue them together for the finished spitz.

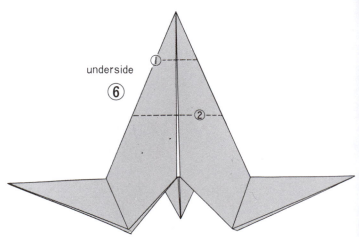

underside
⑥
①
②

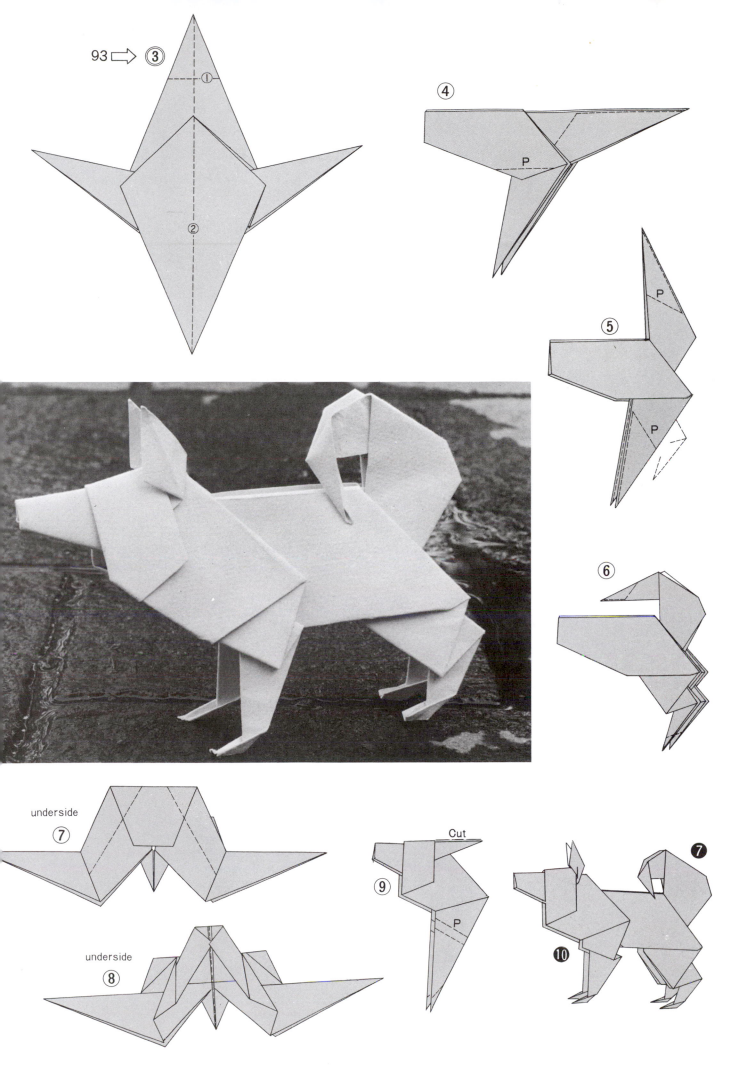

93 ➡ ③

underside ⑦

underside ⑧

Cut
⑨

139

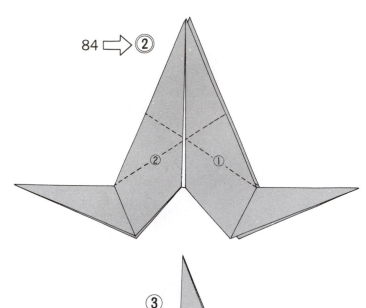

84 ⇨ ②

104. Seal (II)

Use two crane bases made from six-inch squares of black paper.

Front Section

1. Fold as for the horse (84) to step 2.
2. Valley fold on the dotted lines in numerical order. Fold line 1, then unfold it. Fold line 2, and leave it folded.
3. Valley fold the model in half. Peak fold the center line of the triangular section, and as you fold, pull it into the position in step 4.
4. Valley fold the ears and the legs for reverse folds inside out.
5. Peak and valley fold the muzzle in. Valley fold the flippers on the dotted lines.

Rear Section

1. Fold the lower tips out as shown.
2. Pull the under top point down as the arrow indicates for step 3.
3. The figure should look like this.
4. Peak and valley fold the tail section for a reverse fold outside in.
5. The figure should look like this.
6. Peak and valley fold the trunk section inward. Valley fold the center section of the tail into the position indicated by the dotted lines.
7. Peak and valley fold the back as shown for a reverse fold outside in. Valley fold the rear flippers into the position in step 8.

▶ Join the two sections, and glue them together for the finished seal.

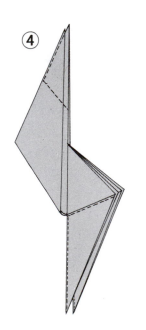

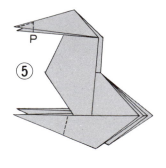

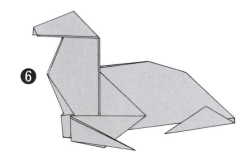

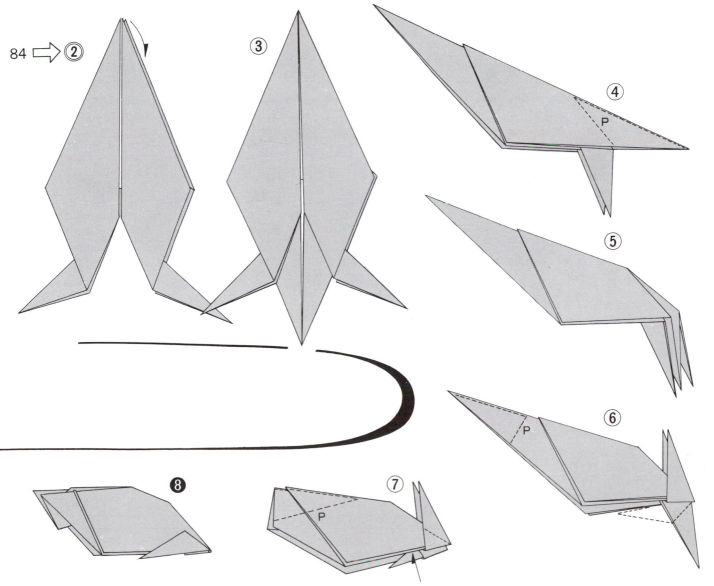

84 ⇨ ②

③

④

⑤

⑥

⑦

❽

141

105. Bear

Use two crane bases made from six-inch squares of black paper.

Front Section

1. Valley fold the top layer only on the dotted line in the direction the arrow indicates.
2. Fold the tip of the inner triangle down as shown, and return the long point to its original position.
3. Peak and valley fold the top layer only on the dotted lines in numerical order. Peak and valley fold the lower points as shown to form the legs.
4. Valley fold the top layer only on the dotted line.
5. Peak fold the point on the dotted line. The tip of the point after you fold it should come to the bottom of the model at the spot you see in step 7.
6. The model should look like this. Turn it over.
7. Valley fold the top layer only on the dotted lines.
8. Valley fold the model in half on the dotted line.
9. Cut the ears as indicated. Peak and valley fold the legs into the position in step 10. Peak and valley fold the tips of the feet.

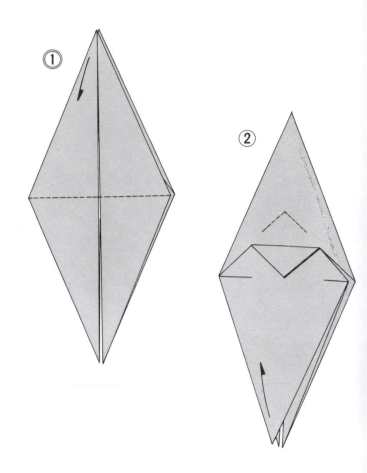

Rear Section

1. Open the crane base out from the sides by valley folding on the dotted line.
2. Peak and valley fold the lower points on the indicated lines to reverse fold them into the position in step 3.
3. Valley fold the top flap only on the dotted line.
4. Cut the top layer of the upper point only on the dotted lines.
5. Open the flaps out to the position shown. Valley fold the top point on the dotted line.
6. Valley fold the model in half on the dotted line.
7. Peak and valley fold the tail for a reverse fold outside in.
8. Valley fold the tail for a reverse fold inside out.
9. Peak fold the belly section under.
10. Peak and valley fold the tail as indicated. Fold one flap of the belly section around the other as the arrow shows. Peak and valley fold the legs into the position in 11.
11. Peak fold the tip of the tail under. Peak fold the front of the body as shown in the inset.

▶Join the two sections, and glue them together for the finished bear.

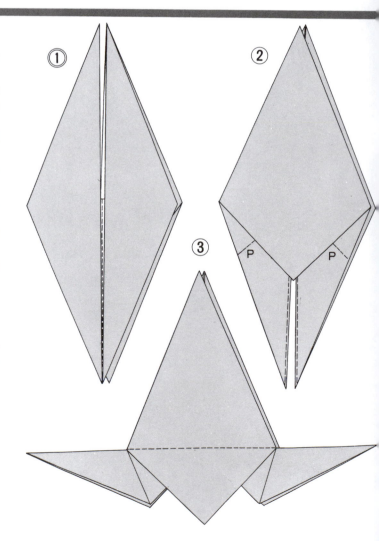

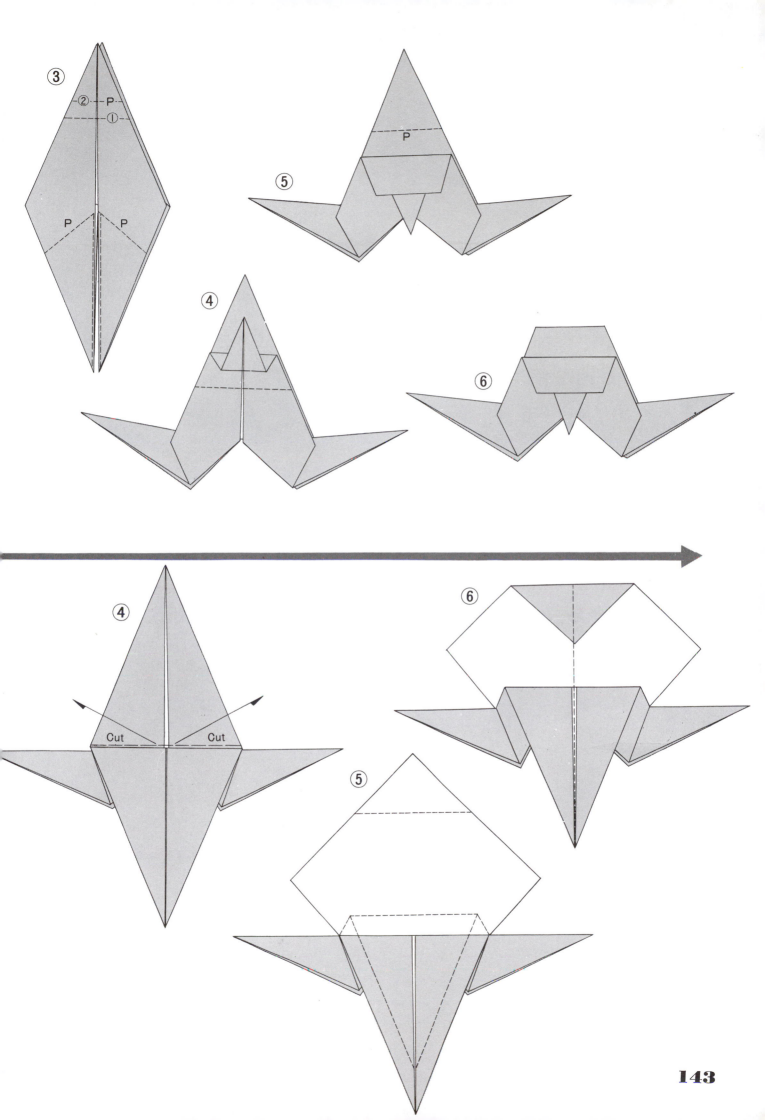

③

②···P
①

P   P

⑤   P

④

⑥

④

Cut   Cut

⑥

⑤

P

143

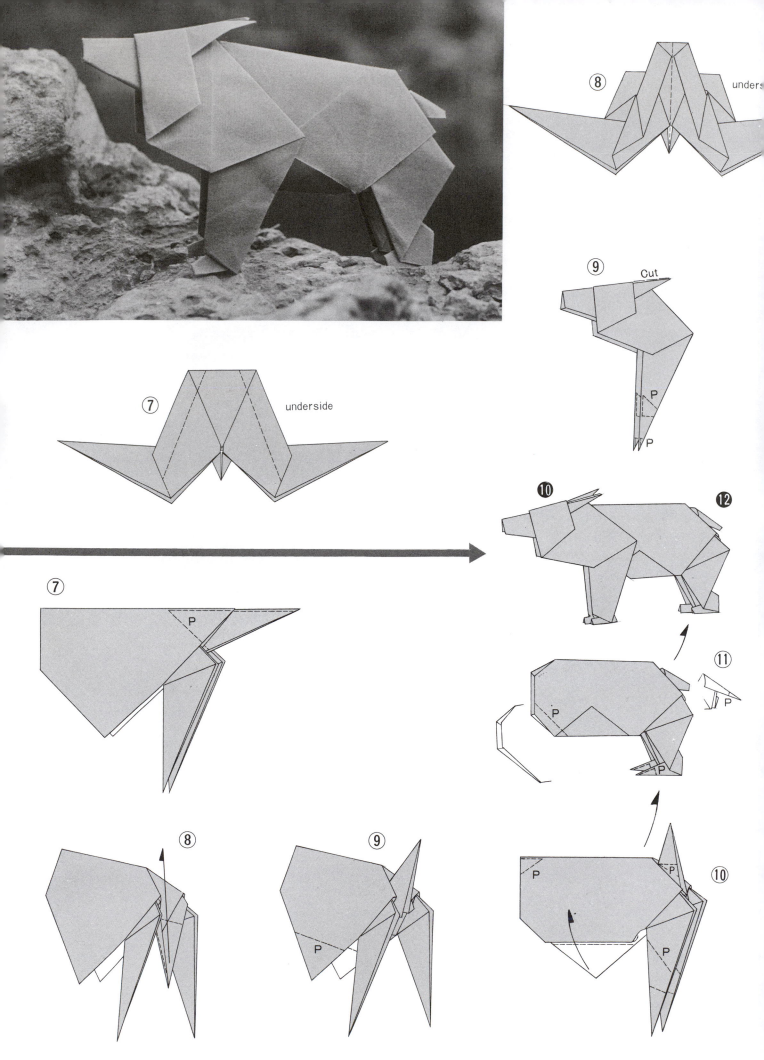

⑧ unders[ide]

⑨ Cut

P

P

⑦ underside

⑩ ⑫

⑪ P

⑦ P

⑧

⑨ P

⑩ P P

P

144

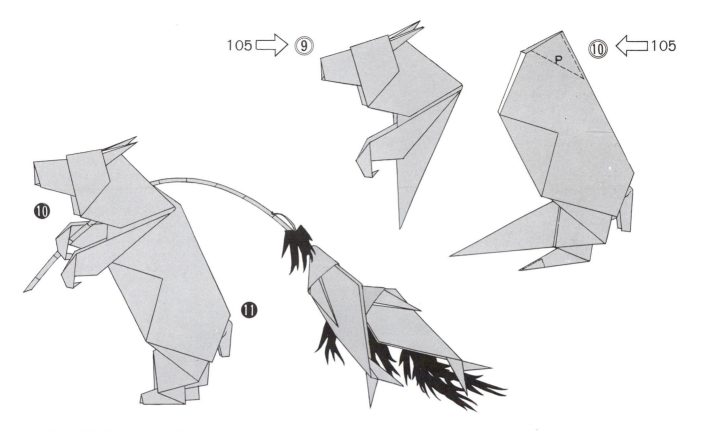

105 ⟹ ⑨   ⑩ ⟸ 105

⑩   ⑪

106. Fisherman Bear

Make a bear according to the steps in (105) Follow
the minor variations shown in this chart so that
your bear will be standing. Make two fish (68),
attach them to a fishing pole, and decorate the
pole with bamboo leaves cut from green paper.

This model makes a charming picture for your
wall if you back it with a suitable paper back-
ground suggesting a pond in the forest.

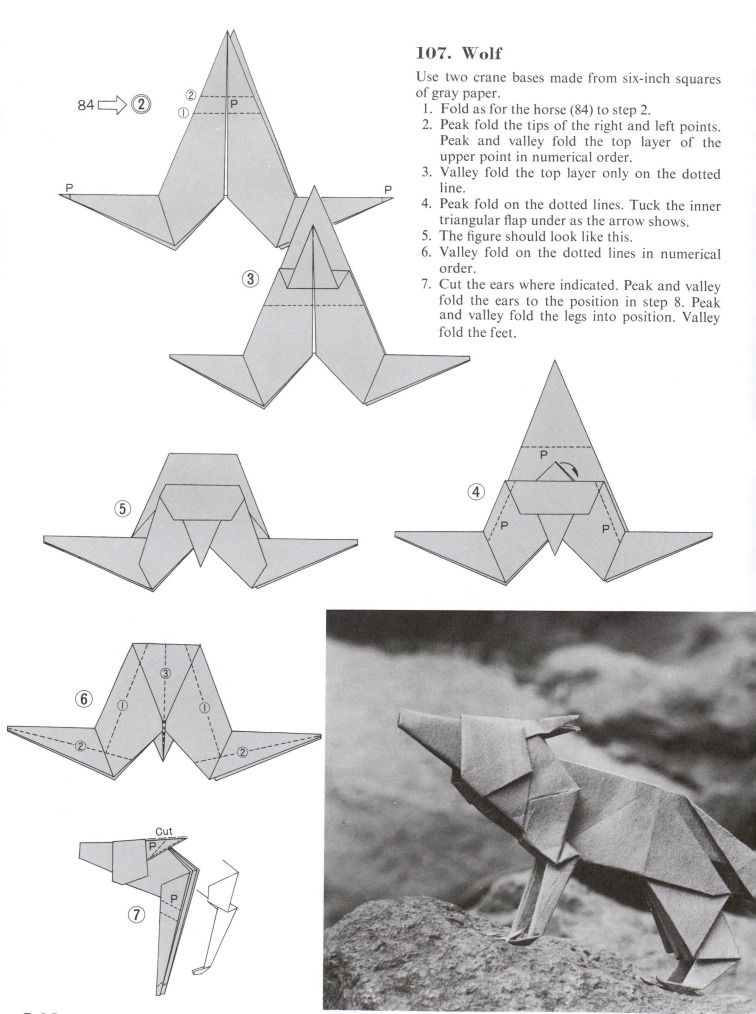

107. Wolf

Use two crane bases made from six-inch squares of gray paper.

1. Fold as for the horse (84) to step 2.
2. Peak fold the tips of the right and left points. Peak and valley fold the top layer of the upper point in numerical order.
3. Valley fold the top layer only on the dotted line.
4. Peak fold on the dotted lines. Tuck the inner triangular flap under as the arrow shows.
5. The figure should look like this.
6. Valley fold on the dotted lines in numerical order.
7. Cut the ears where indicated. Peak and valley fold the ears to the position in step 8. Peak and valley fold the legs into position. Valley fold the feet.

84 ➡ ②

③

④

⑤

⑥

⑦

Cut

146

Rear Section

1~3. Fold as for the horse rear section (84) to step 3. If you peak and valley fold as shown you will squash fold the two sides of the tail section into the position shown in step 4. Be sure that the outer edges of the tail section are parallel. Valley fold the top point down on the dotted line.

4. Valley fold on the dotted lines.

5. Valley fold the model in half on the dotted line.

6. Peak and valley fold the tail into position. Peak and valley fold the legs into position. Peak fold the belly section under.

▶ Join the two sections, and glue them together for the completed wolf.

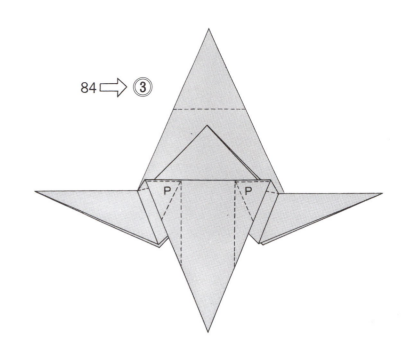

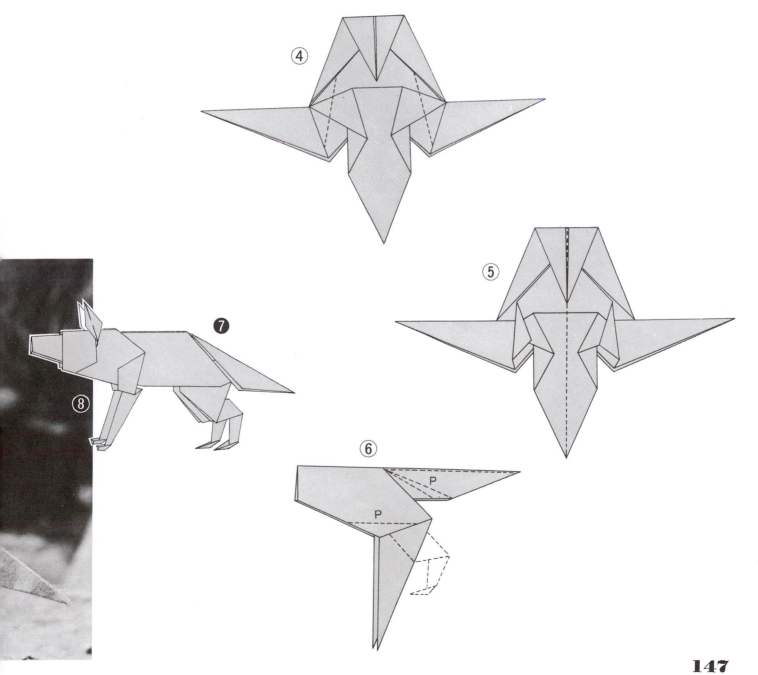

147

108. Elephant

Use two bird bases made of six-inch squares of gray paper.

Front Section

1. Fold as for the horse to step 2.
2. Valley fold the top layer only on the dotted line.
3. Cut on the indicated line. Valley fold on the dotted lines in numerical order.
4. Valley fold the model in half on the dotted line.
5. First fold the tip end of the trunk section under as shown in the inset. Peak and valley fold on the dotted lines for a reverse fold outside in. Valley fold on the dotted lines on the two right points.
6. Valley fold on the dotted lines in the trunk and in the ear sections.
7. Tuck the ear flaps in where the arrow indicates. Valley fold the ears on the dotted lines. Peak and valley fold the feet into the position in step 8.
8. Valley fold the trunk on the dotted lines for a reverse fold inside out. Valley fold the small corner of the ear as indicated. Valley fold the trunk for a reverse fold inside out.
9. Peak and valley fold the feet into position. Be sure to fold the tips of the feet under as indicated.

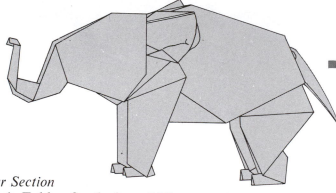

Rear Section

1~4. Fold as for the bear (105) to step 4. Cut on the indicated lines. Peak and valley fold on the indicated lines to bring the outer edges of the lower point in to the center line.
5. Open the flaps you cut to this position, and valley fold on the dotted lines in numerical order.
6. Peak and valley fold the tail for a reverse fold outside in.
7. Valley fold the tail up again on the dotted lines.
8. Peak and valley fold the tail as shown. Peak and valley fold the leg into the position shown in step 9.
9. Peak and valley fold the elephant's back inward. Peak fold the top layer of the belly section.
10. Valley fold the lower layer of the belly section around to the front side.

▶ Join the two sections, and glue them together for the completed elephant.

148

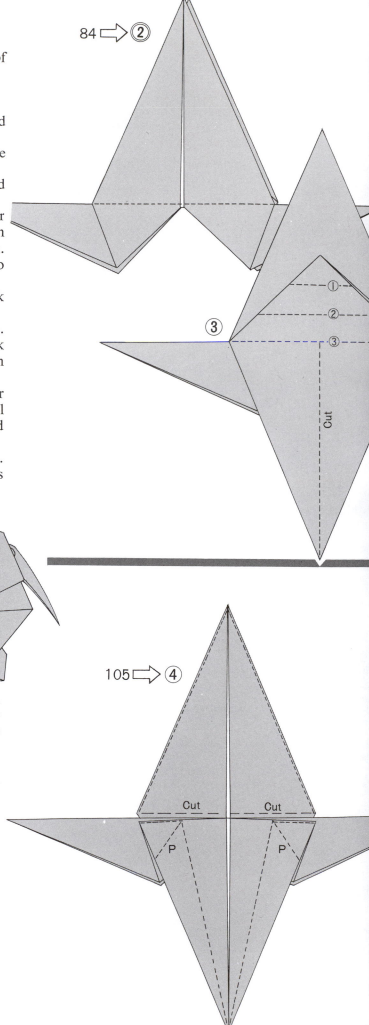

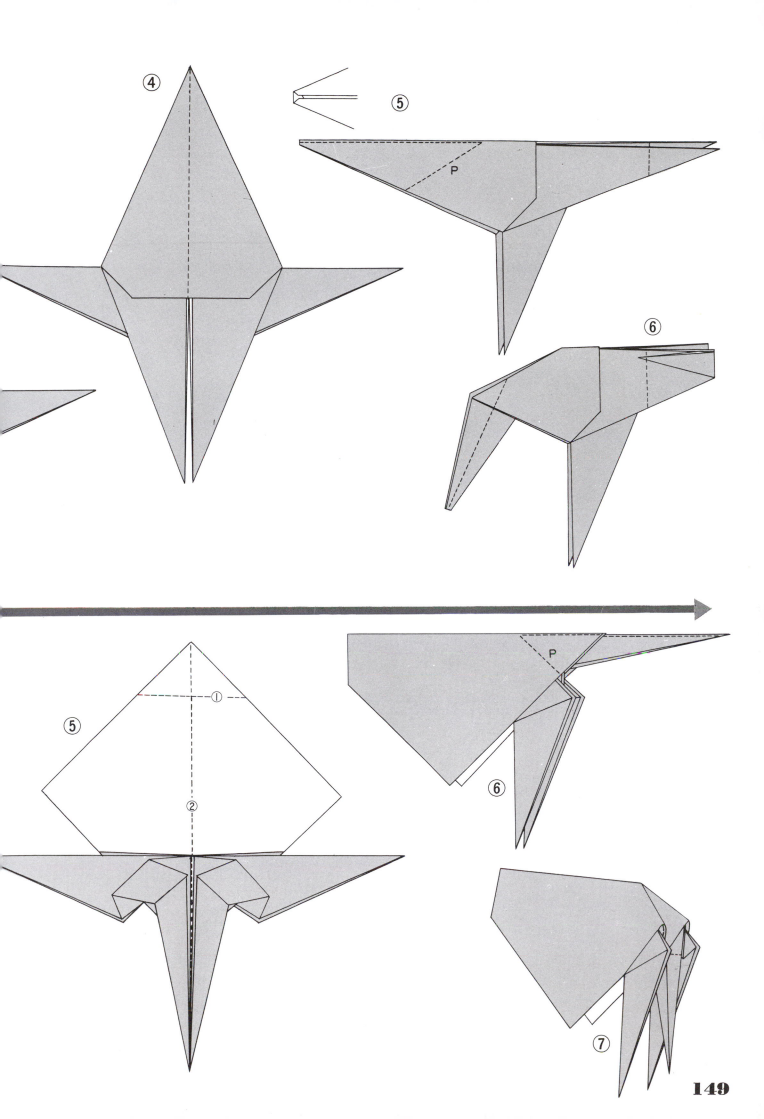

④

⑤

⑥

⑤

① ②

⑥

⑦

P

P

149

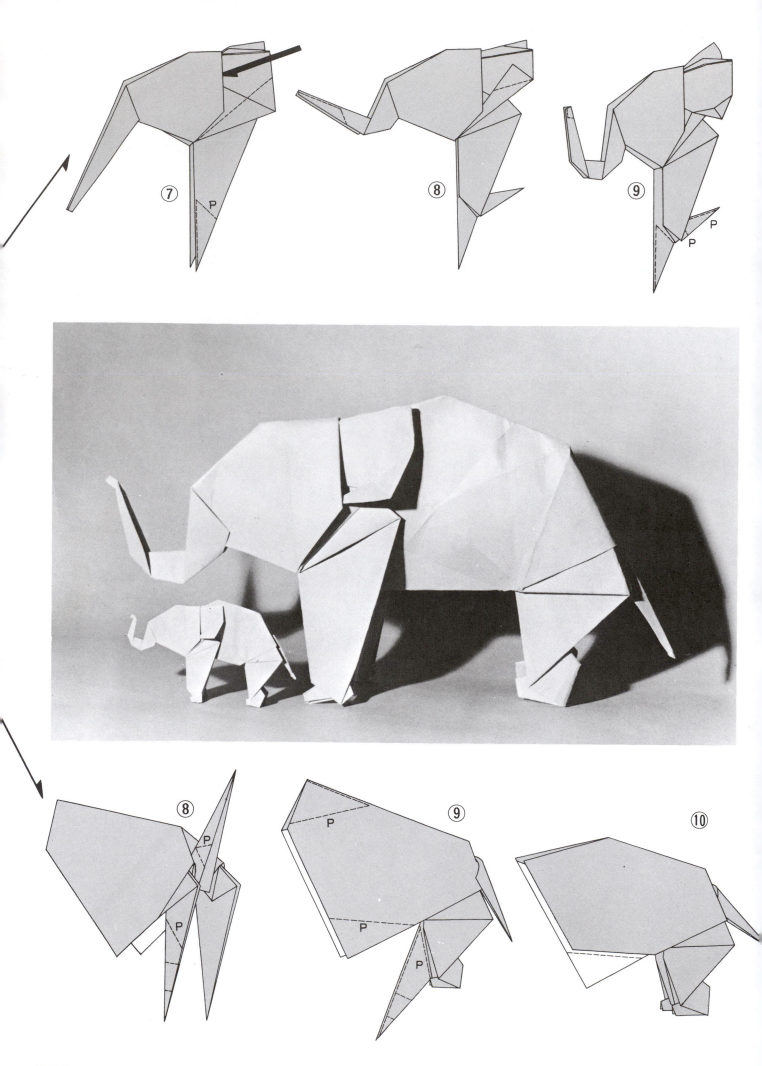

⑦ P

⑧

⑨ P P

⑧ P P

⑨ P P P

⑩

109. Polar Bear

Use two crane bases made from six-inch squares of white paper.

1. Peak and valley fold the points out as shown.
2. Peak and valley fold both layers as indicated.
3. Valley fold the model in half on the dotted line.
4. Peak and valley fold on the dotted line, and crimp inward.
5. Cut on the indicated line to make the bear's ears. Peak and valley fold the legs into place.

Rear Section

1~12. Fold as for the bear (105) to step 12.
▶Join the two sections, and glue them together for the finished polar bear.

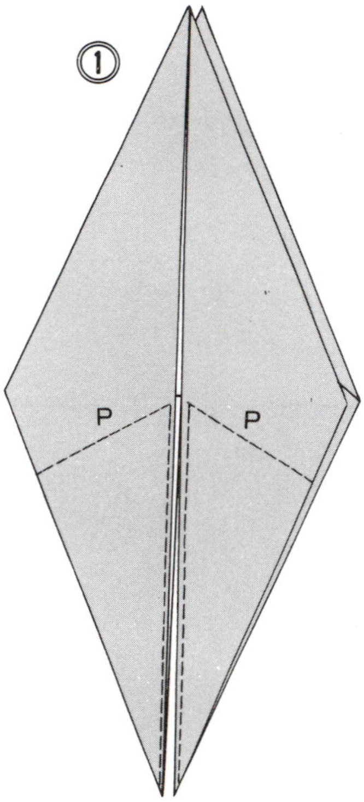

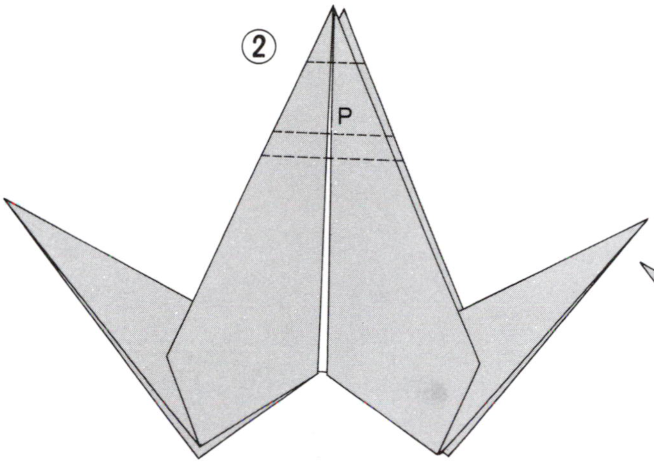

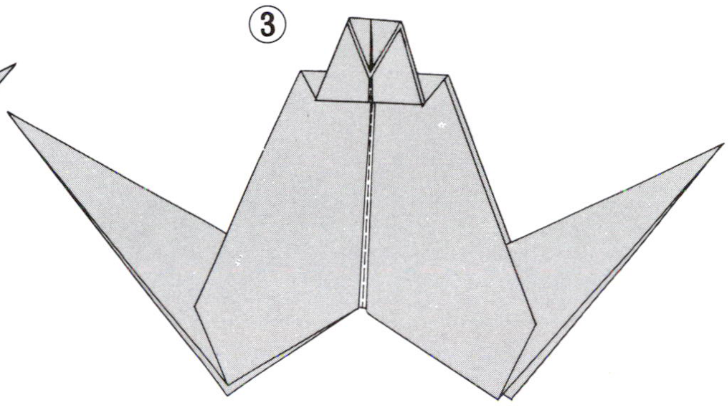

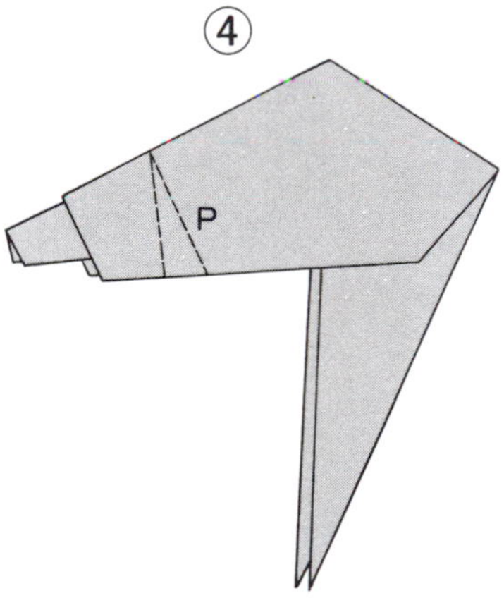

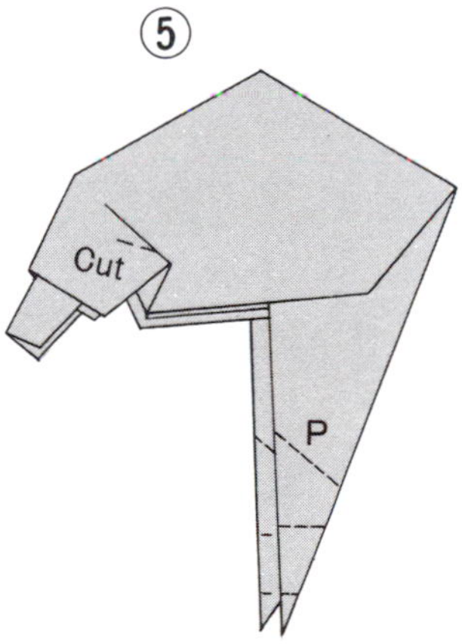

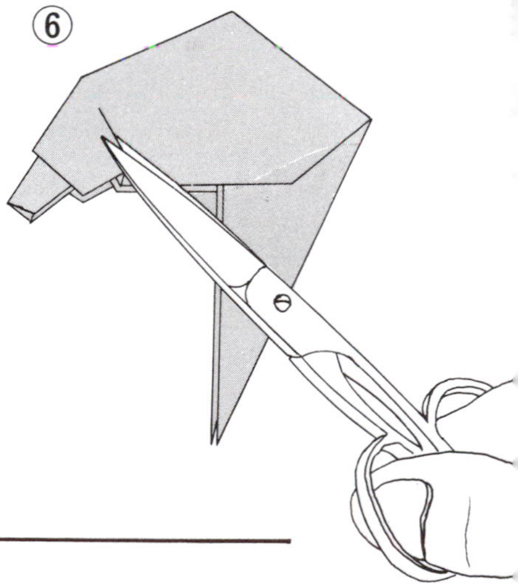

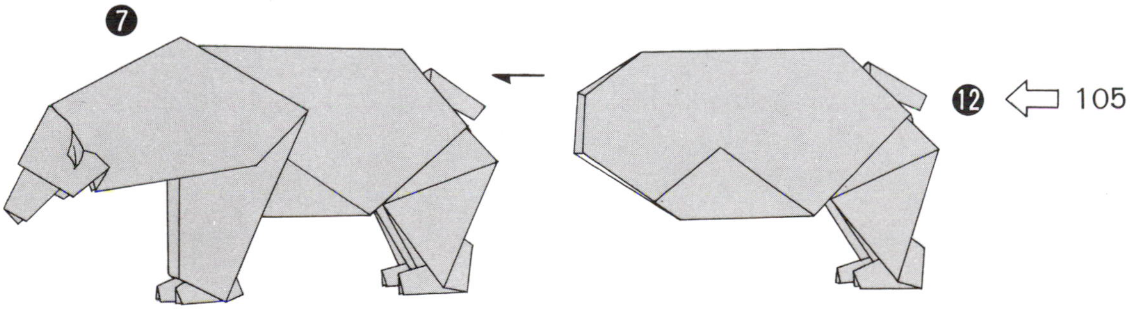

151

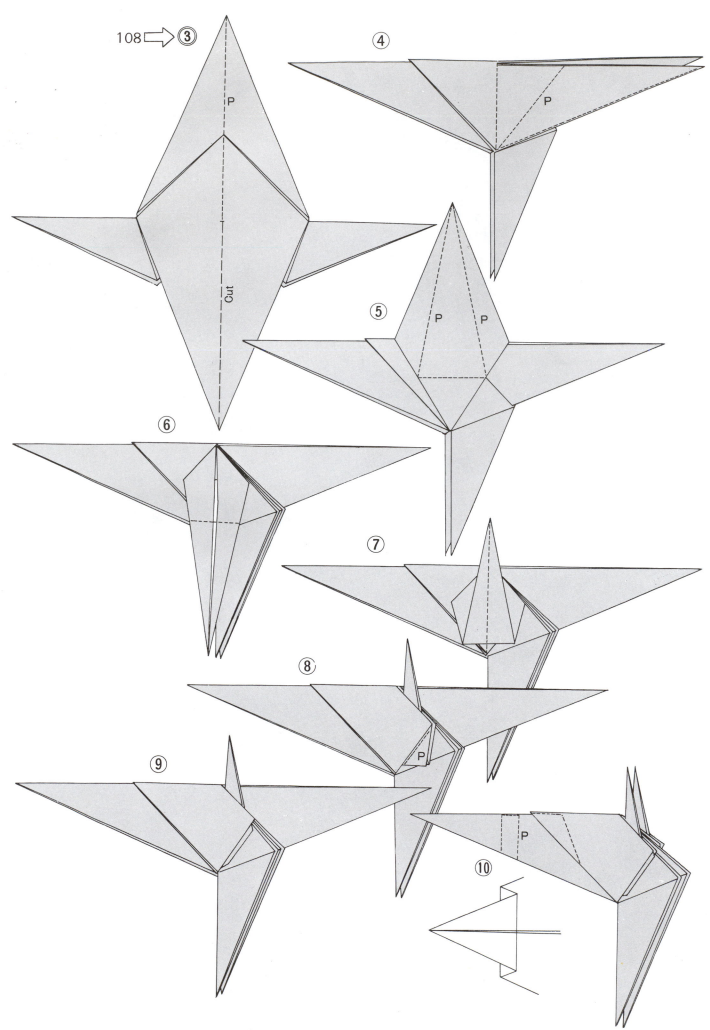

108 ➡ ③

④

⑤

⑥

⑦

⑧

⑨

⑩

P

Cut

110. Rhinoceros

Use two crane bases made from six-inch squares of gray paper.

Front Section

1~3. Fold as for the elephant to step 3. Cut as indicated, and peak fold on the dotted line.
4. Valley and peak fold the top layer only of the right point to the position you see in step 5.
5. Peak and valley fold the resulting flap to the position in step 6. This is easy if you concentrate on bringing the outer edges of the flap to the center line on the underside of the same flap.
6. Valley fold on the dotted line.
7. Valley fold on the dotted line, left side over right.
8. Peak fold on the dotted lines.
9. The figure should look like this. Turn the

model over, and repeat the process from step 5 to make the other ear.
10. Valley fold the top layer for a reverse fold inside out. Peak and valley fold the bottom layer, and crimp it in as you see in the inset.
11. Valley fold the snout on the dotted lines for a reverse fold inside out.
12. Peak fold the jaws under. Peak and valley fold the legs into shape.

Rear Section

1~9. Fold as for the elephant (108) to step 9. Peak and valley fold the legs into shape as shown. Peak fold the top belly flap, and valley fold the lower one around to the top side.

▶Join the two sections, and glue them together for the completed rhinoceros.

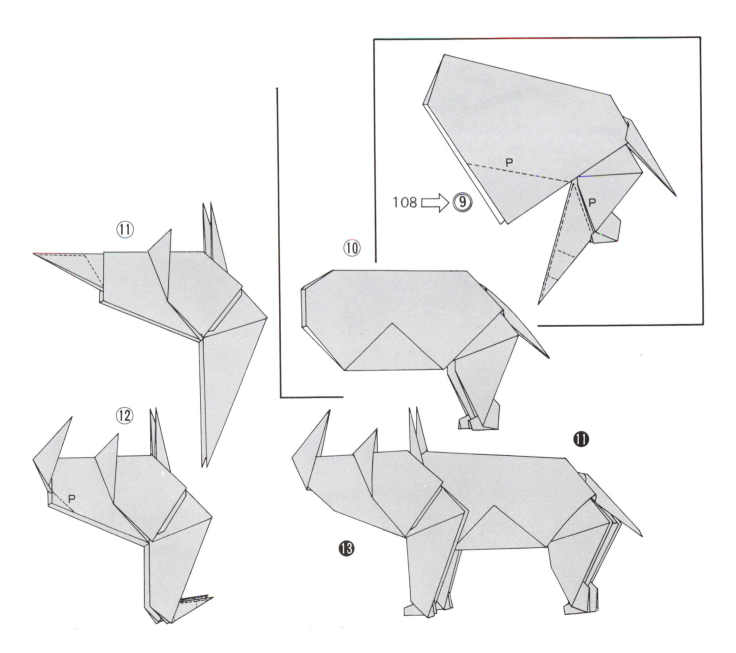

153

111. Pig

Use two crane bases made from six-inch squares of white paper.

Front Section

1~2. Fold as for the bear front section (105) to step 2. Valley fold the top layer of the lower point upward on the dotted line.

3. Crimp the top layer down as you see in the chart. Peak and valley fold the two lower points outward as shown.

4. Valley fold the top layer only on the dotted line.

5. Peak fold on the dotted line. Narrow the legs by valley folding on the dotted lines, one layer at a time.

6. Valley fold on the dotted line.

7. Peak fold the model in half, and cut on the indicated line.

8. Peak and valley fold the ears as shown, and squash them forward. Peak and valley fold the legs, and crimp them upward.

Rear Section

1~8. Fold as for the rear section of the elephant (108) to step 8.

Peak and valley fold the tail and legs as shown. Peak fold the top layer of the belly section. Valley fold the lower layer of the belly section, and bring it around to the front.

9. Valley fold the crook into the tail, and valley fold the feet.

▶ Join the two sections, and glue them together for the finished pig.

105 ⇨ ②

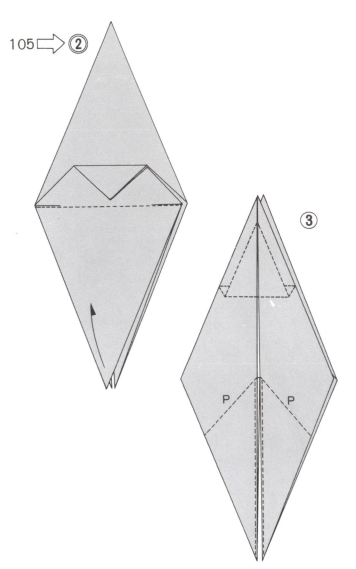

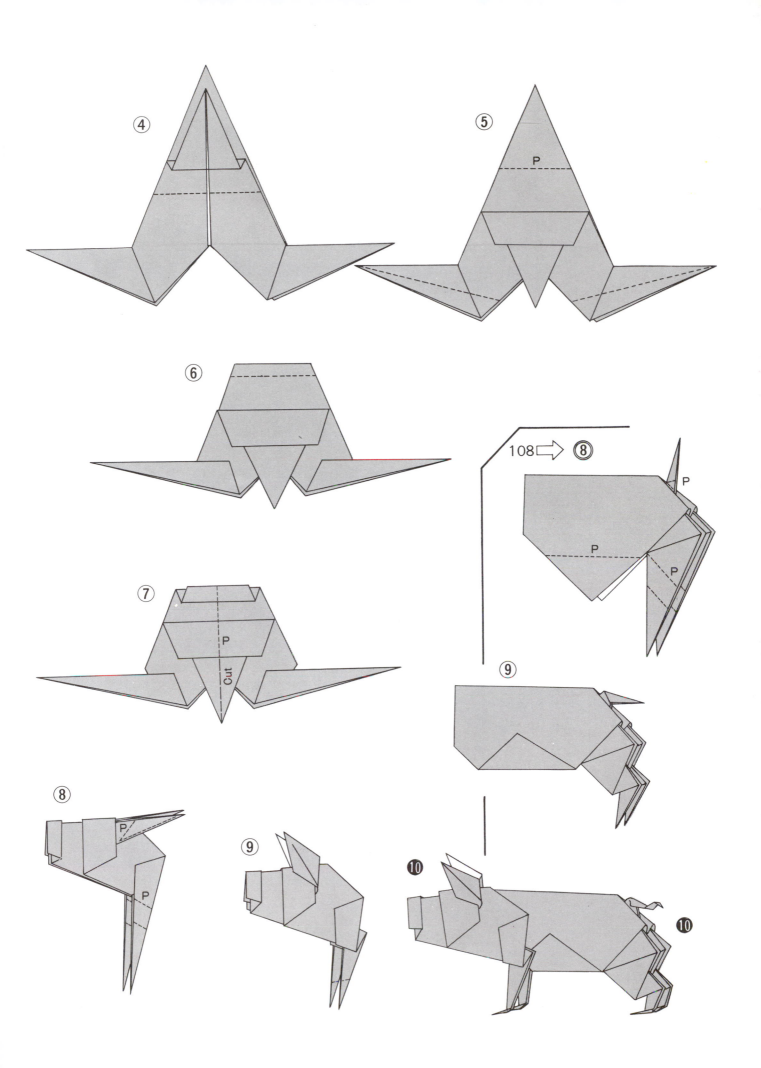

④

⑤ P

⑥

⑦ P Cut

⑧ 108 ⑧ P P P

⑨

⑧ P P

⑨

❿

❿

112. Cow

Use two crane bases made from six-inch squares of paper. You may use brown or black paper or white paper to which you can add spots of black or brown.

Front Section

1~2. Fold as for the horse (84) to step 2. Narrow the leg sections by valley folding on the dotted lines. Peak and valley fold both layers of the upper point on the dotted lines in numerical order.

3. The figure should look like this. Open the top point out again.

4. Cut where indicated, and fold the tip of the point on the dotted lines in numerical order.

5. Return the model to the position in step 3. Valley fold it in half on the dotted line.

6. Valley fold the horns up. Peak and valley fold the ears inward. Peak and valley fold the legs into shape.

Rear Section

1~5. Fold as for the rear section of the bear to step 5. Valley fold on the dotted line.

6. Valley fold on the dotted lines.

7. Valley fold the model in half on the dotted line.

8. Peak fold the belly section under. Peak and valley fold the tail for a reverse fold outside in. Peak and valley fold the legs into shape. Do not forget to valley fold the feet as shown.

▶Join the two sections, and glue them together for the completed cow.

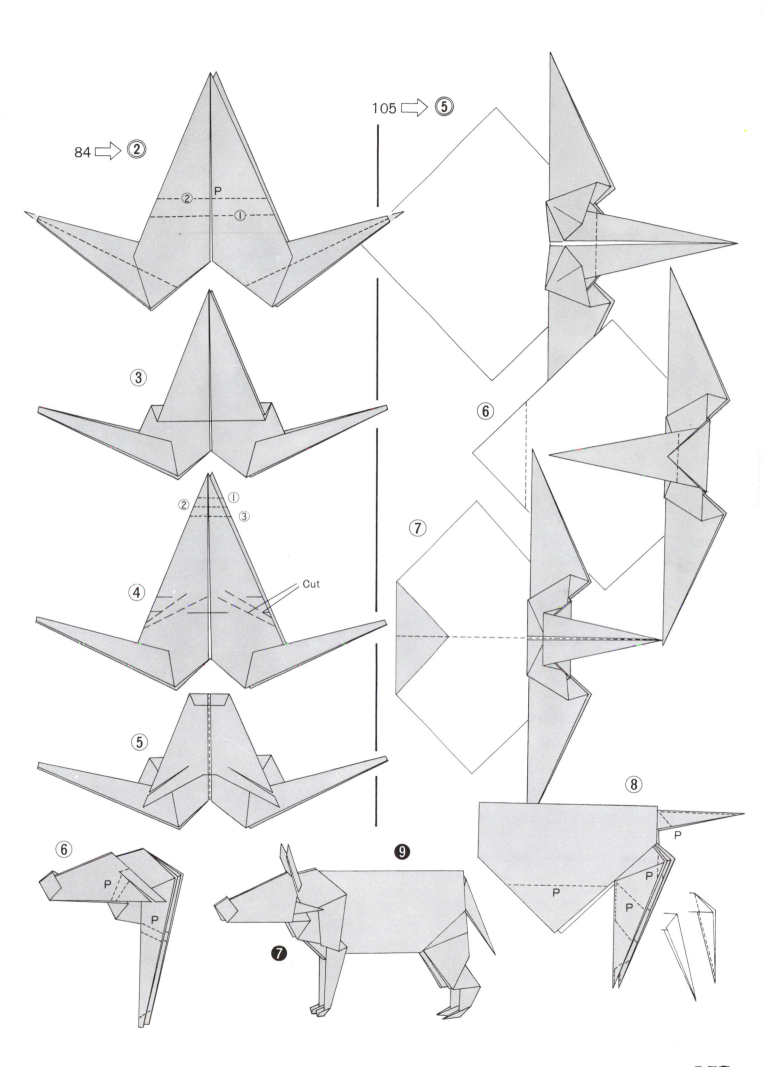

84 ➡ ②

105 ➡ ⑤

P

②
①

③

② ①
    ③

④

Cut

⑤

⑥

⑦

⑥

P

P

⑦

❾

⑧

P

P

P

P

❼

113. Water Buffalo

Use two crane bases made from six-inch squares of black paper.

Front Section

1~2. Fold as for the horse (84) to step 2. Narrow the leg sections by valley folding on the dotted lines.

3. Valley fold the model in half.

4. Valley fold both layers of the point for a reverse fold inside out.

5. Valley fold only the outer layer of the point for a reverse fold inside out.

6. Cut where indicated for the horns. Peak and valley fold the ears. Peak and valley fold the tip of the muzzle in.

7. Peak fold the horns as indicated. Peak fold the tip of the muzzle.

8. Valley fold the tips of the horns into the indicated position. Peak and valley fold the legs into position. Valley fold the feet as shown.

Rear Section

1~9. Fold as for the horse (84) to step 9.

▶ Join the two sections, and glue them together for the finished water buffalo.

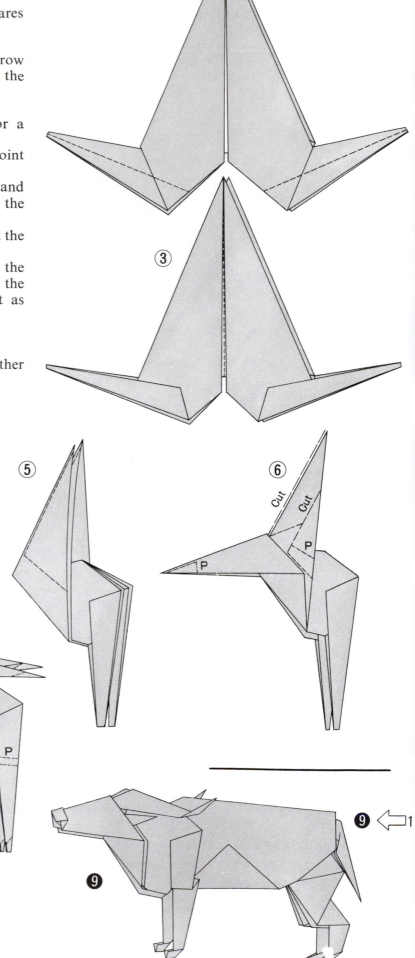

158

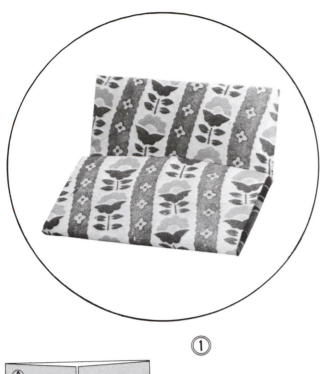

114. Wallet

Use three sheets of six-inch square paper.

1. Prepare the paper by folding two sheets (A & B) so that the outer edges fall along the vertical center line. Fold the third sheet into quarters. Valley fold on the dotted lines: in A the fold is one quarter of the height of the paper, in B, fold almost in half, in C fold so that the upper and lower edges fall on the horizontal center line.
2. Slip C under the flap in A as shown.
3. Put B on top of A as shown with the longer side on the bottom. Valley fold the longer side of B on the dotted line. Valley fold both layers of B on the upper dotted line. Valley fold A on the dotted line. Wrap the flaps of C around by valley folding on the dotted lines.
4. The figure should look like this.
5. Tuck the flap of A in as the arrow indicates.
6. The finished wallet with a pocket in front and one in back.

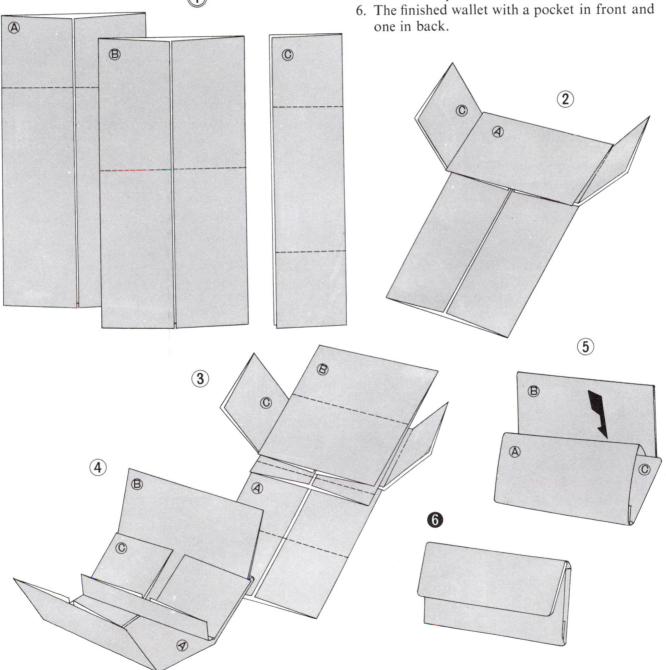

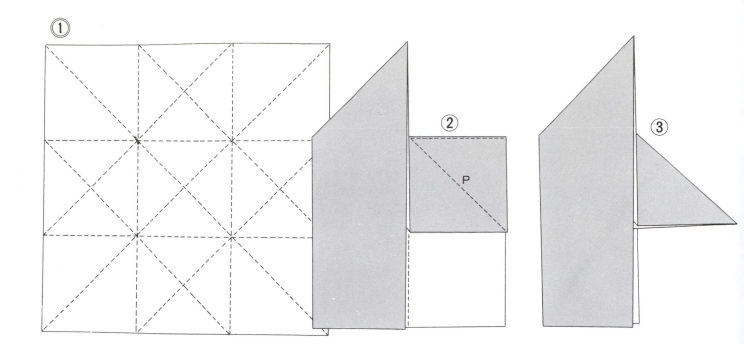

115. Thread Container

Use one six-inch square of paper. Pay particular attention to this square fold because it is the basis for several of the following folds.

1. Prepare the paper by making the creases you see in the chart. This can be done by first folding the square into thirds, both the height and the width. Use a perfect six-inch square, and make two-inch marks with a pencil. Unfold the paper and fold in the diagonal lines by beginning with the diagonals of the top and bottom square in the middle vertical and horizontal rows.
2. Fold the top horizontal third down, and bring the left horizontal third over leaving a projecting point at the top.
3. Repeat this procedure all around the figure for the shape you see in step 4.
4. Valley fold each of the points on the dotted line.
5. Insert the points one under another.
6. The finished thread container.

116. Cubical Box

Use six square folds in six different colors.

1~6. Fold as for the square fold to step 6. Turn the models over, and cut on the indicated lines.
7. The front and the back of the figure.
8. Insert the triangular flaps of four of the models as you see it done in the chart.
9. Add the remaining two for the top and bottom of the box.
10. The completed box.

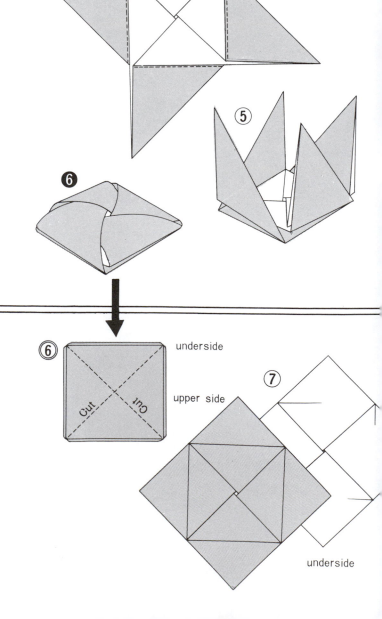

117. Six-sided Box

Use six square folds.

1~7. Fold six square folds. Turn them face up.
8. Join them in sets of three as you see in the chart.
9. Join the two sets of three, gluing all of them together as you go along. Finally, open the top section, and glue that together.
10. The finished six-sided box.

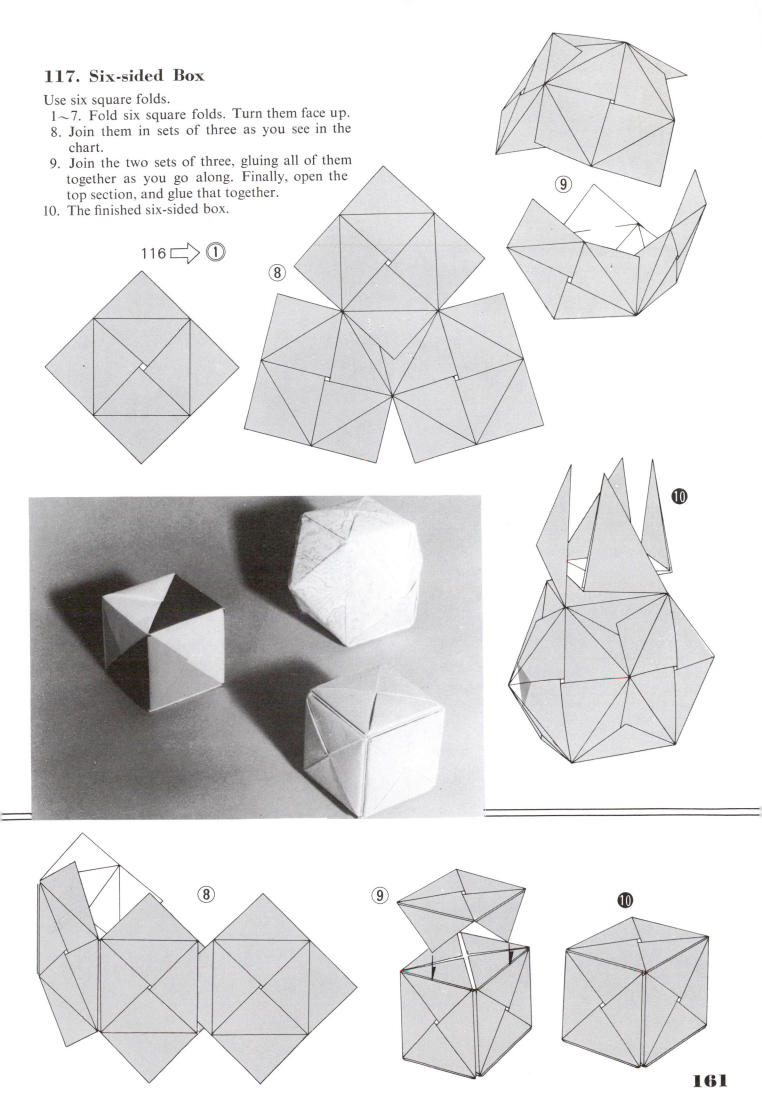

116 ➡ ①

⑧

⑨

⑧

⑨

⑩

⑩

161

118. Hanging Ornament

Use a six-sided box (117).

To fold the tassel, use four strips of colored paper 3/8 of an inch wide and 24 inches long.

1. Weave the four strips together as you see in the chart.
2. Bring one layer only of each section around, and weave again.
3. The figure should look like this. Crease it well, and using a piece of string and two large beads complete the ornament so that it looks like the figure in step 4.
4. The completed ornament.

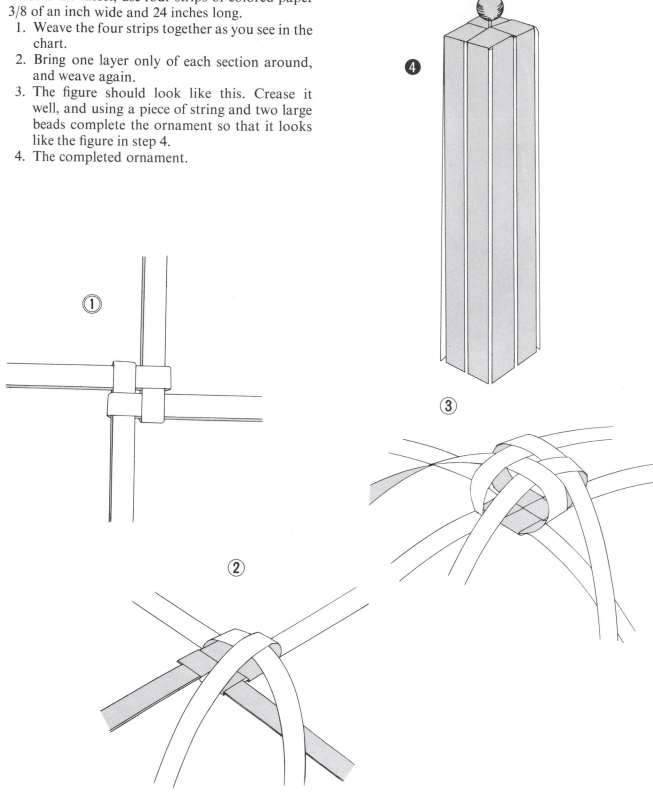

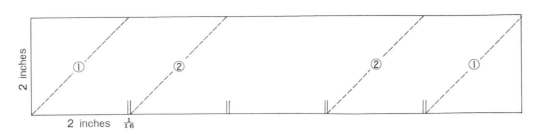

① Valley fold on the dotted lines in numerical order.

2 inches

2 inches $\frac{1}{16}$

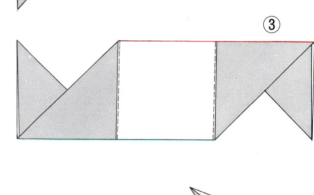

119. Mystery Box

Use six sheets of different colored paper cut to the dimensions you see in step 1.

1. Valley fold on the dotted lines in numerical order.
2. Peak fold on the dotted lines.
3. Valley fold on the dotted lines.
4. The model should look like this. Make six of them.
5. Join the figures so that A and B are in the relationship you see in the chart.
6. Join C and D as indicated.
7. Add the last two models as the arrow shows. They should slide into the spaces between the models you have already joined.
8. The completed box.

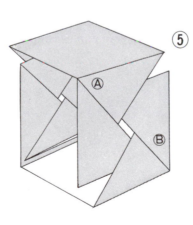

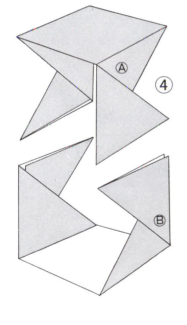

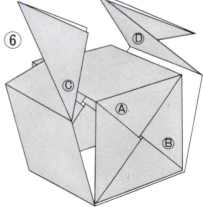

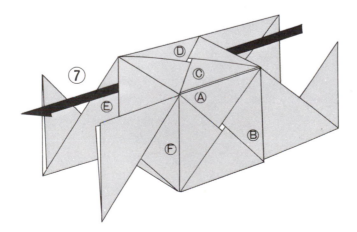

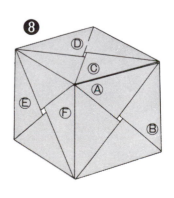

163

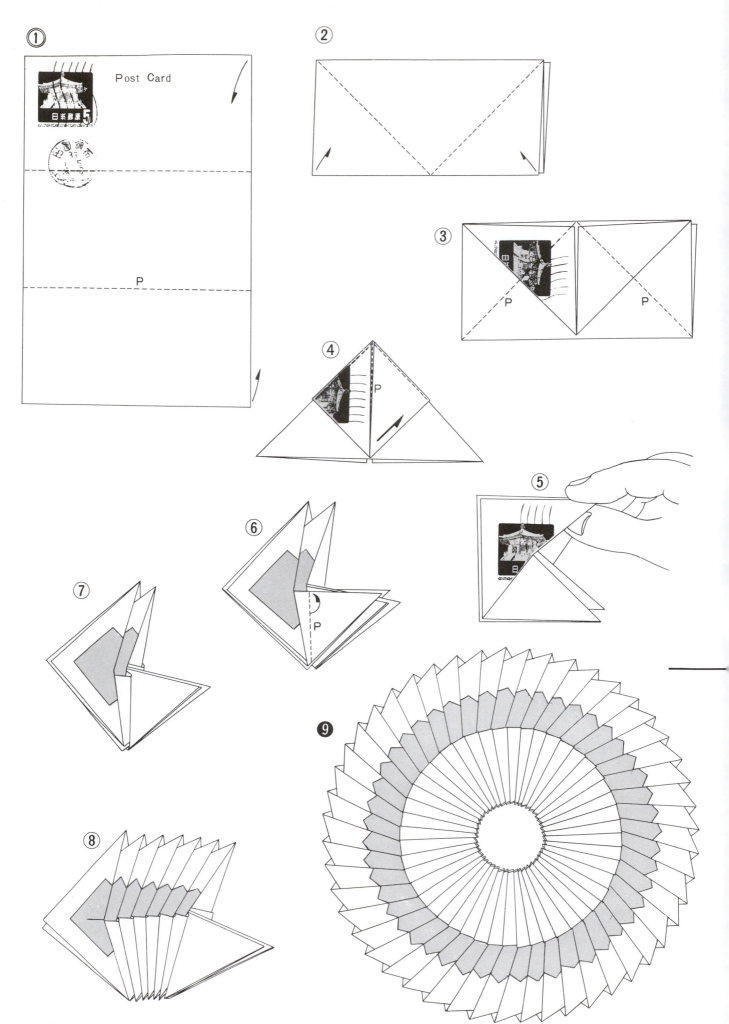

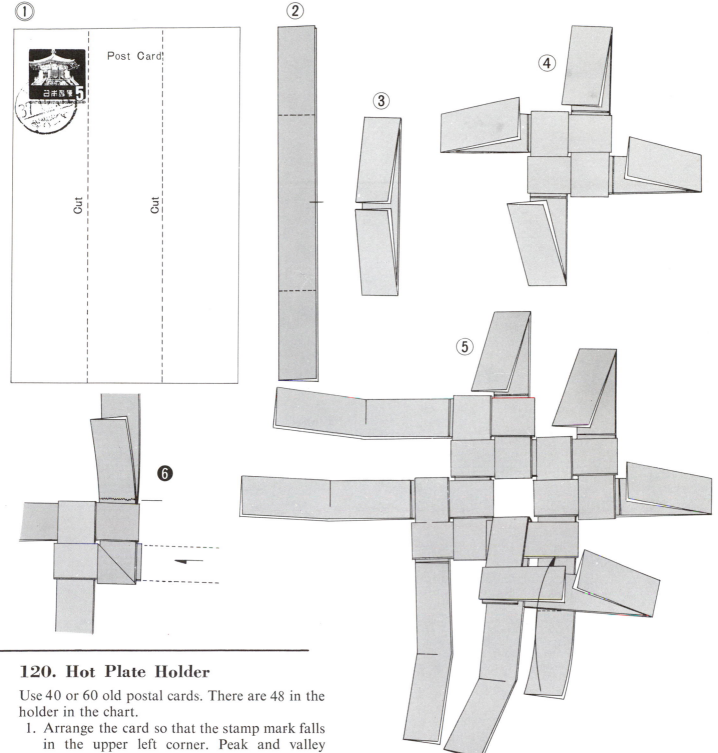

Post Card

白末郵便5

Cut　　Cut

① ② ③ ④ ⑤ ⑥

120. Hot Plate Holder

Use 40 or 60 old postal cards. There are 48 in the holder in the chart.

1. Arrange the card so that the stamp mark falls in the upper left corner. Peak and valley fold on the dotted lines.
2. Valley fold the top layer only on the dotted lines.
3. Peak fold both layers on the dotted lines.
4. Take the lowest point of the inner square in your fingertips, and pull straight out till the model assumes the shape in step 5.
5. The model should look like this. Make as many of them as you have postal cards.
6. Join the individual sections as you see in step 6. Peak fold the top section's triangular flaps into the pocket in the under section.
7. Two sections joined should look like this.
8. Continue adding sections until you form a ring.
9. The completed holder.

121. Woven Mat

Use any suitable number of old postal cards.

1. Cut the cards lengthwise into thirds as you see in the chart.
2. Valley fold on the dotted lines.
3. The fold should look like this. Fold a number of them.
4. Weave four of them together as you see in this step.
5. Weave a number of these sections of four, and join them as you see in this step.
6. When you have a mat the size you want fold the ends under as you see in this step, and cut off the projecting ends.

RIGHT TRIANGULAR PAPER

In some folds we use a right triangle, though we could use a square, to eliminate bulk.

Preparing the Paper for
{
An Equilateral Triangle
A Rhombus
A Right Triangle
}

1. All you need to to make a right triangle, of course, is to fold a square piece of paper diagonally in half and cut along the diagonal. In origami, however, we use the equilateral triangle more, and the right triangle is limited to certain special folds.
2. An Equilateral Triangle. (Chart 1) To make an equilateral triangle fold a piece of square paper in half from top to bottom. Unfold the paper. Bring one of the bottom corners up so that it touches the center line. Be sure you bisect the angle in the opposite botom corner. Mark the point A with a pencil, and then cut the·triangle out on lines AB and AC, as you see in step 2.

(Chart 2.)

A. Another method for obtaining an equilateral trinagle. Fold a piece of square paper in half from top to bottom. Measure a 60-degree angle at the lower right corner, and draw a line with a straight edge. Cut along that line, and open the paper out.
B. For a rhombus, fold a rectangular piece of paper in fours and cut just as in A. Open the paper out and you will have two right triangles joined to form a regular rhombus. You may also make a right triangle or a rhombus pattern of heavy paper and use them as models for cutting other basic triangles and rhombuses as you see in A and B below.

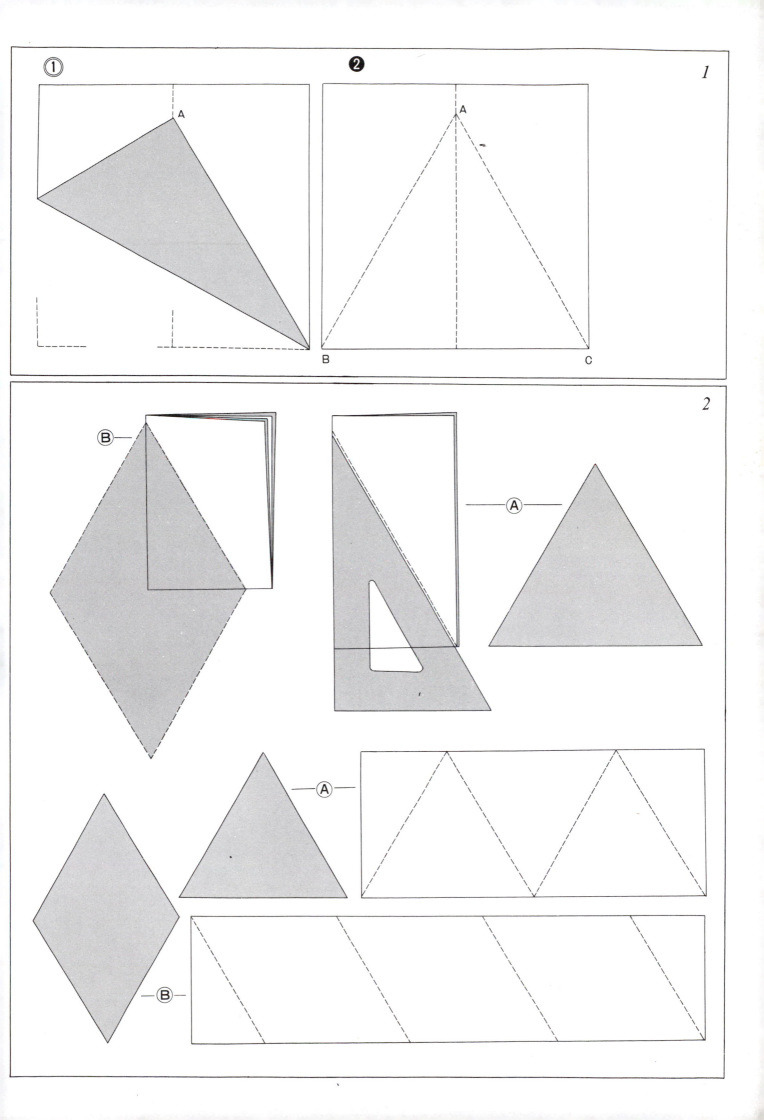

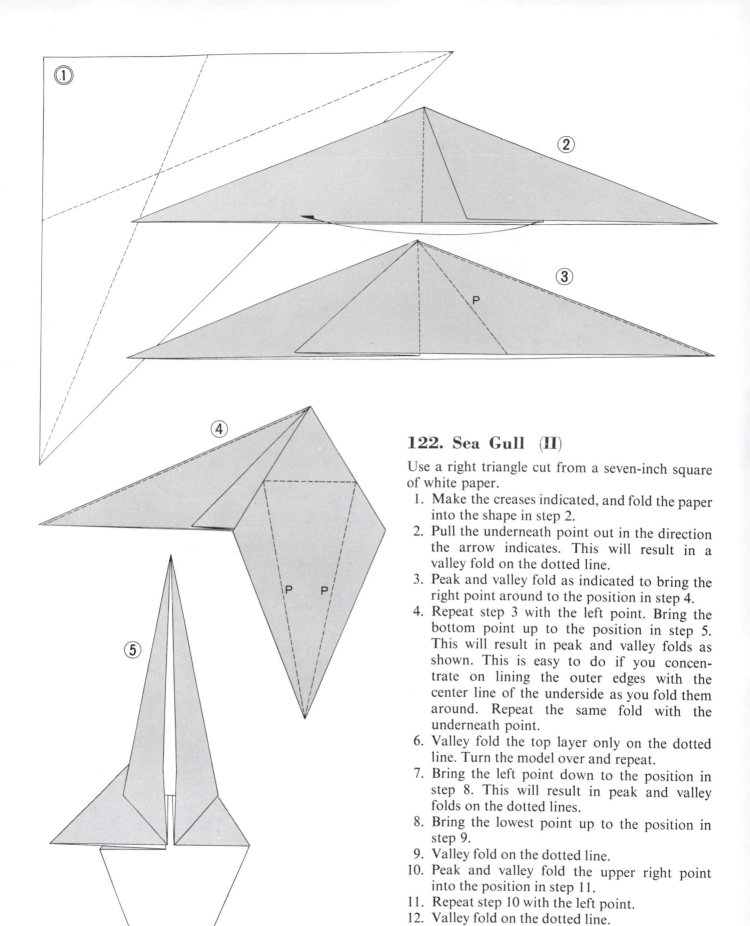

122. Sea Gull (II)

Use a right triangle cut from a seven-inch square of white paper.

1. Make the creases indicated, and fold the paper into the shape in step 2.
2. Pull the underneath point out in the direction the arrow indicates. This will result in a valley fold on the dotted line.
3. Peak and valley fold as indicated to bring the right point around to the position in step 4.
4. Repeat step 3 with the left point. Bring the bottom point up to the position in step 5. This will result in peak and valley folds as shown. This is easy to do if you concentrate on lining the outer edges with the center line of the underside as you fold them around. Repeat the same fold with the underneath point.
6. Valley fold the top layer only on the dotted line. Turn the model over and repeat.
7. Bring the left point down to the position in step 8. This will result in peak and valley folds on the dotted lines.
8. Bring the lowest point up to the position in step 9.
9. Valley fold on the dotted line.
10. Peak and valley fold the upper right point into the position in step 11.
11. Repeat step 10 with the left point.
12. Valley fold on the dotted line.
13. Valley fold the wings on the dotted lines. Peak and valley fold the head section, and crimp it in.
14. The completed sea gull.

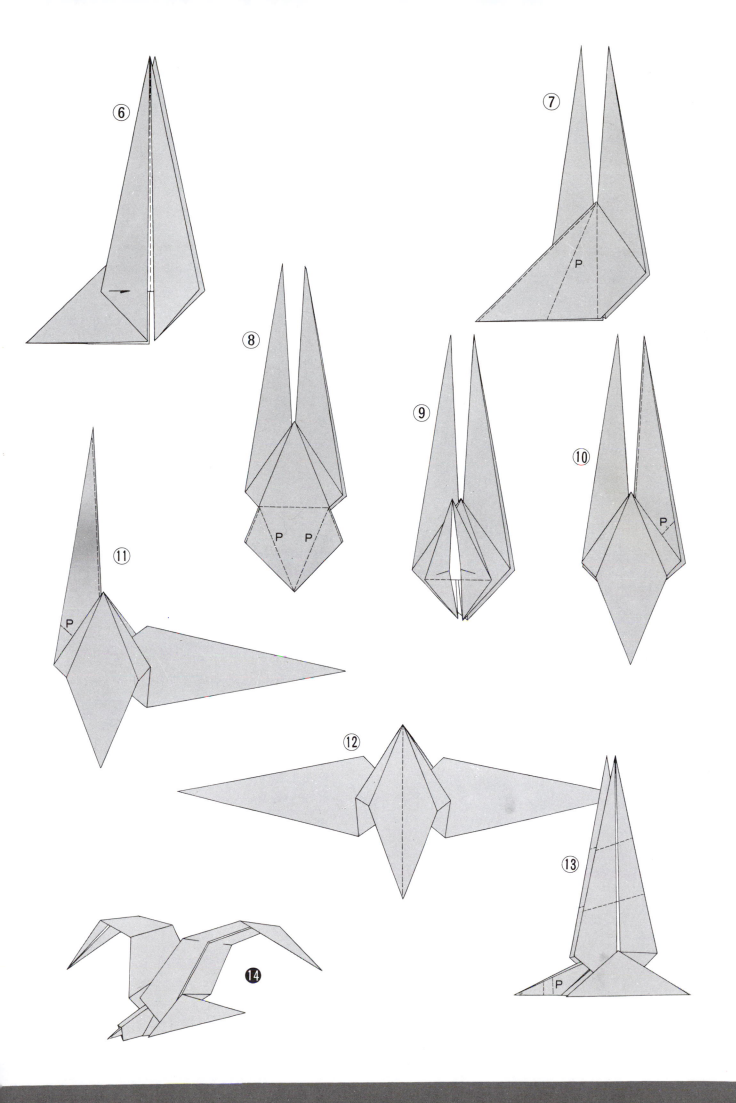

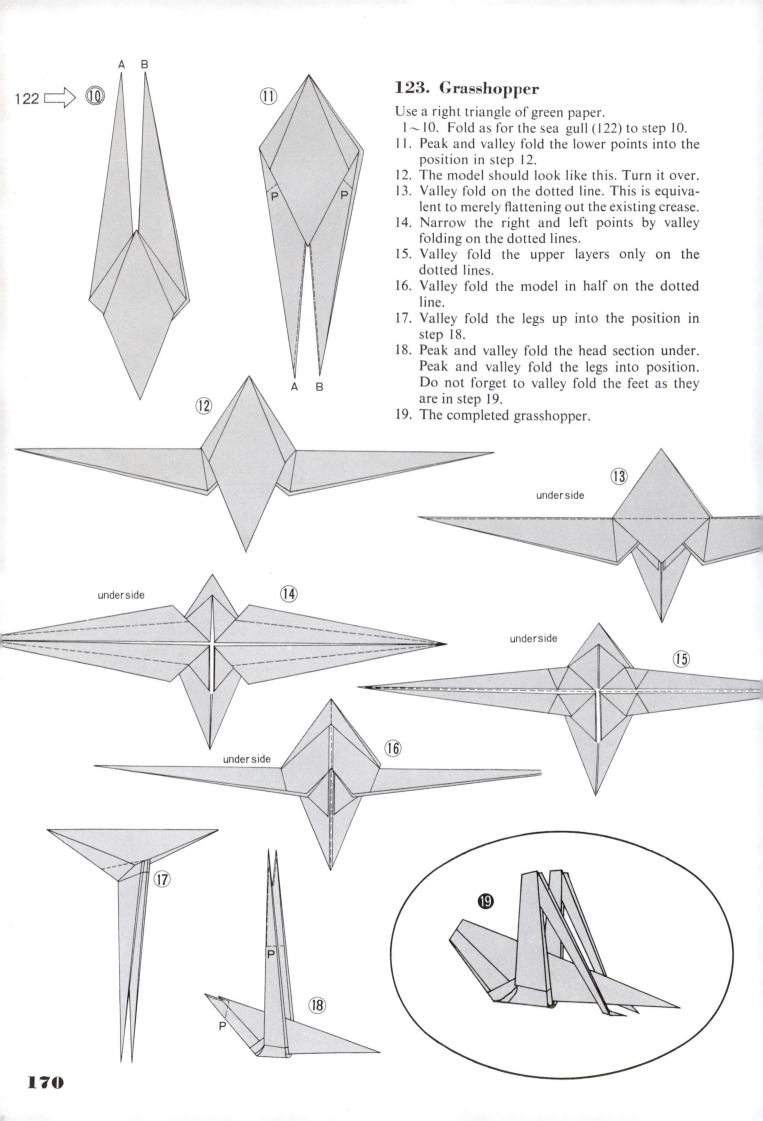

122 ⟹ ⑩

A   B

⑪

P   P

A   B

123. Grasshopper

Use a right triangle of green paper.
1~10. Fold as for the sea gull (122) to step 10.
11. Peak and valley fold the lower points into the position in step 12.
12. The model should look like this. Turn it over.
13. Valley fold on the dotted line. This is equivalent to merely flattening out the existing crease.
14. Narrow the right and left points by valley folding on the dotted lines.
15. Valley fold the upper layers only on the dotted lines.
16. Valley fold the model in half on the dotted line.
17. Valley fold the legs up into the position in step 18.
18. Peak and valley fold the head section under. Peak and valley fold the legs into position. Do not forget to valley fold the feet as they are in step 19.
19. The completed grasshopper.

⑫

⑬
under side

⑭
under side

⑮
under side

⑯
under side

⑰

⑱
P

P

⑲

TRIANGULAR PAPER

124. Wild Goose

Use an equilateral triangle of brown paper with a base seven inches long.

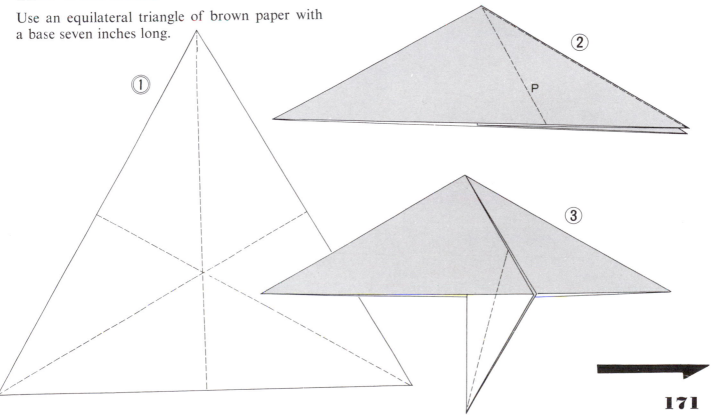

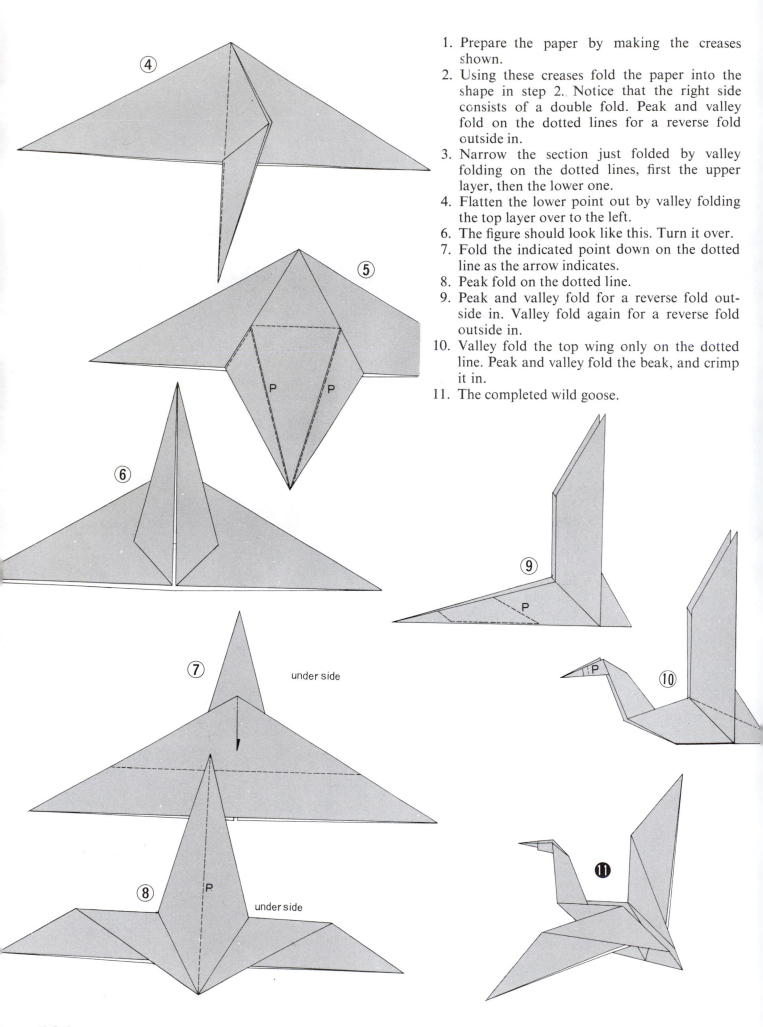

1. Prepare the paper by making the creases shown.
2. Using these creases fold the paper into the shape in step 2. Notice that the right side consists of a double fold. Peak and valley fold on the dotted lines for a reverse fold outside in.
3. Narrow the section just folded by valley folding on the dotted lines, first the upper layer, then the lower one.
4. Flatten the lower point out by valley folding the top layer over to the left.
6. The figure should look like this. Turn it over.
7. Fold the indicated point down on the dotted line as the arrow indicates.
8. Peak fold on the dotted line.
9. Peak and valley fold for a reverse fold outside in. Valley fold again for a reverse fold outside in.
10. Valley fold the top wing only on the dotted line. Peak and valley fold the beak, and crimp it in.
11. The completed wild goose.

172

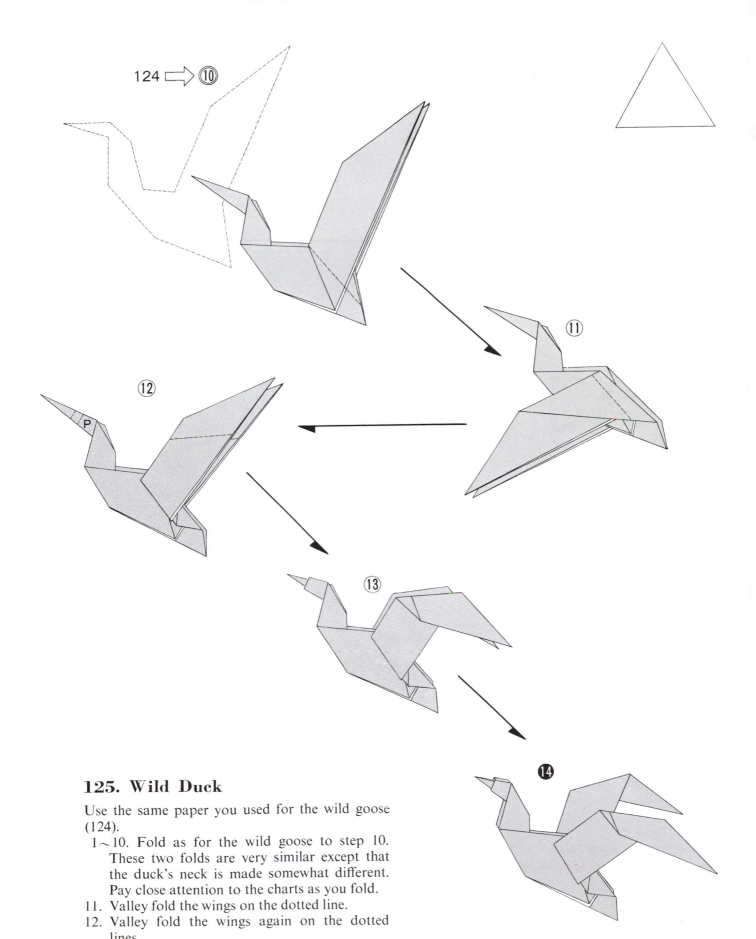

124 ⇨ ⑩

125. Wild Duck

Use the same paper you used for the wild goose (124).

1~10. Fold as for the wild goose to step 10. These two folds are very similar except that the duck's neck is made somewhat different. Pay close attention to the charts as you fold.

11. Valley fold the wings on the dotted line.
12. Valley fold the wings again on the dotted lines.
13. Adjust the wings to suggest flight.
14. The finished wild duck.

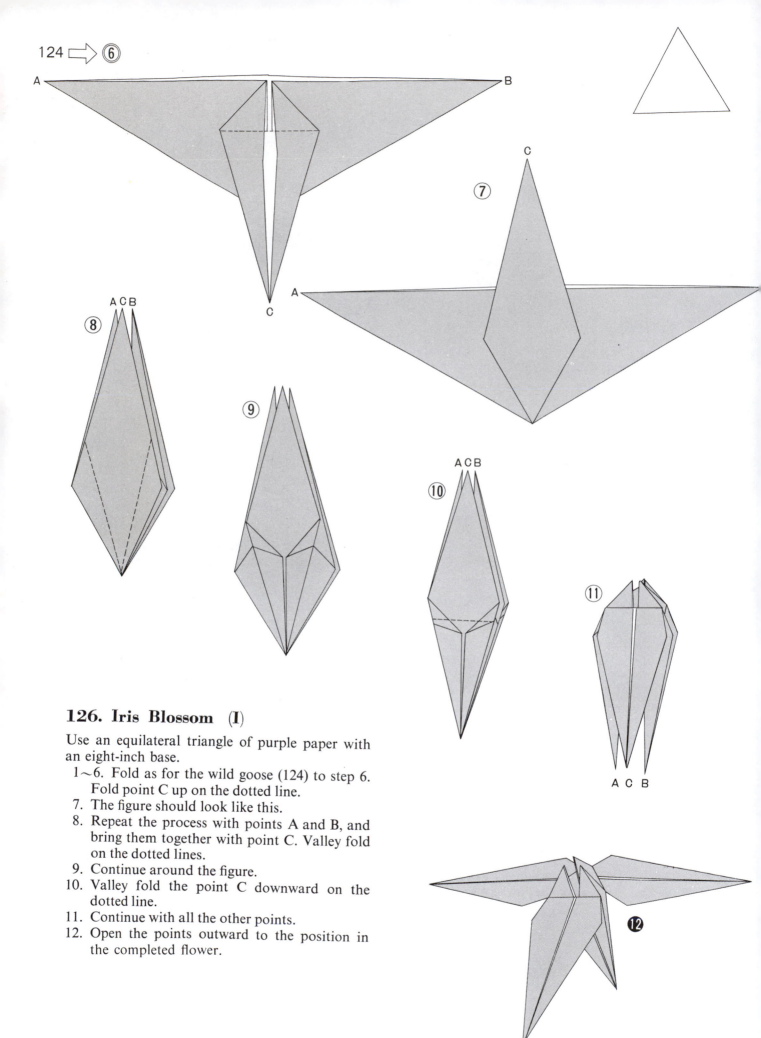

126. Iris Blossom (I)

Use an equilateral triangle of purple paper with
an eight-inch base.

1~6. Fold as for the wild goose (124) to step 6.
    Fold point C up on the dotted line.
7. The figure should look like this.
8. Repeat the process with points A and B, and
    bring them together with point C. Valley fold
    on the dotted lines.
9. Continue around the figure.
10. Valley fold the point C downward on the
    dotted line.
11. Continue with all the other points.
12. Open the points outward to the position in
    the completed flower.

174

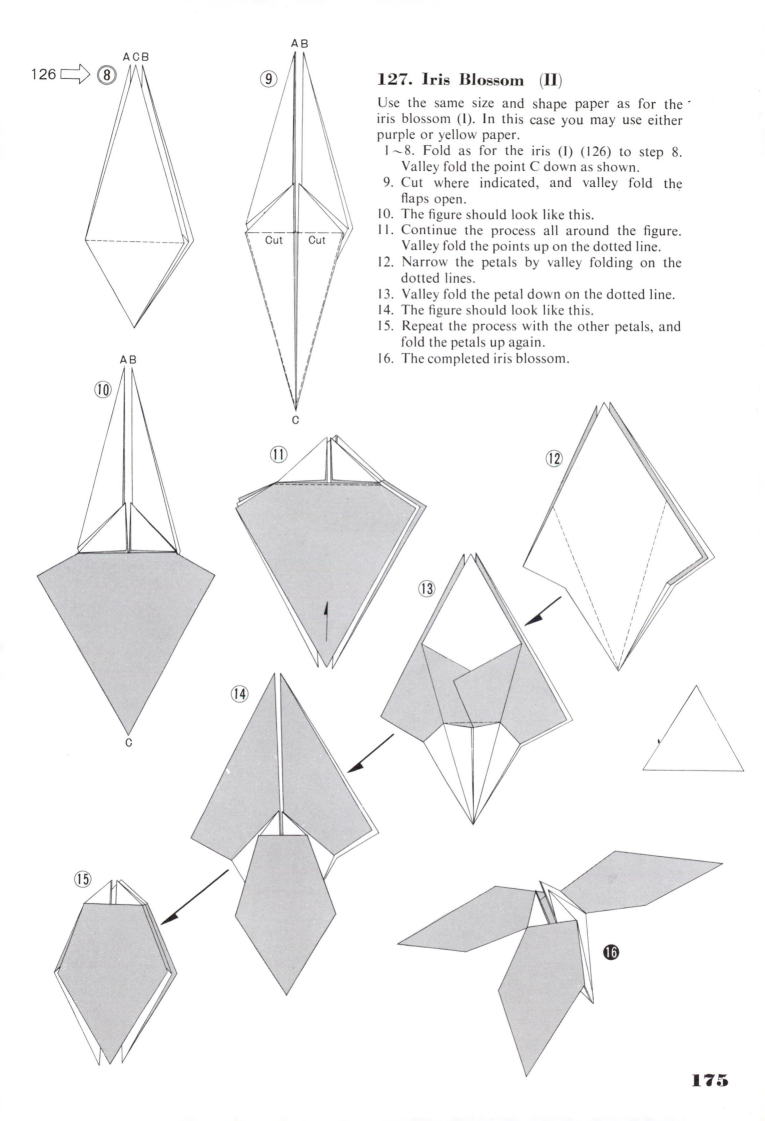

127. Iris Blossom (II)

Use the same size and shape paper as for the iris blossom (I). In this case you may use either purple or yellow paper.

1~8. Fold as for the iris (I) (126) to step 8. Valley fold the point C down as shown.

9. Cut where indicated, and valley fold the flaps open.

10. The figure should look like this.

11. Continue the process all around the figure. Valley fold the points up on the dotted line.

12. Narrow the petals by valley folding on the dotted lines.

13. Valley fold the petal down on the dotted line.

14. The figure should look like this.

15. Repeat the process with the other petals, and fold the petals up again.

16. The completed iris blossom.

128. Swallow

Use an equilateral triangle of black paper with a base eight inches long.

1~7. Fold as for the wild goose (124) to step 7. Bring the top point down in the direction the arrow indicates to the position in step 8.
8. Valley fold so that the right point comes down on top of the right lowest point.
9. Valley fold all layers of the right lower point to the position in step 10.
10. Valley fold on the dotted line.
11. Valley fold on the dotted line.
12. Repeat the same process to make a left wing.
13. Peak and valley fold for the head and for the beak.
14. Peak fold the model in half on the dotted line.
15. Valley fold the wing as indicated. Cut the tail, and valley fold the top layer only.
16. The finished swallow.

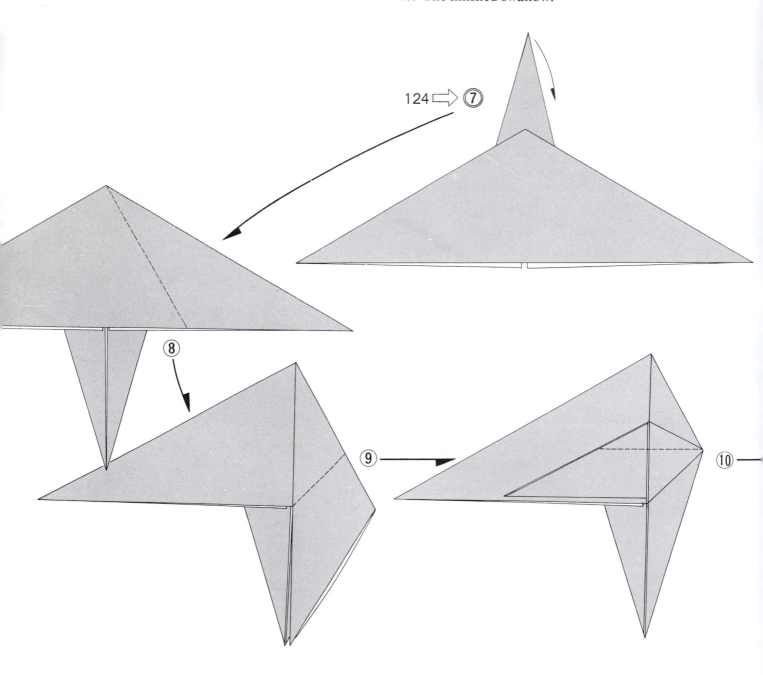

124 ⇨ ⑦

⑧ ⑨ ⑩

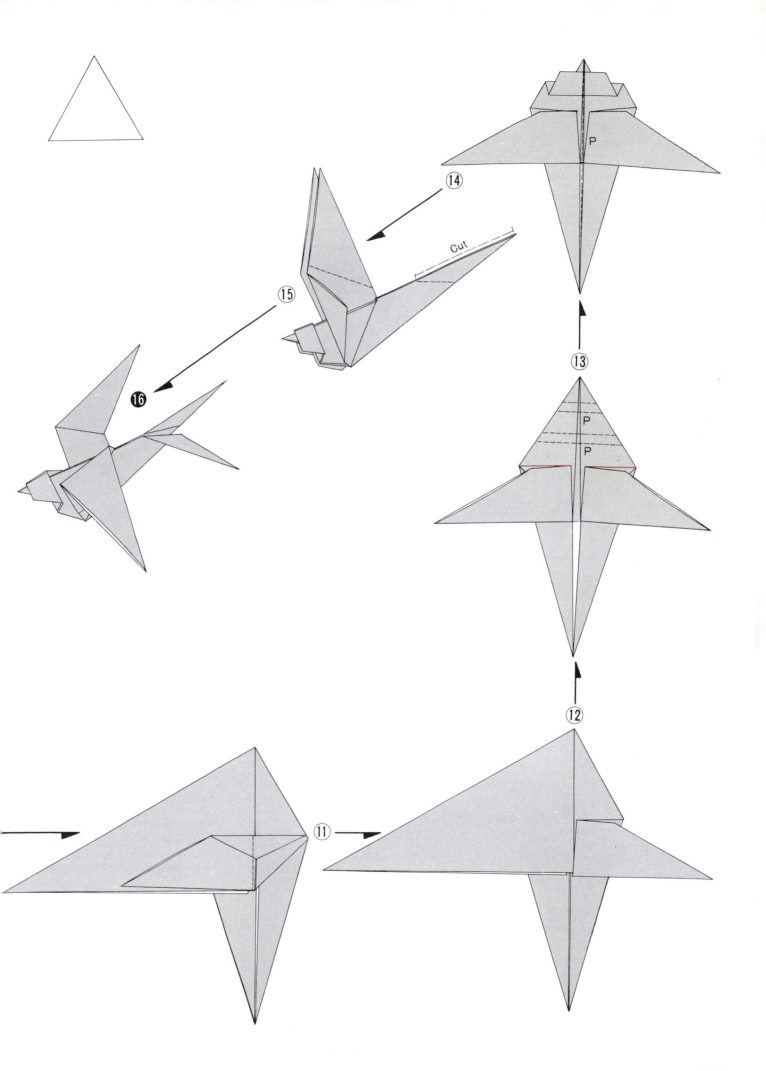

Cut

P

⑭

⑮

⑯

⑬

P
P

⑫

⑪

177

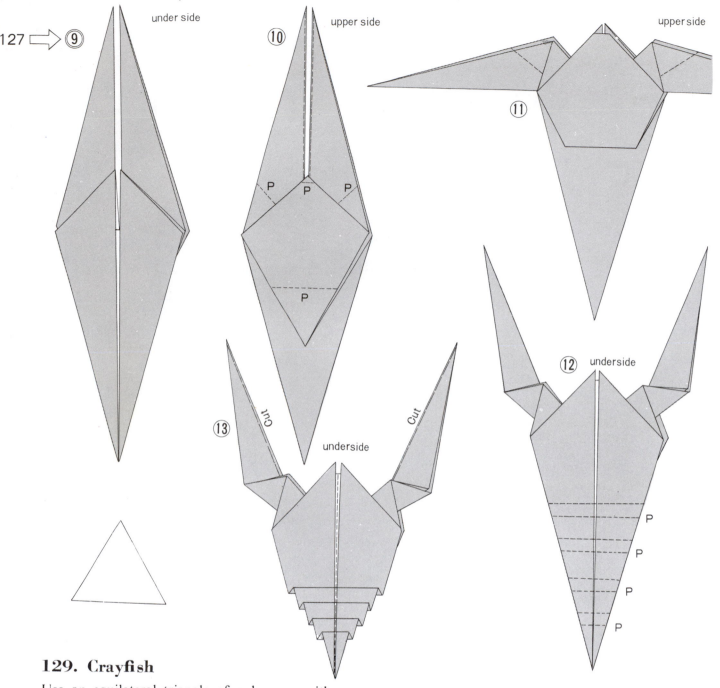

127 ⇨ ⑨

129. Crayfish

Use an equilateral triangle of red paper with a base eight inches long.

1~9. Fold as for the iris blossom (II) (127) to step 9. The figure should look like this. Turn it over.

10. Peak and valley fold the right and left points into the position in step 11.

11. Valley fold the right and left points again for a reverse fold inside out.

12. Turn the model over. Valley and peak fold the tail section starting at the bottom and crimping each fold inward.

13. Cut the claws where indicated, and valley fold the figure in half on the dotted line.

14. Valley fold each claw, one layer only on the dotted line. Pull the tail sections gently outward to curve them into the position in step 15.

15. The finished crayfish.

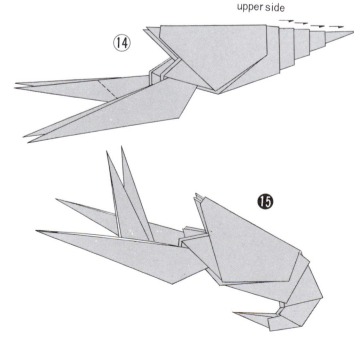

178

130. Duck

Use an equilateral triangle with a base eight inches long.

1. The point on the left will be the duck's beak. Tuck it slightly under as you see in the inset. Crease both sides of the triangle along the lines you see indicated in only the lower side of the chart. Fold the figure into the position shown in the upper half of step 1. Pull the underneath point out in the direction the arrow shows into the position shown in step 2.
2. Repeat with the bottom point.
3. Peak and valley fold the upper right point into the position in step 4.
4. Bring the point just folded up to the position in 5. This will result in peak and valley folds on the lines indicated.
5. Repeat with the lower point. Valley fold on the dotted lines.
6. Valley fold the model in half on the dotted line.
7. Peak and valley fold the neck for a reverse fold outside in. Valley fold the same section again for a reverse fold outside in.
8. Peak and valley fold the beak and the feet into shape.
9. The completed duck.

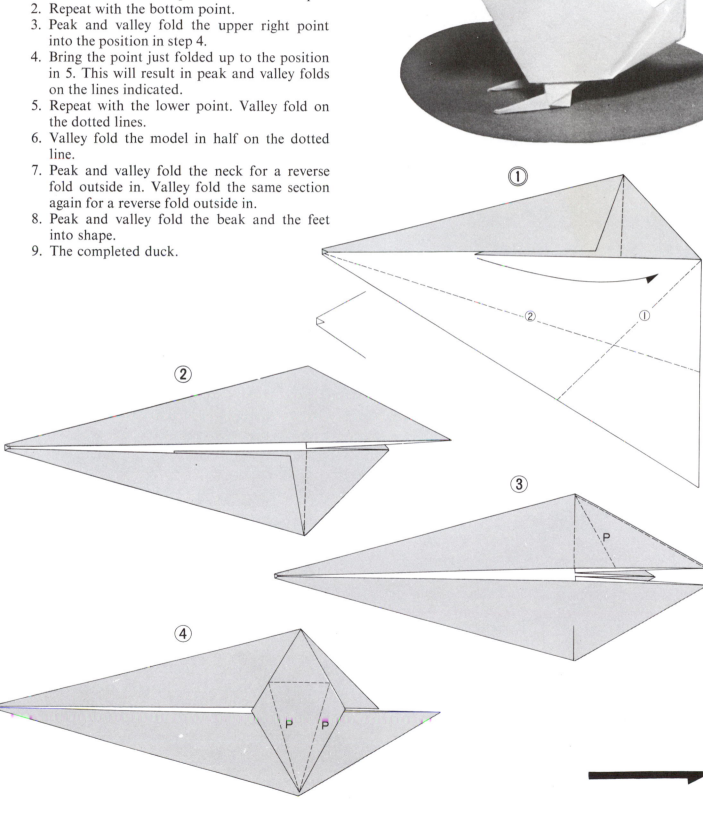

179

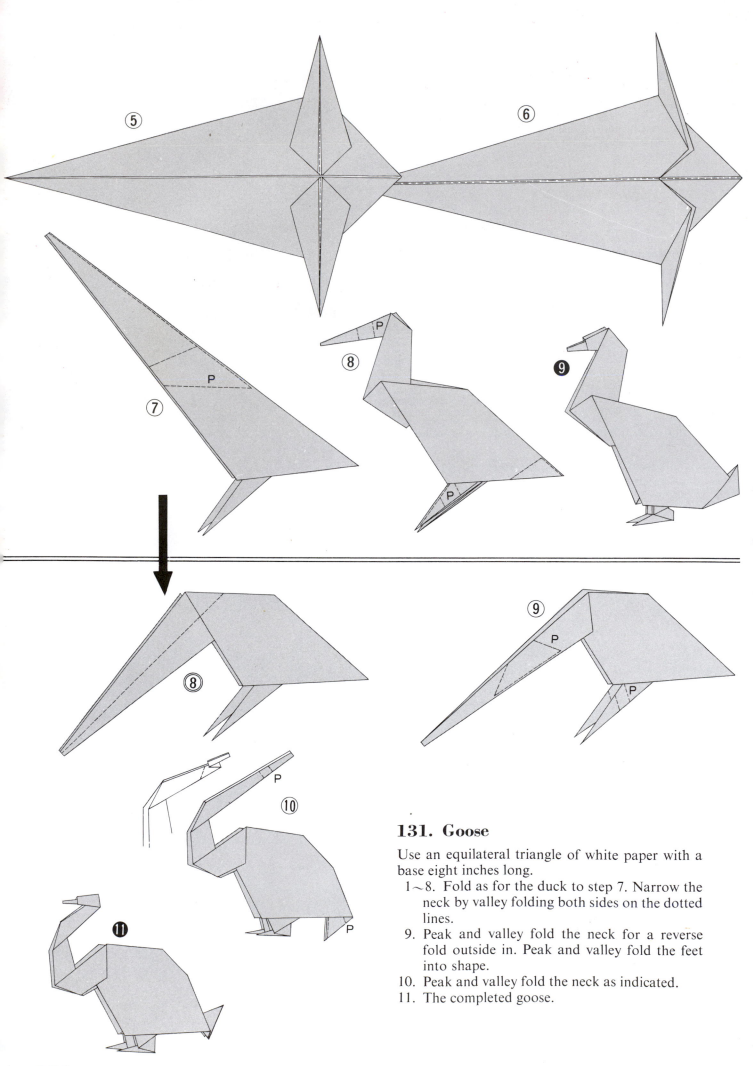

131. Goose

Use an equilateral triangle of white paper with a base eight inches long.

1~8. Fold as for the duck to step 7. Narrow the neck by valley folding both sides on the dotted lines.

9. Peak and valley fold the neck for a reverse fold outside in. Peak and valley fold the feet into shape.

10. Peak and valley fold the neck as indicated.

11. The completed goose.

INDEX OF FOLDS

Numerals are page numbers.

Animals Folds

Plant Folds